The Reich Chancellery
and Führerbunker Complex

The Reich Chancellery and Führerbunker Complex

*An Illustrated History
of the Seat of the Nazi Regime*

STEVEN LEHRER

McFarland & Company, Inc., Publishers
Jefferson, North Carolina

ALSO BY STEVEN LEHRER AND FROM MCFARLAND: *Hitler Sites: A City-by-City Guidebook (Austria, Germany, France, United States)* (2002; paperback 2005); *Wannsee House and the Holocaust* (2000; paperback 2009)

Frontispiece, top: Reichskanzlerpalais before 1937, when Albert Speer added a front entrance portico (Ullstein Bilderdienst). *Bottom:* Ruins of Reichskanzlerpalais 1945 (Walter Frentz)

The present work is a reprint with corrections of the illustrated case bound edition of The Reich Chancellery and Führerbunker Complex: An Illustrated History of the Seat of the Nazi Regime, *first published in 2006 by McFarland.*

LIBRARY OF CONGRESS CATALOGUING-IN-PUBLICATION DATA

Lehrer, Steven, 1944–
The Reich Chancellery and Führerbunker complex :
an illustrated history of the seat of the Nazi regime / Steven Lehrer.
    p.   cm.
Includes bibliographical references and index.

ISBN 978-0-7864-7733-3
softcover : acid free paper ∞

1. Reichskanzlei (Berlin, Germany : Building) — History.
2. Berlin (Germany) — Buildings, structures, etc.
3. Public buildings — Germany — Berlin.
4. Architecture and state — Germany — Berlin.
5. Germany — Politics and government — 1933–1945.
6. Hitler, Adolf, 1889–1945 — Homes and haunts.
I. Title.
DD896.L44   2014   943'.1552 — dc22   2005036405

BRITISH LIBRARY CATALOGUING DATA ARE AVAILABLE

© 2006 Steven Lehrer. All rights reserved

No part of this book may be reproduced or transmitted in any form or by any means, electronic or mechanical, including photocopying or recording, or by any information storage and retrieval system, without permission in writing from the publisher.

Cover photograph: Voß Straße 6 entrance, New Reich Chancellery, from *Die Neue Reichskanzlei*, Zentralverlag der NSDAP, Franz Eher Nachfolger, Munich, 1939

Manufactured in the United States of America

*McFarland & Company, Inc., Publishers
Box 611, Jefferson, North Carolina 28640
www.mcfarlandpub.com*

Acknowledgments

I wish to thank the following: Hanns Peter Frentz and Bernd Schnarr, Bildarchiv Preußischer Kulturbesitz; Thomas Binder and Ilona Wirsing, Geheimes Staatsarchiv Preussischer Kulturbesitz; Olaf Hamann and Verena Nickel, Preußische Staatsbibliothek; Regina Müller and David Price-Hughes, Archiv für Kunst und Geschichte; Jörg Lampertius, Ullstein Bilderdienst; Sabine Klingbeie, Staatsbibliothek zu Berlin Preussischer Kulturbesitz; Nora Psoula; Andreas Grunwald, Bundesarchiv Berlin; Klaus-Dieter Pett, Landesarchiv, Berlin; Peter Zeug, Heidelberg; Henrike Kämpfer, Bayerische Staatsbibliothek, Munich.

Contents

Acknowledgments v
Introduction 1

    I. Wilhelmstraße 3
    II. Hitler in the Chancellery 30
    III. The New Reich Chancellery 63
    IV. Bunkers and Führerbunker 117

Appendix A. King Friedrich Wilhelm I Presents Wilhelmstraße 77 to Graf von der Schulenburg 161
Appendix B. Reich Chancellors 1871–1945 162
Appendix C. Paul von Hindenburg 175
Appendix D. Interior Renovations to the Reichskanzlerpalais 1875–1878 177
Appendix E. Further Renovations to the Reichskanzlerpalais 1890–1925 179
Appendix F. Notable Gatherings in the Reichskanzlerpalais Before 1914 180
Appendix G. Hitler's Speech at the Topping-Out Ceremony of the New Reich Chancellery in the Deutschlandhalle, August 2, 1938 182
Appendix H. Hitler's Speech in the Berlin Sportpalast, January 9, 1939, on the Occasion of the Completion of the New Reich Chancellery 186
Appendix I. Adolf Hitler Describes His Chancellery Renovations 189
Appendix J. Text of Hitler's Agreement to Occupy Czechoslovakia, Signed in the New Reich Chancellery 192
Appendix K. Heinrich Himmler's Heydrich Eulogy 193
Notes 197
References 199
Index 203

Introduction

Of the many sites associated with Adolf Hitler, the Reich Chancellery and Führerbunker excite intense interest, though not a stone of them endures. Yet their former location, at Wilhelmstraße and Voß Straße in central Berlin, continues to attract tourists, just as it did during the Nazi era. Many visitors leave disappointed. What was once Berlin's government quarter, and later Hitler's last subterranean refuge, is now the site of dreary apartment houses. A children's sandbox occupies the spot where aides incinerated the bodies of Hitler and his mistress, Eva Braun, after their double suicide, April 30, 1945.

The site still has immense historic significance. From 1933 until 1945, it was not only a seat of government but, in Winston Churchill's words, the hub of "a monstrous tyranny never surpassed in the dark, lamentable catalogue of human crime." Hitler intended that his fame be enshrined forever in marble. He called his buildings "words of stone," which were meant to be "eternal."[1] Munich, Nuremberg, Linz, and Hamburg, but above all, Berlin, were to be rebuilt as "Führer cities," with architecture that was "gigantic," "monumental," "overpowering," "smashing." "We will use granite," Hitler averred, so that stone monuments to the Nazi movement would be like cathedrals in the millennia to come. Some of his buildings still make a powerful impression. Examples are the Führerbau in Munich (a matched pair of buildings) and the Zeppelin Tribune (Führertribune) in the Reich Party District of Nuremberg. Most powerful of all was the New Reich Chancellery.

After the war, Germans had no interest in Hitler. He had reduced their country to corpses and rubble, and the survivors, mortified that their erstwhile leader had gulled them so completely, focused only on rebuilding. They had made a formerly homeless, penniless, half-educated vagrant their Führer, had cheered him wildly, and obeyed him faithfully. He in turn had propelled them into a cataclysmic disaster, unparalleled in history, and had committed unspeakable crimes in their name. Germans are still ashamed and do not want to talk about Hitler. Mentioning him is considered impolite. But others, in particular Americans, have a legitimate interest. What sort of person was Hitler?

There is no better embodiment of Hitler than the New Reich Chancellery and Führerbunker. The cavernous Chancellery, with its Brobdingnagian rooms and blood-red marble, incarnated Hitler's megalomania, and his need to cow his visitors, especially diplomats. The Führerbunker was his last troglodyte's refuge, a place from which he could decree the total destruction of Germany, then commit suicide rather than face the hangman's noose.

This book is intended as a virtual tour of the Chancellery and bunker. For visitors to the site, it can serve as a guide to the location of events and rooms. For others, it is a topographical biography of history's most prolific mass murderer.

Was glänzt, ist für den Augenblick geboren,
Das Echte bleibt der Nachwelt unverloren.

(Whatever shines is born for the moment,
The genuine endures for future generations)

—*Faust*, "Prelude in the Theater,"
Johann Wolfgang von Goethe

I. Wilhelmstraße

If they could talk, some streets could tell a story that would fill a book, a story of famous residents, political developments, and power. One such street is Berlin's Wilhelmstraße. From the Anhalter Station to Pariser Platz, Wilhelmstraße is a veritable historical treatise.[1]

The number of celebrated Wilhelmstraße buildings, still standing or destroyed, is so large that an account of them could fill a book in itself. On this one street were the Prussian State Ministry (Wilhelmstraße 63, today 52), the Palace of the Reich President (Wilhelmstraße 73), and the Reichskanzlerpalais (Wilhelmstraße 77). The writer Wilibald Alexis (1798–1871), author of *The Trousers of Herr von Bredow*, lived in Wilhelmstraße 97. Friedrich Schleiermacher (1768–1834), whose book *On Religion* is a classic of Protestant theology, lived at Wilhelmstraße 73. The Nazis published a newspaper, *Der Angriff*, in Wilhelmstraße 106. The Reich Ministry for Enlightenment of the People and Propaganda was at Wilhelmplatz 8/9.

"I live here in paradise," newlywed Bettina von Arnim wrote to Johann Wolfgang von Goethe, describing her garden house, Wilhelmstraße 78. "The nightingales flutter in the chestnut trees outside my bedroom window, and the moon, which never shined so brightly, awakens me with his rays." Bettina Brentano and Achim von Arnim were married on May 11, 1811, and their passionate letters are part of German literature. Among the men who worked in Wilhelmstraße were Reich Chancellor Otto von Bismarck (1815–1898), the founder of the German Empire; Reich President Friedrich Ebert (1871–1925); and Reich Chancellor Gustav Stresemann (1878–1929), Nobel Peace Prize winner.

Joseph Goebbels, Hermann Göring, Reinhard Heydrich, and Heinrich Himmler instigated their reign of terror from Wilhelmstraße. Under the Ministry garden, deep within his Führerbuker, Hitler committed suicide in 1945.

Many of the historical buildings are long gone. Drab apartment houses and a playground have replaced the Reich Chancellery. The new British Embassy is at Wilhelmstraße 70-71. The old embassy was built in 1868 and demolished in 1950.

Still standing at Wilhelmstraße 81-85 is Göring's mammoth Air Ministry, now the Finance Ministry. At Wilhelmstraße 49 is the Labor Ministry. At Wilhelmplatz 8-9, the Nazi-era extensions of the Propaganda Ministry are government offices.[2] In 1947, the Soviet "Kommandatura" used them for their headquarters.

A walk down Wilhelmstraße today, with its rich diversity of building styles, is almost a march through history. And a foundation, Topographie des Terrors, has placed plaques on sites that were associated with atrocities during the Nazi era.

Topographie des Terrors plaque. The author stands next to the plaque at the corner of Wilhelmstraße and Voß Straße, which explains the significance of the site.

Nazi-era extensions to Joseph Goebbels' Propaganda Ministry on Wilhelmplatz. This building now houses social welfare offices.

Schulenburg Palais

The Schulenburg Palais, 77 Wilhelmstraße, was in private hands for more than a century before it became the Reichskanzlerpalais, the Old Reich Chancellery. It was built at the behest of King Friedrich Wilhelm I, an oafish, uncouth monarch, whose only known passion was for a regiment of tall soldiers. When his son, Crown Prince Friedrich, tried to flee the kingdom with his friend (and probably lover) Hans Hermann von Katte, Friedrich Wilhelm had Katte beheaded in front of Prince Friedrich (later Frederick the Great), who fainted.

The king conferred money, plots of land, and building materials on privileged favorites. The choicest parcels were in the north section of Wilhelmstraße and were quite large. Between the lots granted to Major General Wolff Adolf von Pannewitz (Wilhelmstraße 76), and State and War Minister Samuel von Marschall (Wilhelmstraße 78), the king awarded Wilhelmstraße 77 to his esteemed Lieutenant General Count Adolf Friedrich von der Schulenburg. To enrich the gift, the king granted Count Schulenburg a permit to "brew white and brown beer."

The architect of Schulenburg's Palais is uncertain. In his 1768 work, *The Royal Residences of Berlin and Potsdam*, Friedrich Nicolai wrote that the architect was C.F. Richter (1701–1766), member of a family of architects from Thuringia.[3] Richter, a mediocrity, had built many houses in Berlin, but even before 1933 few survived. Richter also formulated "a description of a machine, with which a piling could be cut underwater."

Architectural historian Melanie Mertens disputes Nicolai's information. Nicolai wrote that the Schulenburg Palais was designed in an Italian style typical of Richter. In fact, the building was unlike anything Richter had ever built, and resembled a rural chateau, rather than a Berlin or Italian building from the period.

Copper engravings, drawn by Court Architect C.H. Horst and executed by Jean George Ringlin, show that the Schulenburg Palais consisted of a middle portion with three floors and two two-story wings enclosing a courtyard. Beside both wings on Wilhelmstraße were low one-story additions, with corridors that allowed passage from front to back. Behind both these structures was a market court, which had stables and sheds facing a park.

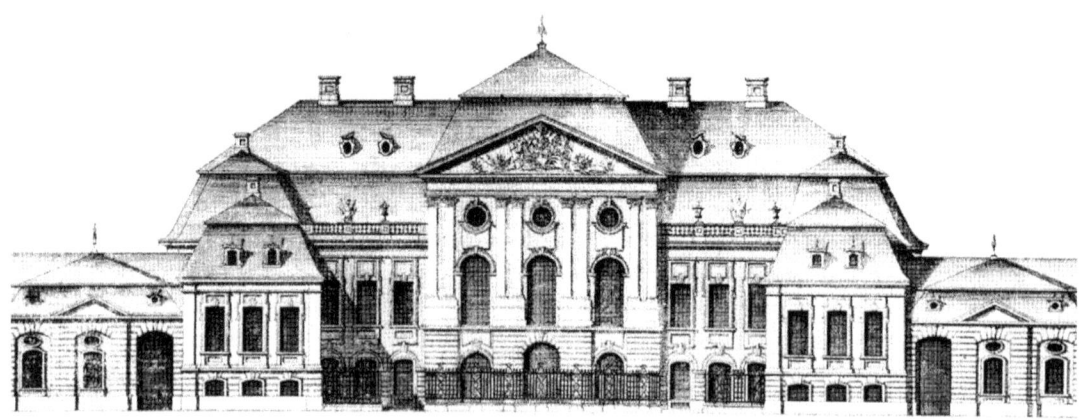

Top: Friedrich Wilhelm I. King Friedrich Wilhelm I ordered the building of the Palais at 77 Wilhelmstraße for Count Adolf Friedrich von der Schulenburg (portrait by Antoine Pesne, Deutsches Historisches Museum).
Bottom: Palais Schulenburg in the eighteenth century.

I. Wilhelmstraße

The park extended on the west side to Friedrich Ebert Straße. There was an alleyway though the middle, broken at intervals by benches. An oval riding track was at the end. In the middle of the second floor of the palais was the huge ballroom, 300 square meters. On the north side of the building, near the ballroom, was a larger room, probably originally a gallery for paintings. In 1786, Nicolai wrote in *The Royal Residences of Berlin and Potsdam* (p 849):

> In Count Schulenburg's palace in the Wilhelmstraße there was an impressive collection of paintings. But now there are far fewer, to wit,
> P. Veronese, Christ with the literary scholars at mealtime
> P. Veronese, A storm and a conflagration
> [Francesco] Trevisani, Pero suckles her father Simon in prison
> [Anthony] Van Dyck, Christ with the crown of thorns
> Th. Roosgen von Tivoli, Four landscapes with cattle.

In the uppermost floor of the side wings of the palais were servants' rooms. The top floor of the central building was not completed.

Construction of the Schulenburg Palais began in 1738. In 1739, in the presence of King Friedrich Wilhelm I, the palais was festively dedicated. But during the festivities, the king became severely chilled in one of the icy rooms and died in Potsdam the following year as a result. The offending room, two stories high on the garden side, was given a second, lower, ceiling. Count Schulenburg died in battle not long afterward.

Adolf Friedrich von der Schulenburg-Wolfsburg auf Betzendorf, Osterwohle, Klosterrode, Detzel und Ramstadt was born in Wolfenbüttel in 1685. He attended the Ritterakademie, studied three years in Utrecht, journeyed to England in 1704, and

Adolf Friedrich Graf von der Schulenburg was the first owner of the future Reichskanzlerpalais, Wilhelmstraße 77 (Geheimes Staatsarchiv Preußischer Kulturbesitz).

joined the Army of Hanover in 1705. After fighting at Oudenaarde as a major, he was wounded at the battle of Malplaquet. He entered Prussian military service after the Peace of Utrecht in 1713. He took part in the attack on Stralsund, the landing at Rügen, and was promoted to commander of the Derfflinger Grenadier Equestrian Regiment. In 1729 he was ennobled and elevated to count. He was in special favor of King Friedrich Wilhelm I, who entrusted him with many sensitive tasks. Schulenburg hated smoking, but in order not to offend the king and his smoking society, the *Tabakskollegium*, he kept an empty pipe in his mouth.

In 1732, with the announcement of the engagement of Crown Prince Friedrich to Princess Elizabeth Christine of Braunschweig-Beyern, Schulenburg was sent to Vienna, to the court of Emperor Charles VI. He returned from his mission with a rich treasure of diamonds the emperor and empress had given him.

Upon the death of his patron, Friedrich Wilhelm I, Schulenburg hurried to Berlin from Friedeberg, to wish good luck to the crown prince. But the young King Friedrich II was quite annoyed because Schulenburg had taken French leave from his regiment. Red faced at the reception he received, Schulenburg asked for permission to depart Berlin. Friedrich II quickly forgave Schulenburg because of the impending conflict with Austria. He awarded Schulenburg the Order of the Black Eagle and sent him off to war. At Mollwitz, April 10, 1741, Schulenburg, commanding ten squadrons of Prussian cavalry, found himself at a disadvantage facing the Austrians, who had fielded 30. Thrown back twice by the Austrians, King Friedrich vented his fury upon the hapless Schulenburg, with harsh words about the bravery of his cavalry. Pained at this smear upon his valor and the reputation of his regiment, Schulenburg threw himself into battle. Enemy horses thundered in at full gallop to hit Schulenburg's ranks with lance and saber.[4] His lines broke. Schulenburg was wounded, and standing in the saddle, sword in hand, he furiously wheeled his foaming horse to curse his confused squadrons into attack formation. But the enemy continued to hit hard. A saber slashed Schulenburg's face, and one eye fell from its socket. Schulenburg held his cheek together with one hand, remained mounted, and continued forward. An Austrian bullet killed him.

Just before his death, Schulenburg had added to his will that his "house with contents" should go to his eldest son as *Fideikomiß*, that is, inalienable and indivisible family property. However, Schulenburg stipulated that the house could be sold and the proceeds held as *Fideikomiß*.

The eldest son, Count Gebhard Werner von der Schulenburg, who had studied at the universities of Helmstedt and Leipzig, was a Prussian government official. In 1745 he had gone to France as part of the Elector's Embassy and in 1750 he became a Lord High Steward. In 1764 he was the second ranking diplomat in the embassy at the court of Joseph II in Vienna. Then King Friedrich II sent him as his minister and representative to Stuttgart, assigning him to settle the festering quarrel between Duke Karl and the Würtemberg council.

The Countess Chesterfield called Schulenburg to London and made him her heir. Upon his return in 1776, the king named him a state minister. When the House of the Margraves of Bayreuth was dissolved, Schulenburg took possession of their lands and conveyed them to the Margrave of Ansbach. When Friedrich Wilhelm II, King Friedrich's successor, contemplated a second marriage, Schulenburg was elevated to the rank of councilor.

Like his father, Gebhard Werner von der Schulenburg enjoyed the special trust of King Friedrich II, and was among those chosen few invited to stay at Potsdam with the king every year. The few were invariably men, since Frederick the Great was gay and generally avoided

Gebhard Werner von der Schulenburg is shown with his wife, Sophie Charlotte, née Veltheim. Anna Dorothea Therbusch (1721–1782), who painted this portrait, was one of the few women artists in the Prussian Court. She was the daughter of a portrait painter and went to Paris in 1765 to study. She returned to Berlin in 1769 and became court painter to Frederick the Great (Staatsbibliothek zu Berlin).

the company of women.

Schulenburg, traveling as he did, spent little time in his palais on Wilhelmstraße. In 1757 he rented the building to Prince August Ferdinand of Prussia, youngest brother of Frederick the Great, who was married to Princess Anna Elisabeth Louise, daughter of Margrave Friedrich Wilhelm of Brandenburg-Schwedt. The prince and princess remained rental tenants until 1762, when August Ferdinand was named head of the Johanniter Orden and moved into the Ordenspalais on nearby Wilhelmplatz. This building later served as Joseph Goebbels' propaganda ministry and was blown to bits during a British air raid on March 13, 1945.

After Prince August Ferdinand moved out of the Schulenburg Palais, a succession of others passed through. From 1762 to 1787, Baron Ernst Ludwig Julius von Lenthe, the Hanoverian ambassador, was in residence. In 1788, the representative of the Electoral Palatinate, Count von Schall, moved in.

In 1788, Gebhard Werner von der Schulenburg died. In his will, he stipulated that the palais and contents, as per the will of his father, should pass as *Fideikomiß* to his eldest son, Count Karl Friedrich Gebhard von der Schulenburg. But he also stated that it would be better for his descendants to sell the palais for a cheap price, because of the danger that at any time the building could burn to the ground. The older a building became, wrote Gebhard Werner, the less it was worth, and a fire would wipe out virtually all equity. The proceeds of the sale should be used, among other things, for the amortization of debt with which a *Fideikomiß* from a grandmother was burdened.

Count Karl Friedrich Gebhard von der Schulenburg, after studies at Göttingen, was chosen by Duke Karl Wilhelm Ferdinand von Braunschweig to accompany his eldest son on a three-year journey to the German Royal Courts and Switzerland. On May 19, 1790, Karl Friedrich Gebhard sold the Wilhelmstraße Palais to Chamberlain Chevalier Adrian de Verdy du Vernois for 30,000 Thalers in gold. The money came from the chevalier's rich wife, the former Charlotte Eleanor Baroness von Keller. The chevalier and his wife had been living in the palais with Count von Schall.

On April 30, 1792, Chevalier Adrian and his wife sold the palais for 40,000 Thalers to Countess Sophie Julie Friederike Wilhelmine von Dönhoff, the morganatic wife of King Friedrich Wilhelm II. Frederick the Great had died childless, and his nephew Friedrich Wilhelm II succeeded him to the throne.

Countess Sophie's father, Friedrich Wilhelm Graf von Dönhoff, was a major in the Prussian Army and had a large estate in Mecklenburg. Friedrich Wilhelm II met 21-year-old Sophie in Berlin's City Palace. Sophie's beauty, her piano playing and singing, quickly ensnared the music-loving monarch.[5] But he had already married and divorced Princess Elisabeth von Braunschweig-Wolfenbüttel (both spouses were cheating on each other), and was in a morganatic union with the "beautiful Wilhelmine"—Wilhelmine Encke—Madame Rietz (later Countess Lichtenau). No matter. On April 11, 1790, in Charlottenburg Palace, the king entered into a second morganatic union with Countess Sophie. On January 24, 1792, the union produced a son, named Friedrich Wilhelm after his father.

When Chevalier Adrian de Verdy du Vernois sold the Palais Schulenburg to Countess Sophie, the money, not surprisingly, had come from the king, who ordered that the palais be completely renovated. Doorways, roof, planking, attic rooms, stables, side wings and housing for coachmen were repaired, and a bathhouse was built. Chairs, sofas, commodes, candelabras, silk tapestries, curtains, beds, and fireplace curtains were repaired or replaced. But the work was never completed because of Sophie's treachery. Not only smart and talented, Sophie was materialistic and, worse, allied with a group of reactionary noblemen opposed to the king and his reforms.

By the time Sophie produced a second child, a daughter Julie, January 4, 1793, the marriage had gone sour. The king had discovered Sophie's scheming with his adversaries. The frustrated Sophie decided to go out with a bang rather than a whimper. On November 19, 1793, the king hosted a concert at Potsdam and played the viola himself. In the middle of the performance, Sophie rushed into the room and dumped her infant daughter at the King's feet. "Here," Sophie shouted, "take back your property!" Never had there been such a scandal. Even Sophie's reactionary friends

Countess Sophie Julie Friederike Wilhelmine von Dönhoff was the morganatic wife of King Friedrich Wilhelm II, who bought the Palais Schulenburg for her. (Bildarchiv Preußischer Kulturbesitz)

turned their backs on her. The king exiled Sophie to Angermünde with 8000 Thalers yearly alimony. He kept the two children, who, much to Sophie's dismay, were raised by her rival, Countess Lichtenau. The king had to send two official commissions to Angermünde to persuade Sophie to relinquish her ownership of the Palais Schulenburg.

Radziwill Palais

The new tenants the king chose for the palais were affianced. Princess Friederike Dorothée Luise Philippine of Prussia was the daughter of Prince August Ferdinand, the king's brother. Prince Anton Radziwill had become a Prussian subject after the three partitions of Poland, which in 1795 ended the existence of Poland as a sovereign state. The immensely wealthy Radziwills had intermarried twice with the Prince Electors of Brandenburg. But the thrifty Friedrich Wilhelm II informed the couple that he could not ask his ministers to pay for the engagement festivities of a prince who did not come from a ruling house. After long, tedious negotiation of the marriage contract, the wedding took place March 17, 1796.

In the meantime, Prince Anton's father, Prince Michael Radziwill, bought the Palais Schulenburg for 60,000 Thalers. By the terms Prince Michael set, Princess Luise would have life use of the property, but her interest in it would terminate with her death. The Radziwills made few changes to the palais. They built a small greenhouse, bought some new carpet and furniture, and added the family coat of arms to the gable. The inscription beneath read "Hotel de Radziwill." This inscription gave Heinrich Clauren (1771–1854) the inspiration for his comedy, *The Wool Market*, in which a landed nobleman turns his palace into a hotel. Prince Radziwill, as a joke, liked to play the role of the nobleman, while his servants waited on his guests.

Prince Anton Radzwill, a convivial aristocrat, maintained an open house. Because of his devout Catholicism, the palais was a gathering place for bishops and Catholic clergy in stoutly Protestant Berlin. Pious Protestants were highly suspicious of the palais and its inhabitants, but the prince's open door attracted many people who were less religious and far more interesting.

The Palais Radziwill became a pre-eminent Berlin salon. Frederick Chopin performed in the ballroom, and Prince Anton was a generous patron of the Berlin Vocal Academy. The prince himself owned a Stradivarius cello, on which he played masterfully his own compositions and those of others. Johann Wolfgang von Goethe said of him that he was the first real troubadour he had ever met. Heinrich von Treitschke, historian and anti–Semite ("the Jews are our misfortune"), praised the palais, the only gathering place for intellectuals among the high nobility in Berlin.

To the palais came the heroes of the wars of liberation against Napoleon: Field Marshal Count August Wilhelm Neidhardt von Gneisenau and Carl von Clausewitz, whose treatise *On War* is still widely studied and quoted. Philosopher-Educator Wilhelm von Humboldt was a frequent guest. Other visitors were composer Felix Mendelssohn, sculptor Christian Daniel Rauch, architect Karl Friedrich Schinkel, and composer Gaspare Luigi Spontini.

Prince Anton Radziwill devoted himself energetically to musical composition. During a visit to Weimar, the prince met and befriended Goethe. The prince subsequently composed music for Goethe's *Faust*, and Goethe wrote two new spirit-choruses in his play especially for the prince's music. In 1816 the Berlin Vocal Academy performed the premiere of the prince's *Faust* music in the Palais Radziwill.

The aged Goethe had no use at all for Franz Schubert's settings of his poems, especially Schubert's exquisite "Gretchen at the Spinning Wheel." Yet Schubert's Goethe Lieder are now considered sublime masterpieces, while no one remembers Radziwill's music. Some critics of the immortal Goethe have called him a sycophant with a tin ear.

After the French defeated the Prussians at Jena and Auerstadt in 1806, Napoleon entered Berlin. In 1807 he appointed his marshal, Claude Victor-Perrin, governor of the territory between the Elbe and the Oder. Berlin remained the seat of government.

Prince Anton Radziwill (Bildarchiv Preußischer Kulturbesitz).

Marshal Victor refused to reside in the home of the state minister, Count Carl Otto Friedrich von Voß. Napoleon's governor wanted something grander: the royal residence. Prince Ferdinand, the king's brother, begged Marshal Victor not to inflict this disgrace on the Prussians, and instead to occupy his son-in-law's home, the Palais Radziwill. Marshal Victor moved in to the palais with his family, but used the nearby Voß house as his offices. He remained until 1808, when he went to Spain to fight in the Peninsular War.

Victor found that the Radziwill Palais was expensive to light. During a ball, December 6, 1807, the entire building was illuminated, even the Radziwill coat-of-arms under the gable. The weather was bad, and the rain extinguished all the lights within the first hour. But the bill came to 2,000 Thalers, 1,600 of which went to pay for oil.

During the wars of liberation, the palais, situated between a courtyard and a garden, offered more protection than buildings that fronted directly on the street. In early 1813, many Radziwill friends and acquaintances sought shelter in the spacious rooms. After the battles of Großbeeren and Leipzig, wounded soldiers joined them.

Prince Anton Radziwill's beautiful daughter, Princess Elisa Radziwill, was involved in one of the tragic romances that ensnared nineteenth century European royalty. Because of

Opposite: Victor, Maréchal Claude (Perrin), Duc de Bellune (painting by Antoine Jean Gros, Art Resource). Victor was not one of the French Emperor's better warriors. On February 18, 1814, Napoleon relieved him of command on account of dilatory behavior before Montereau. Victor threatened to fight as a private if necessary, and Napoleon relented, giving him command of two young guard divisions. Victor embraced the Bourbon restoration and held important military positions until 1830, when he retired after 49 years' military service.

the close relations between the Radziwills and the Prussian royal family, Elisa and Prince Wilhelm of Prussia became acquainted at a very early age. In 1820 they fell passionately in love. Wilhelm's father, King Friedrich Wilhelm III, initially was against the union because the Radziwill family was Polish, but as the ardor of Wilhelm and Elisa grew, the king gave the couple his blessing. The king's ministers were adamantly opposed because Elisa did not have royal blood. The king accepted this reasoning and in the winter 1823/24 declared a marriage impossible. But the lovesick Prince Wilhelm was disconsolate.

One minister, Prince Ludwig Adolf Peter Wittgenstein, suggested that arranging for a nobleman with royal blood to adopt Elisa could circumvent her own lack of royal blood. On February 12, 1826, Prince Wilhelm wrote to his father, suggesting that Prince August of Prussia should adopt Elisa.

While these machinations were in progress, Prince Wilhelm obtained permission from his father to visit Elisa in Posen. There he spent joyful days with his beloved, but as the time approached for him to leave, he became despondent and severely injured himself in a fall. He was transported to Berlin in a critical state, made worse by the ministers' decision that an adoption was no substitute for royal blood. The government was in constant fear of revolution and could not tolerate any deviation from the time-honored rules of royal succession.

In June 1826 the king sent his son a sympathetic letter setting forth his refusal to permit the marriage. Wilhelm wrote an equally sensitive response, thanking his father for his graciousness. In 1829 Wilhelm, later Kaiser Wilhelm I, married Princess Augusta of Saxe-Weimar. Elisa frequently visited the home of Wilhelm and his new wife, and there in 1833 suffered a lung hemorrhage, the result of pulmonary tuberculosis. She died the following year.

Prince Anton spent the years just before his death in 1833 in a dispute with the Berlin police over the cobblestones in both entrances to the palais entry court. The bureaucrats insisted that the prince replace the cobblestones with flat granite plates. Prince Radziwill pointed out that the entrances to the royal palace were paved with cobblestones. The dispute escalated until it finally reached the Lord High Steward's office. The police prevailed.

On the death of Princess Luise, December 7, 1836, the

Princess Elisa Radziwill. (Ullstein Bilderdienst)

Palais Radziwill passed to Prince Anton's three children, Prince Wilhelm, Prince Boguslav, and Princess Wanda, wife of Adam Constantin Count Czartoryski. A dispute over the inheritance the following year left the two brothers with sole ownership. Prince Wilhelm had married Countess Mathilde Clary-Aldrigen in 1832, and Prince Boguslav married her sister, Countess Leontine. Both brothers moved into the Palais Radziwill with their spouses and proceeded to fill it with children.

In 1837 the princes applied for a building permit to construct a gallery with a stone framework and flat roof. The gallery was to be placed in the southern market courtyard, was to be one story tall, and was to connect the main building with another building nearby. The gallery was never built, and its purpose is unclear.

In 1869, the stable on the north side of the building was demolished. A residential addition was erected which extended to the street front and had three rows of windows. Servants' quarters were added to the main building and a new stable built. Prince Wilhelm died in 1869 and Prince Boguslav died in 1873. They left 14 squabbling heirs with an interest in the Palais Radziwill, which had become enormously valuable. In 1875, the Radziwill heirs offered to sell their property, Wilhelmstraße 77, to the Reich.

Reichskanzlerpalais

With extraordinary intelligence, cunning, guile, and world-class conniving, Otto von Bismarck defeated the armies of Denmark (1864), Austria (1866), and France (1870) and combined the German states into the German Empire, a union the major European powers had struggled for centuries to prevent. Bismarck was highly emotional, a promiscuous lover, a passionate gambler, a voracious reader, and a glutton. He cried frequently, was subject to emotional outbursts, cholecystitis, jaundice, and convulsions. The historian Golo Mann called him "a nervous barbarian."

As Reich Chancellor

Otto von Bismarck (painting by Franz von Lenbach, Deutsches Historisches Museum).

Above: Proclaiming the Kaiser. On January 18, 1871, the Prussian Army surrounded Paris, whose citizens were reduced to eating rats. In the Hall of Mirrors at Versailles, King Wilhelm reluctantly accepted the title of Kaiser Wilhelm I. Wilhelm is at center on the dais, Crown Prince Friedrich at left. Bismarck (in white) is at center of the painting, Field Marshal Helmuth von Moltke just to the right (painting by Anton von Werner, AKG Images).

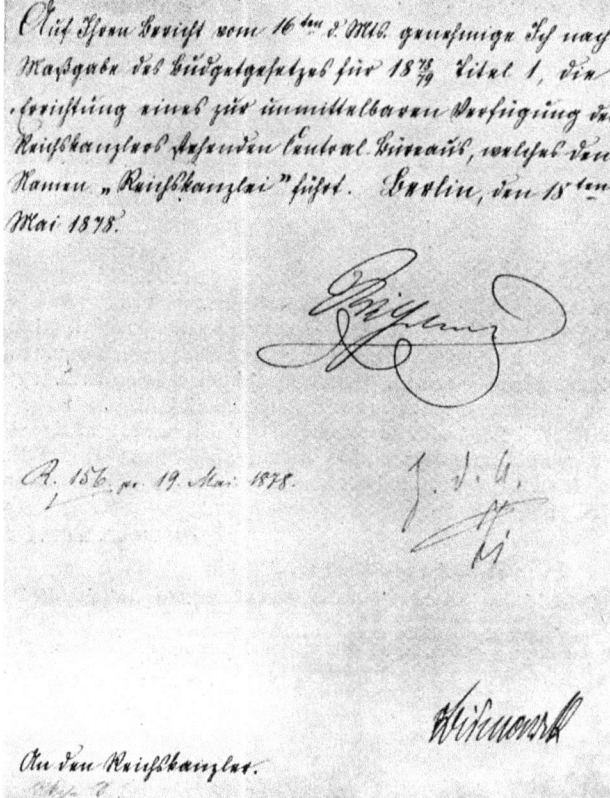

Left: Royal order for the establishment of a Reich Chancellery. *Auf ihren Bericht von 16ten d. Monats genehmige ich nach Maßgabe des Bundesgesetzes für 18 Titel 1. die Einrichtung eines zu unmittelbaren Verfügung des Reichskanzlers stehenden Central Bureaus, welche den Namen "Reichskanzlei" führt. Berlin den 18ten Mai 1878.* [According to your report of the 16th of the month, I authorize, according to federal law 18 title 1, the immediate establishment of a central bureau at the disposal of the Reich Chancellor, called the Reich Chancellery. Berlin, May 18th, 1878.] The large upper signature belongs to the Kaiser. Bismarck signed at bottom right.

and minister president of the newly created empire, Bismarck thought that contiguous buildings for the chancellor's offices, foreign office, and president's office, (Wilhelmstraße 77, 74–76, and 73, respectively) would be convenient.

At the time, Bismarck was living in Wilhelmstraße 73, the Presidential Palace. Victor Tissot, a former chief editor of the *Gazette de Lausanne*, visited Bismarck and recorded his impression (Demps, 2000): "A blue silk wall tapestry surrounds the gigantic marriage bed. A small table serves as a washstand. On the table I discover half a dozen combs, many more than the chancellor has hairs on his head — he has only three. In Frau von Bismarck's room, instead of the usual glass cabinet there is a safe."

Bismarck showed Tissot more of the Presidential Palace: "When we left the salon, my guide, with a majestic gesture, opened a door to the right and announced, 'the ballroom.' This ballroom, the walls covered with mirrors, had been a chapel. Since the Chancellor has jailed so many bishops, he probably has no scruples about allowing couples to dance in a church."

On January 25, 1875, Bismarck was legally empowered to purchase the Radziwill Palais, along with land sold in 1869, which separated it from Königgrätzer Straße. Although the Palais was a middling example of German baroque architecture, it became the chancellor's new residence. The Reich paid six million marks. The money came from war reparations the Germans had forced on the French after the calamitous French defeat in the Franco-Prussian War of 1870. The French never forgot this stinging humiliation, and had their revenge at Versailles in 1919. ("The hour has come for the weighty settlement of our accounts," French premier Georges Clemenceau announced to the cowed German delegates compelled to sign the onerous peace treaty of World War I.)

Bismarck's baldness delighted cartoonists. "The barometer which should be on the desk of every minister," is the comment on this drawing from *Kladderadatsch,* a German political satirical weekly.

Kaiser Wilhelm I approved the six million-mark purchase on February 4, 1875. The Princes Radziwill had to vacate the Palais by April 1. They were hard pressed to find suitable princely living accommodations on such short notice. Kaiser Wilhelm, who felt an attachment to the Radziwill family because of his memories of Princess Elisa, wrote to Bismarck (Pünder, 1928): "I confess that I would have wished for more compassionate handling of this unpleasant matter, which has been painful for me. I am quite dumbstruck by the very quick eviction."

Bismarck gave the Radziwills more time, and they were gone by the end of May. They took with them the coffins, buried in the park, of Princess Lulu, burned to death in a fire in 1808, and her sister, who had died before her at the age of one-and-a-half. Johann Gottfried Schadow, the sculptor of the Quadriga atop the Brandenburg Gate, had carved the grave marker. Coffins and marker were moved to the family mausoleum in the Radziwill Palace Mysliwski in Antonin (now Poland, 80 km northeast of Wroclaw, formerly Breslau).

The Reich wasted no time renovating the palais according to the wishes of its new tenant. The architect was Georg Joachim Wilhelm Neumann, who also built the Reich Finance Office and Reich Justice Office. Bismarck took a particular interest in the park, which he wanted to have a wild appearance. Thick shrubs were planted to shut out the neighbors. Bismarck wished to create the illusion of a refreshing piece of wilderness, away from the stresses of the big city.

Removal of the Radziwill coat of arms and inscription *Hotel de Radziwill* from the gable required the assent of the Kaiser. The Reich eagle with the Kaiser's coat of arms replaced them.

The chancellor and his officials had their offices on the ground floor. The chancellor's residence was on the second floor, and was separated from the official rooms and offices. One room of Bismarck's apartment had a bathtub, a rarity for the time. (When Kaiser Wilhelm I wanted a bath, he had a tub brought to his palace from a nearby hotel.) See appendix D for a detailed description of the interior renovations.

In 1878 the remodeling of the Reichskanzlerpalais was completed. The work had cost 892,000 marks. During the first formal reception in March 1878, Bismarck is said to have remarked that he liked his old quarters in the Presidential Palace better.

The official event inaugurating the Reichskanzlerpalais was the Congress of Berlin, June 15 to July 13, 1878, which was held in the enormous second floor ballroom. To this international gathering came representatives of the major European powers to resolve a conflict over the Balkans. The impetus for the congress was the Treaty of San Stefano, March 1878, by which Russia, after its victory over Turkey, had expanded its influence in the Balkans. Great Britain and Austria-Hungary felt threatened.

Bismarck was chairman of the conference. He was not eager to play mediator, but accepted the job when acclaimed an "honest broker."

On July 13, 1878, the feuding powers signed the Treaty of Berlin, which only served to perpetuate international tensions. Bismarck characterized the agreement as "holding open the Oriental sore." Russia was forced to accept a reduction of its Balkan influence. The rivalry between Russia and Austria-Hungary grew, while the people of the Balkans yearned for independence. The yearning reached a crescendo on June 28, 1914, when a Bosnian Serb terrorist, Gavrilo Princip, assassinated Austrian Archduke Ferdinand in Sarajevo, igniting World War I. Historian A.J.P. Taylor described Princip, a dreamy poet and spasmodic nationalist, as a character out of Chekhov who unfortunately knew how to shoot.[6]

View of Reichskanzlerpalais park from Bismarck's office window.

The Congress of Berlin, 1878. The delegates met in the second floor ballroom of the Reichskanzlerpalais. The Congress of Berlin put Wilhelmstraße on the map. Henceforward the Reich Chancellery was a force to be reckoned with. Until 1945 the former Radziwill Palais was the residence of the chancellors of Germany (painting by Anton von Werner, Deutsches Historisches Museum).

After the death of Wilhelm I, his son Friedrich III ruled for 99 days before dying of laryngeal cancer. In 1888, Wilhelm II succeeded him. Wilhelm was a man totally unsuited to rule a major industrial state. He believed his power came from Heaven and God inspired his decisions. "From Friedrich I he inherited a love of display, vanity, and an autocratic nature," wrote Bismarck, "from Friedrich Wilhelm I a taste for tall fellows; from Frederick the Great only the love of interfering in his officials' business; from Friedrich Wilhelm II a mystic turn and a strong sexual impulse, from Friedrich Wilhelm IV the compulsion to talk too much." Though outwardly bellicose, Wilhelm II feared war. Historians consider him a major cause of World War I.

On March 19, 1890, foreign ambassadors and many of Bismarck's colleagues came to the Lehrter Station to say goodbye. Bismarck described his departure as "a first-class funeral." Wilhelm II had fired his grandfather's chancellor, and replaced him with a series of much weaker men.

See Appendix F for noteworthy meetings in the Reichskanzlerpalais before World War I.

The Chancellery Annex

Kaiser Wilhelm II

In 1913, discussions had begun about the need for an

Bismarck leaves Berlin after Wilhelm II cashiered him.

extension of the Reichskanzlerpalais. The original plans called for the extension to be completed in 1915, and the money for the project was set aside. The new building was in the planning stages when World War I broke out and sidelined civilian construction. After the German defeat, political changes made a larger chancellery an acute necessity. Wilhelm II abdicated and fled to Holland, November 10, 1918. Germany was abruptly transformed from a monarchy to a democracy. With no Kaiser, the Reich Chancellery became the seat

Germany signs the peace treaty ending World War I, June 28, 1919. Hermann Müller and Dr. Johannes Bell sign for Germany in the Hall of Mirrors at Versailles. President Woodrow Wilson, British Prime Minister Lloyd George, and French President Georges Clemenceau look on. The vindictive, punitive, humiliating treaty, "a sad story of complicated idiocy," in Winston Churchill's words, made possible the rise of Adolf Hitler (painting by William Orpen, AKG Images).

of government.

The officials required more office space. First to be sacrificed were the chancellor's apartments in the south wing of the Chancellery, which became offices. See Appendix E for a description of the renovations.

The bureaucrats were now spread through both floors and the attic rooms of the Reichskanzlerpalais. The office of the chancellor with its outer office was in the north wing on the second floor. Some of the offices of the chancellery director were in the main building, some on the first floor of the south wing. The delegates' rooms in the south wing of the building were isolated and could only be reached via the massive staircase. The willy-nilly dispersal of offices in the huge building impaired the efficient functioning of the government. The rooms on the first floor were underused, while the second floor rooms were always crowded. These circumstances prompted Chancellery officials to proceed with the building of an annex (*Erweiterungsbau*). The only possible location was on the adjacent lot, formerly the Palais Marschall, Wilhelmstraße 78a, between the Reichskanzlerpalais, Wilhelmstraße 77, and the Borsig Palais at the corner of Wilhelmstraße and Voß Straße.

Wilhelmstraße 78 was a corner lot, divided into sections, also called Voß Straße 1/2, and Wilhelmstraße 78a. In the eighteenth century a single building, the Palais Marschall, occupied the entire property. After this structure was razed in 1870, Prince of Pleß Hans Heinrich XI, Count of Hochberg-Fürstenstein, had a new palais built at Wilhelmstraße 78a. A French architect, Hippolyte Destailleur, designed the building to resemble a French chateau. Because of the many chimneys, Berliners called Pleß's Palais the "chimney sweep academy." Pleß was a friend of Kaiser Wilhelm II, who spent much of World War I at Pleß's castle in Upper Silesia, far from the western front, where German soldiers were being slaugh-

Palais Marschall, Wilhelmstraße 78. The Palais Marschall was designed by the architect Philipp Gerlach and built in 1736. Samuel von Marschall (1685–1749), state and war minister, was of bourgeois origin. Friedrich Wilhelm I ennobled him and presented him with Wilhelmstraße 78 because in the early years of his rule the king relied on him extensively. Marschall was also a trusted advisor of Frederick the Great. The large size of the Wilhelmstraße 78 lot was in direct relationship to Marschall's influence. In 1800 state minister Karl Friedrich von Voß acquired the palais, and in 1820 willed it to his son, Count Karl Otto Friedrich von Voß. In 1870 Voß's heirs sold the palais to the Berlin Bank Union, which razed it. A new street, Voß Straße, was built through the garden. The remainder of the lot was divided into two lots, Wilhelmstraße 78a and Voß Straße 1/2.

The Pleß Palais, Wilhelmstraße 78a. In 1909 the Union Bank Society bought the property, and razed the Pleß Palais in 1913. The German government bought the lot the same year.

tered.

Just before World War I, a building was erected at Wilhelmstraße 78a that served as a press office for the Chancellery and a residence for the state secretary of the Reich Colonial Office. After the war, the Versailles Treaty stripped Germany of its colonies. The Colonial Office became superfluous.

In summer 1927, the Chancellery announced a competition for the Annex design. One hundred twenty-eight architects submitted plans. In 1928 the winners were declared. Three architects were given second prizes of 5,000 marks, and four got third prizes. The first prizewinner was Berlin architect Professor Eduard Jobst Siedler of the Berlin Institute of Technology. In the presence of Reich President Paul von Hindenburg, May 18, 1928, the cornerstone for Siedler's Annex was laid. This date was chosen because it was 50 years to the day since the Reich Chancellery had been established. Hindenburg whacked the cornerstone with a hammer and solemnly intoned, "always and in all things, the Fatherland first."

(Siedler complained to the finance ministry that he had been underpaid for his work on the Chancellery Annex and a considerable correspondence ensued. In the end he never received more money.[7]

The annex, completed in 1930, provoked controversy in political circles because its starkly modern façade was in jarring contrast to its 18th century neighbors. In fact, Siedler was making a political statement. The Reichskanzlerpalais was closely associated with the first Reich Chancellor, Otto von Bismarck, and a potent symbol of the German Empire. The starkly modern annex signaled a clear break with the old Reich and the emergence of the Weimar Republic.

The ground floor of Siedler's new annex had a large hall behind its main entrance. There was an apartment for the concierge, a room for the telephone switchboard, offices for criminal officials, diplomats, and the inspector general. A waiting room and corridors led to the staircases.

The second floor of the annex was level with the Reichskanzlerpalais. In the front were the offices of the Reich Chancellor and state secretary, as well as waiting rooms and antechambers. In the rear of the building was the cabinet room with an antechamber and a hall for the deputies. The ornate Red Room was directly in front of meeting rooms for the state representatives, with access to the rooms in front and the main

Eduard Jobst Siedler (Ullstein Bilderdienst).

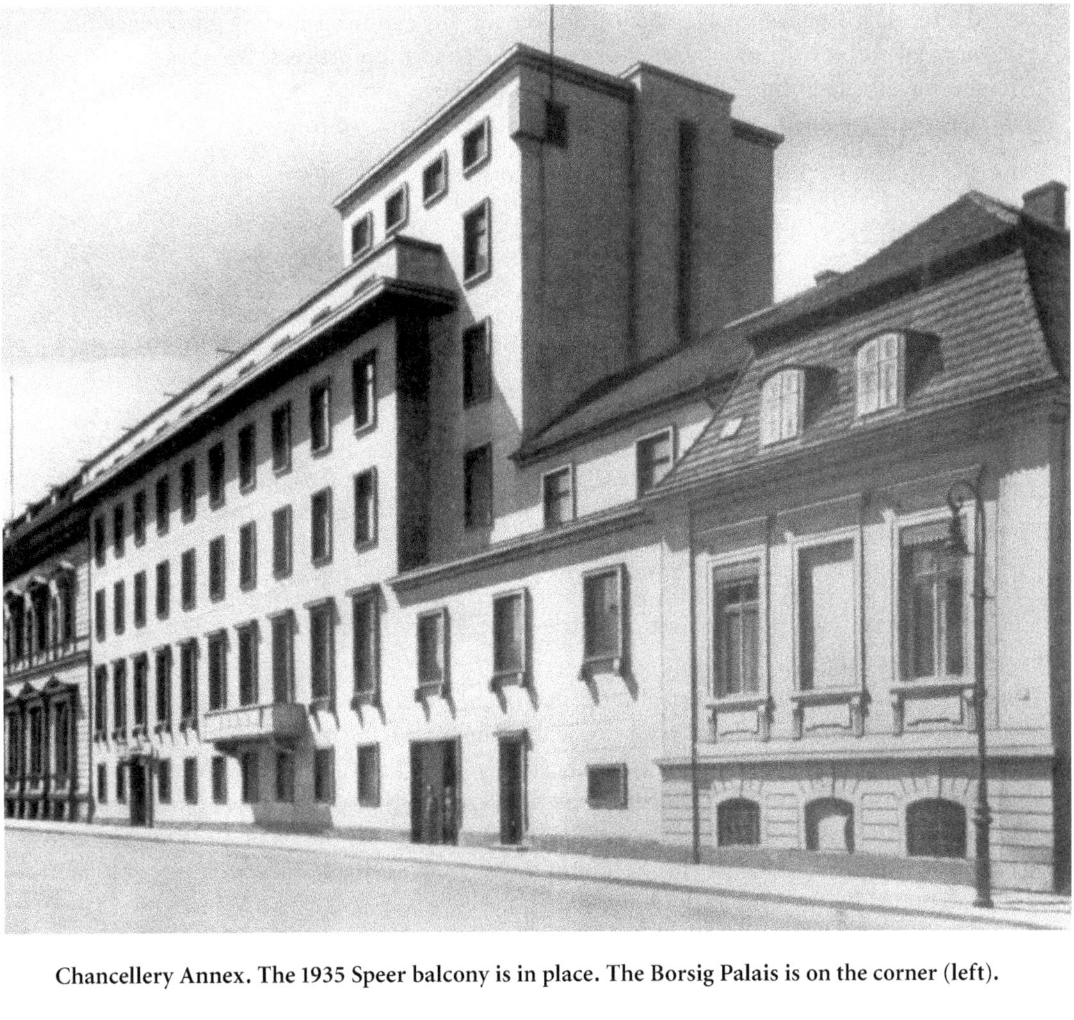

Chancellery Annex. The 1935 Speer balcony is in place. The Borsig Palais is on the corner (left).

stairs. A staircase led from the Red Room to the park. The arrangement of rooms allowed for the accommodation of very large gatherings.

On the third floor of the annex were assorted offices of the Reich Chancellery. Above the Red Room and the state representatives' room was a library and file room.

The fourth floor held the 10-room apartment of the state secretary and the six-room apartment of the office manager. Three of the office manager's rooms were on the floor above and connected to the three lower rooms by a plank stairway. The two apartments had roof gardens. The annex was built of heavy brick, with a façade of travertine marble. The window frames were also travertine. The interior was tastefully appointed with fine wood and stone.

Hermann Pünder

Hermann Pünder, state secretary in the Reich Chancellery from 1926 to 1932, was the official most responsible for building the annex, due to his relatively long tenure in office. During this time, three chancellors came and went. Pünder's influence increased further because between 1930 and 1932, Chancellor Heinrich Brüning and his cabinet ruled by emergency decree. Parliament was for the most part shut out of the governing process. Because the state secretary was in effect the managing director of the government, Pünder had extraordinary power, paving the way for the authoritarian state that was to follow.

The Bismarck Museum

The freeing-up of space in the Reichskanzlerpalais suggested to Pünder that a Bismarck Museum could be placed in Bismarck's former offices. On March 21, 1930, the *Kölnische Volkszeitung* reported:

> It [the Bismarck museum] will be opened in Bismarck's former ground floor offices to celebrate the completion of the new Chancellery Annex. Three rooms will be used:
> 1. The pre-salon, in which Bismarck, as Prussian Minister-President, held his state ministerial meetings
> 2. Bismarck's office
> 3. The garden room at the rear, where Bismarck went to relax or converse privately
>
> The rooms will be arranged to appear exactly as they did when Bismarck was Chancellor.

The Bismarck Museum was not opened immediately, and after 1933 the idea was permanently shelved. The official reason was that the former Bismarck rooms were necessary for other purposes. In fact, the new chancellor, Adolf Hitler, did not want a shrine in the middle of his home and office for the man who created the Imperial German Empire, and whom most Germans regarded as the greatest German statesman of all time. Franz von Lenbach's Bismarck portrait and Reinhold Begas' bust of Bismarck were quite sufficient.

Rebuffed by the Chancellery, Pünder inquired whether Berlin's Märkisches Museum might want the Bismarck objects for a memorial. On November 9, 1935, Walter Stengel, the museum director, politely rejected the request on account of a shortage of rooms and the size of Bismarck's furniture. But, Stengel added helpfully, "I suggest you consider placing the objects in the Evangelisches Gymnasium zum Grauen Kloster, in Klosterstraße, where Bismarck was a [high school] student. I think the school director and the mayor would be very receptive to this idea."

On November 26, 1935, the office manager of the Chancellery wrote an extremely polite letter of protest to Berlin's Mayor, Dr. Heinrich Sahm, which began:

> We have expressed our desire to place a little Bismarck Museum in the Reichskanzlerpalais, using Bismarck articles still in the Reich Chancellery, which were in Bismarck's offices during his tenure. We were never able to do this because the building has become home and office for our Führer and Reich Chancellor.

The letter had two attachments, with a detailed list of Bismarck objects. Sahm replied on December 3, 1935, that he was pleased "that the capital, Berlin, had been chosen as the home for the Bismarck objects, which are on loan. Herr Director Stengel has been able to secure a room in the Märkisches Museum for exhibiting them." Bismarck's furniture remains in the Märkisches Museum.

Erich Salomon Visits the Chancellery

Erich Salomon was an erudite photographer of diplomats and heads of state in the first half of the twentieth century. Now we are accustomed to seeing such images whenever statesmen meet, but at the time, before anyone had heard the words "photo opportunity," pictures like Salomon's were astounding. Other photojournalists, such as Margaret Bourke White, are today better known, but magazines and newspapers in the 1920s and 1930s covered Salomon's short, tragic career with profound respect. His photographs appeared in illustrated newspapers in Berlin and Munich, in England in *The Graphic* and *Daily Telegraph*, and in the United States in *Life* and the *New York Times*.

Salomon visited the Reich Chancellery July 27, 1931, to photograph a dinner Reich Chancellor Heinrich Brüning organized for British Prime Minister Ramsay MacDonald. At a banquet for Brüning in London, MacDonald had heaped honor on his guest by placing George Bernard Shaw beside him at table. Brüning, when he entertained the British leader in Berlin, returned the compliment with interest by giving him for dinner companions the illustrious scientists Albert Einstein and Max Planck. Salomon's photograph shows MacDonald and Einstein in eager talk, Planck listening. MacDonald is speaking with hand spread wide in an eloquent gesture. Salomon was too far away from the table to catch any words. Later he asked MacDonald what he had been expounding so earnestly to Einstein. "I don't just remember," said MacDonald, "but I presume I was telling him all that I don't understand about relativity."

Erich Salomon was born in Berlin, April 28, 1886. His early interests were divided between carpentry and zoology. Later, he took a doctorate in law from the University of Munich but practiced only briefly. His career as a free-lance photographer began in 1928, when he bought one of the first miniature cameras, an Ermanox, equipped with a high-speed lens that enabled him to photograph in dim light. He concealed his camera and secretly made photographs of a sensational murder trial. These sold so well that he became a professional photojournalist. Salomon, dressed impeccably in evening attire, could walk

Above: In the Reich Chancellery, July 27, 1931. Visible faces, left to right: Max Planck, British prime minister Ramsay MacDonald, Albert Einstein, Hermann Schmitz (Ullstein Bilderdienst).

Left: Erich Salomon, 1930. Salomon is in working attire and holds his Ermanox camera. The Nazis murdered Erich Salomon July 7, 1944, along with his wife and youngest son, at Auschwitz (Ullstein Bilderdienst).

in unannounced to highly exclusive gatherings. He had such an uncanny ability to get around restrictions that Aristide Briand, a premier of France, called him the king of indiscretion. Salomon's presence at state functions eventually became customary, and Briand later stated that nobody would believe a meeting was important unless Salomon photographed it. Among Salomon's subjects were some of the most important and influential men of his day (women seldom appear) — France's Briand and Pierre Laval, England's MacDonald and Anthony Eden, America's Herbert Hoover and William Randolph Hearst, and Italy's

Benito Mussolini. Salomon took pictures of these men at conferences and meetings convened to decide the fate of the world. At the time, Salomon's audience could well believe that it was seeing the future being decided by earnest leaders. Today, the high seriousness of Salomon's diplomats seems ironic, since we know that their efforts for peace ended in war, just as Salomon's charmed life ended during the Holocaust. When Hitler came to power, Salomon moved to Holland. During World War II Salomon and his family went into hiding, but a Dutch Nazi betrayed them. In May 1944 they were deported to Auschwitz. The Nazis murdered Erich Salomon July 7, 1944, along with his wife and youngest son. The oldest son, Peter Hunter (né Salomon) escaped to England. After the war he was able to retrieve many of his father's negatives, some of which had been buried in a chicken yard.

II. Hitler in the Chancellery

Hitler Named Reich Chancellor

Just after noon, January 30, 1933, the members of Hitler's cabinet marched into the Reich president's rooms in the Reichskanzlerpalais (the Reich Presidential Palace, Wilhelmstraße 73, was being renovated). The aged president, Paul von Hindenburg, annoyed at being kept waiting, made a brief welcoming speech, expressing satisfaction that the nationalist Right had finally come together. Former Chancellor Franz von Papen then made the formal introductions. Hindenburg nodded his approval as Hitler solemnly swore to carry out his duties without party interests and for the good of the whole nation. Hindenburg again approvingly acknowledged the sentiments expressed by the new Reich Chancellor after Hitler unexpectedly made a short speech emphasizing his efforts to uphold the constitution, respect the rights of the president, and, after the next election, to return to normal parliamentary rule. Hitler and his ministers awaited a reply from the Reich president, which was brief.

"And now, gentlemen, forward with God," said Hindenburg.

"Hitler is Reich Chancellor. Just like a fairy-tale," noted Goebbels in his diary. As Ian Kershaw wrote, the extraordinary had happened. What few beyond the ranks of Nazi fanatics had thought possible less than a year earlier had become reality. Against all odds, Hitler's aggressive stubbornness, born out of lack of alternatives, had produced results. The vagrant from Vienna, obscure World War I corporal, beer hall demagogue, leader of what was for years no more than a party on the lunatic fringe of politics, was now the head of a government of one of the major states in Europe. Yet Hitler was a man with no credentials for running a sophisticated state-machine. His sole qualification was the ability to muster the support of the nationalist masses, whose base instincts he showed an unusual talent for rousing. And the future Führer had not kept his intentions secret. Heads would roll, he had said. Marxism would be eradicated. Jews would be removed. A world catastrophe had begun.

On the night of January 30, 1933, a torchlight parade of Hitler's legions, the SS, SA, and steel helmets, marched from Charlottenburger Chaussée, through the Brandenburg Gate, past the French, American, British, and Soviet embassies, to Wilhelmstraße 77/78. Only victorious soldiers at the end of a war had ever before staged such a march. The new chancellor wanted to trumpet not only a regime change, but the emergence of a new power in the land. "There was a longing in Europe for Fascism before the name was ever invented," says historian Fritz Stern, "for a new authoritarianism with some kind of religious orientation and above all a greater communal belongingness."[1] Hitler saw himself as "the instrument of providence" and fused his "racial dogma with a Germanic Christianity. Some

Chancellor Hitler asks the Nationalist members of his cabinet to join him for a photograph, January 30, 1933. With Hitler are his Nazi appointees, Prussian Prime Minister Hermann Göring and Wilhelm Frick, Minister of the Interior.

people recognized the moral perils of mixing religion and politics, but many more were seduced by it."

Before becoming chancellor, Hitler and his *alte Kämpfer* had occupied the Hotel Kaiserhof on Ziethenplatz, across the street from the Reich Chancellery. Now the Nazis moved in. "Wilhelmstraße has become ripe," wrote Joseph Goebbels in his diary, and published a book, *From Kaiserhof to Reich Chancellery*, in which he declared war on democracy and the workers' movement. When Goebbels relocated his propaganda ministry to the former Ordenspalais, Wilhelmplatz 8/9, directly across Wilhelmstraße from the Chancellery, the building had been the government press office. On March 12, 1933, Goebbels began literally cleaning house.

> The civil servants made many difficulties with renovation and furnishing, even my own office. I finally took matters in hand. With some construction workers from the SA, during the night I threw out old plaster and wood coverings. Ancient newspapers and files vegetating on the shelves forever suddenly went rumbling down the stairs like thunder. Only dark clouds of dust remained of the bureaucratic splendor.

Sounding like a revolutionary, Goebbels heralded a new beginning: "We are going to rebuild this city. We are eager to give it a German face." The "German face" appeared on Wilhelmstraße in the form of banners. Before 1933, the only flags and banners in evidence were the service flags and standards on government buildings when the occupant was in residence. For example, when Kaiser Wilhelm II was in the nearby city palace, Berliners

Germans acclaim Hitler, January 30, 1933. After being named Chancellor, Hitler shows himself to jubilant crowds from a window of the Chancellery Annex, Wilhelmstraße 78.

would say, "*Hängt der Lappen raus, ist der Kerl im Haus.*" (If the rag is hanging out, the fellow's in the house.)

With the arrival of Hitler came swastika banners everywhere. They choked the street, oceans of them, long bolts of cloth that covered the baroque facades of the dignified old buildings. With very little renovation, Hitler had given Wilhelmstraße an entirely new appearance.

But even the plethora of new swastikas did not make Berlin an agreeable place for Hitler. The city's liberal traditions, workers' movement, taste for expressionist art, and sobriety annoyed him. He said many times that he wanted to be in Berlin only during the week. His weekends he would spend in Bavaria. As the war progressed, he spent even less time in the capital and more in his isolated Berchtesgaden aerie, the Obersalzberg.

After Hindenburg's death, August 2, 1934, Hitler took over the office of Reich president. Now he called himself Führer and Reich Chancellor. He needed a new organ of government. The Reich Chancellery, Presidential Chancellery, and Party Chancellery were not enough. He established the new organ, the Private Führer Chancellery, at Wilhelmstraße 55.

Hitler's First Chancellery Renovations

In the autumn of 1933 Hitler commissioned his Munich architect, Paul Ludwig Troost, to renovate the Chancellery. Troost had designed the fittings for the ocean liner *Europa*,

Wilhelmstraße (Walter Frentz)

and during World War I constructed officers' messes and common rooms on German warships. After the war, Troost rebuilt the Brown House, the Nazi Party office in Munich.

Hitler gushed over Troost's work. Hermann Göring had picked out the former official residence of the Prussian minister president on Leipziger Platz for himself, and had elaborately renovated it. When Hitler came to see the place, he sneered, "Dark! How can anyone live in such darkness? Compare this with my Professor's work. Everything bright, clear, and simple."[2]

Göring immediately repudiated the design. He commandeered architect Albert Speer to revamp it, although, Speer wrote, he probably felt comfortable in it, since it corresponded to his disposition. Speer, the son and grandson of architects, was 28 when he met Hitler. Speer had drawn up plans for the first party rally in Nuremberg, and visited Hitler in his Munich apartment on Prinzregentenplatz to go over them.

Paul Ludwig Troost brought his building supervisor from Munich to accomplish the Chancellery renovations. But the supervisor was not familiar with Berlin construction firms or building processes. Hitler assigned Speer to the job. Hitler, Speer, and the building supervisor inspected the chancellor's residence. The necessary work appeared formidable, as Hitler wrote in 1939:

> After the 1918 Revolution the building gradually began to decay. Large parts of the roof timbers were rotted and the attics were completely dilapidated.... Since my predecessors in general could count upon a term of office of only three to five months, they saw no reason to remove the filth of those who had occupied the house before them nor to see to it that those who came after would have better conditions than they themselves. They had no prestige to maintain toward foreign countries since these in any case took little notice of them. As a result

II. Hitler Named Reich Chancellor

Hitler in the Congress Hall of the Reichskanzlerpalais. The Führer receives the diplomats on New Year's Day, 1934.

the building was in a state of utter neglect. Ceilings and floors were moldy, wallpaper and floors rotting, the whole place filled with an almost unbearable smell.

And the drains were plugged. On July 3, 1935, Colonel Josef Beck, Polish foreign minister, arrived in Berlin for a two-day visit. There had been heavy rains, and the entire ground floor of the Reichskanzlerpalais was flooded.[3] (Four years later Beck experienced another German inundation, this time of Wehrmacht troops that overran Poland. Beck fled to Rumania, where he was interned. He died in 1944.)

Like Hitler, Albert Speer found the condition of the Chancellery deplorable. The kitchen had little light and was equipped with antique stoves. There was only one bathroom for everyone, and its fixtures dated from the turn of the century. There were many examples of poor taste: doors painted to imitate natural wood and marble urns for flowers that were actually only marbleized sheet-metal basins. Hitler exclaimed triumphantly: "Here you see the whole corruption of the old Republic. One can't even show the Chancellor's residence to a foreigner. I would be embarrassed to receive a single visitor here." During the inspection, which lasted three hours, Hitler, Speer, and the supervisor went into the attic. The janitor explained:

"And this is the door that leads to the next building."
"What do you mean?"

Opposite: Hitler's office in the Reich Chancellery, renovated by Paul Ludwig Troost.

Hitler and Colonel Joseph Beck, Reich Chancellery, July 3, 1935.

"There's a passage running through the attics of all the ministries as far as the Hotel Adlon."
"Why?"
"During the riots at the beginning of the Weimar Republic it turned out that the rioters could besiege the residence and cut the Chancellor off from the outside world. The passage was created so that in an emergency he could clear out."

Hitler opened the door. Sure enough, wrote Speer, they could walk into the adjacent foreign office. "Have the door walled up," Hitler said. "We don't need anything like that."

After the work had begun, Hitler came to the site at noon almost every day, followed by an adjutant. He studied the progress and enjoyed seeing the rooms as they came into being.

The former chancellor's office, on the second floor of the Reichskanzlerpalais, had three windows that overlooked the Wilhelmplatz. Hitler didn't like the room.

"Much too small," Hitler told Speer. "Six hundred fifty square feet. It might do for one of my assistants. Where would I sit with a state visitor? In this little corner here? And this desk is just about the right size for my office manager."

Worse, a crowd often gathered below the windows, chanting for their Führer. The noise interfered with Hitler's concentration. Hitler ordered Speer to renovate a hall overlooking the garden as a private Führer office. He continued to use this office even after the New Reich Chancellery was completed in 1939.

Speer had already accompanied Hitler 20 or 30 times around the building site when one day the Führer said to him, in the course of a tour: "Will you come to dinner with me today?"

But plaster had fallen on Speer from the scaffolding.

"I must have looked at my stained jacket with a rueful expression, for Hitler commented: 'Just come along; we'll fix that upstairs.'"

In Hitler's apartment the guests were already waiting, among them Goebbels, who looked quite surprised to see Speer, the formerly lowly young architect. Hitler took Speer into his private rooms and sent his valet off for the Führer's own dark-blue jacket.

"There, wear that for the while," said Hitler.

"So I entered the dining room behind Hitler and sat at his side, favored above all the other guests," Speer wrote. "Evidently he had taken a liking to me. Goebbels noticed something that had entirely escaped me in my excitement. 'Why, you're wearing the Führer's badge. That isn't your jacket, then?'"

Although Hitler's jacket did not differ from ordinary civilian jackets, he was the only party member to wear a gold "badge of sovereignty," an eagle with a swastika in its talons. Everyone else wore the round party badge. Hitler spared Speer the reply to Goebbels' rude inquiry: "No, it's mine," said the Führer.

Borsig Palais

Hitler wanted more *Lebensraum* ("living space"). He found it in the Borsig Palais at Voß Straße 1. On the corner of Wilhelmstraße and Voß Straße, adjacent to the Pleß Palais, the locomotive manufacturer August Borsig built a neo-renaissance palais, designed by the

The Borsig Palais, Voß Strasse 1, designed by Richard Lucae. The statues in the niches were of Archimedes, Leonardo da Vinci, James Watt, and other scientists and inventors.

architect Richard Lucae, 1875–77. But the Borsig family never occupied the Borsig Palais. Borsig, a self-made man, had a profound disdain for his next-door neighbor, Prince Pleß, whom he considered an effete aristocrat. The prince reacted in a highly vengeful manner. He built his stable adjacent to Borsig's ballroom. August Borsig died in 1878. Some people thought the stink from Pleß's stable had killed him.

In 1903, the Borsig family sold the Borsig Palais to Wertheim's Department Store, directly across the street. A year later, Wertheim sold the property to the Prussian Mortgage Bank. In 1933, the bank rented the building to the German Reich, and on March 23, 1934, the Reich bought the building. The German vice chancellor, Franz von Papen, moved in, followed by Fritz Todt, the engineer who designed the Autobahn. Hitler then relocated the leadership of the SA, his brownshirt army, from Munich to the Borsig Palais, where he could keep a closer eye on men, some of whom he ordered murdered during the Night of the Long Knives, June 29, 1934. Herbert von Bose, Papen's assistant, was shot in one of the Borsig Palais rooms. Albert Speer, responsible for the building's interior reconstruction, noticed a large pool of Bose's dried blood on the floor.

Hitler may have liked Speer's renovation work on the Borsig Palais, but the building office, the *Reichsbaudirektion*, thought Speer wasteful. On August 22, 1934, a *Reichsbaudirektion* auditor wrote to the Finance Ministry:

> The cost estimates Private Architect Herr Dipl. Engineer Speer prepared in April are so full of holes that no evaluation is possible.[4] There are no clarifications and no grand total. But a few observations can be made:
>
> In column 1, the lumped wall, room, marble, and parquet work, including the removal of debris, could have been done for 12% less. The work was carried out in three shifts, and so payments for overtime and night hours could not be estimated, only the additional costs for work on Sunday, which was included in the totals.
>
> In columns 2–13, the work described could also have been done for less. Again, this work was done in three shifts.

The Annex Balcony

After the work on the Borsig Palais was completed, Hitler commissioned Speer to add a new "historic" balcony to the Chancellery Annex. The construction had to be completed quickly. Hitler wanted to be able to show himself to the crowd. "The window was really too inconvenient," Hitler remarked to Speer. "I could not be seen from all sides. After all, I could not very well lean out."

There was a Prussian precedent for an "historic" window. In the palace of Kaiser Wilhelm I on Unter den Linden, the Kaiser would appear at one window shortly before noon to show himself to his people during the changing of the guard. A new "historic" chancellery window would remind the public of this event, and of the "rebirth" of Germany. A balcony would permit the Führer to present himself in an appropriate pose to the masses streaming into Wilhelmstraße to venerate him, augmenting the effect of the window and displaying the new power of the state.

But how high should the balcony be? How near should the masses be allowed to approach their Führer? On the one hand, Hitler wanted people on the edge of Wilhelmplatz to be able to see him. But on the other, he did not want to be so close to the crowds that he might become familiar and boring. Speer consulted both ancient and modern sources for guidance.

Hitler "practices" displaying himself to a crowd from a balcony of the Presidential Palace. This photograph shows how totally unsuited the reserved, dignified Prussian architecture of Wilhelmstraße was for ostentatious display of power. Hitler looks like a minor visiting diplomat being shown the building and its surroundings.

The architect of the annex, Professor Eduard Jobst Siedler, was upset about the balcony. It constituted "violence" to his work. Hans Heinrich Lammers, chief of the Reich Chancellery, agreed that Speer's balcony was an infringement of an artist's copyright. Hitler pooh-poohed this carping: "Siedler has spoiled the whole of Wilhelmplatz. Why, that building looks like the headquarters of a soap company, not the center of the Reich. What does he think? That I'll let him build the balcony too?" But Hitler appeased the professor with another commission.

Speer finished the annex balcony in summer 1935. It had cost 25,360 reichsmarks, but was worth every pfennig. The structure was a resounding hit. Images of Hitler on the balcony, in his "victor pose," became familiar around the world, the Führer in all his glory with the masses at his feet. According to the *New York Times*, the first large gathering Hitler addressed from the balcony was 15,000 railway men dressed in blue uniforms.[5] The occasion, February 4, 1937, was the return of the railways to the Reich after 16 years under a separate government-controlled company, which paid reparations to the wartime Allies. The Reich Railways' revenues had been garnished for reparation purposes because they afforded one of the few stable sources of income that the Allies could seize.

Hitler gave his stiff-arm salute and was greeted by a loud chorus of "Heils." The new minister of transportation, Dr. Julius Dorpmüller, accompanied him. The Führer announced that the Reich Railways had once again been placed wholly under Reich sovereignty and that he was proud to have been able to free Germany from the shackles of the Versailles Treaty. Then he thanked the railway workers for their cooperation in the work of operating the railways.

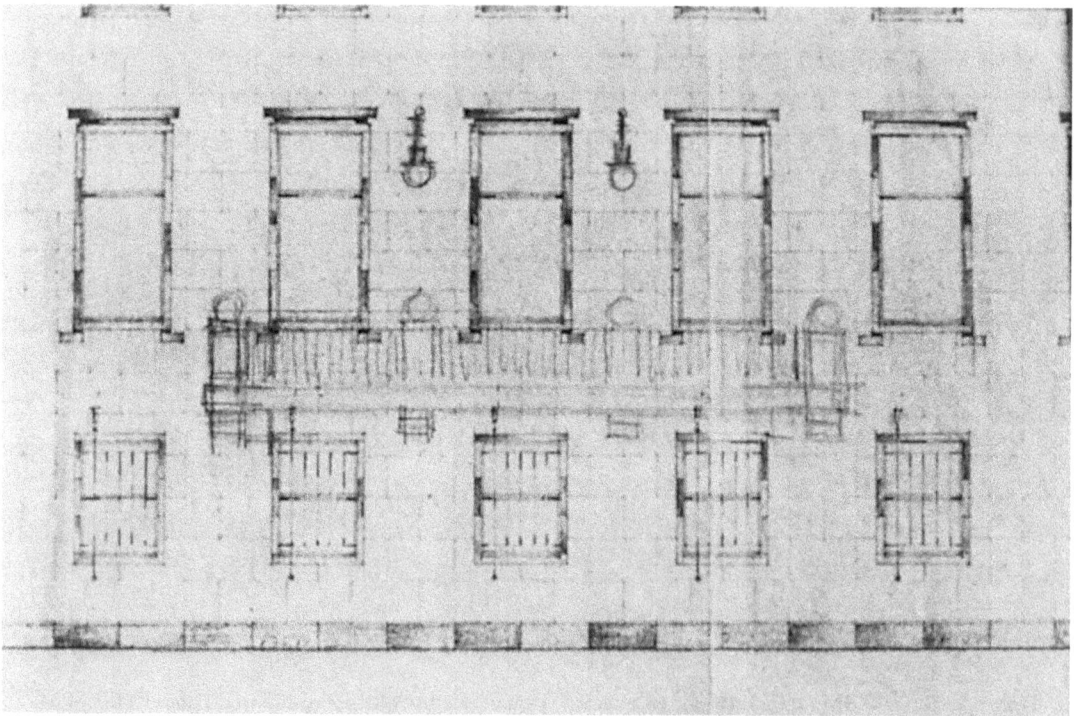

Hitler's pencil sketch of the Chancellery Annex balcony, 1935. The balcony is situated in front of the former office of the Reich Chancellor.

Hitler accepts adulation from a crowd on the Speer Balcony of the Chancellery Annex after the annexation of Austria, March 16, 1938. Hitler looks like the all-powerful Führer he wanted to portray. Hermann Göring stands beside him.

Just over a year later, after the annexation of Austria on March 16, 1938, Hitler spoke again from the same balcony, proclaiming: "You can imagine how I feel. I am so happy that fate has chosen me to unite the German people. I am happy to see how happy the German nation is in all its regions, including that which until a few days ago was the unhappiest of all and that today is the most joyful. Our new unity will never be destroyed." As Hitler spoke, the Gestapo was hunting down and imprisoning Austrian Jews, many of whom were desperately trying to flee.

Reichskanzlerpalais Events 1933–39

THE NEW YORK TIMES INTERVIEWS HITLER

On July 9, 1933, *New York Times* foreign correspondent Anne O'Hare McCormick interviewed Germany's new Reich Chancellor.[6] In a male-dominated profession, McCormick's ladylike manner won her interviews with many world leaders, including Josef Stalin, Franklin D. Roosevelt, Benito Mussolini, Dwight D. Eisenhower, and Harry S Truman.

Fifteen years later, Anne O'Hare McCormick returned to visit Hitler's bombed out Berlin Chancellery.

LENI RIEFENSTAHL LUNCHES WITH HITLER

In the last week of August 1933, Leni Riefenstahl was invited to a luncheon at the Reich Chancellery. After the meal, when the company broke into groups, Wilhelm Brückner, Hitler's adjutant, approached Riefenstahl and said, "The Führer would like to speak to you." She was led to an adjacent room, empty but for a servant serving coffee, tea and mineral water. Hitler came in and greeted her, apparently in high good humor.

His very first question put Riefenstahl in a quandary. "I invited you here today in order to find out how far you've got with your preparations for the film of the party rally, and whether you're getting enough support from the Ministry of Propaganda."

Riefenstahl stared at him in amazement — what was he talking about? Surprised at her reaction, he said: "Didn't the Propaganda Ministry inform you that I want you to make a film about the party rally in Nuremberg?" Riefenstahl shook her head and Hitler was clearly perplexed. "You know nothing about it?" he asked. He summoned Brückner and angrily asked him, "Why wasn't Fräulein Riefenstahl informed?" As he spoke he clenched his fists, glaring with anger.

Riefenstahl herself was by now very agitated, and interrupted Hitler. "My Führer, I cannot accept this—I have never seen a party rally, I know nothing about what goes on there, and I have no experience in making documentaries. It would be better if such films were made by party members who know the material and are happy to be given such assignments." She talked to Hitler almost beseechingly, and slowly he relaxed and calmed down.

Looking at Riefenstahl, Hitler said, "Fräulein Riefenstahl, don't let me down." Leni Riefenstahl didn't let her Führer down. She went on to make two classic documentaries now considered triumphs of cinematic art.

Leni Riefenstahl had first seen Hitler in 1932, and wrote to him asking for a meeting. The instant she heard his voice, she tells us in her autobiography, "I had an almost apocalyptic vision that I was never able to forget. It seemed as if the earth's surface were spreading out in front of me, like a hemisphere that suddenly splits apart in the middle, spewing out an enormous jet of water, so powerful that it touched the sky and shook the earth. I felt quite paralyzed."

In fact, Hitler was a fan of hers, had seen her films, admired her as an artist and flattered her as a person. She soon became aware of what she saw as the rift in his personality: rabble rouser but modest private person and, either way, endowed with charisma. Riefenstahl's early training as a dancer, painter, and actress served her well, as she turned a bumptious Nazi rally into a breathtaking spectacle, *Triumph of the Will* (1934). Her sound cinematic instincts let her come up with a variety of shots never before used in documentaries, such as those made by cameramen on roller skates. Most ingenious were the stratagems by which she kept Propaganda Minister Joseph Goebbels out of her hair, and the minister's hands out of her pants.

Leni Riefenstahl and Hitler, Nuremberg, 1934 (Bayerische Staatsbibliothek).

Even more remarkable was her next masterwork, *Olympia* (1938), a two-part film about the 1936 Berlin Summer Olympics. The technical difficulties to be overcome, given the primitive state of film and the cantankerousness of both sports officials and Joseph Goebbels, were in the end minor obstacles. Commissioned by the German Olympic Committee, the film was intended as a documentary, but once again Riefenstahl produced an *oeuvre d'art*. *Olympia* became a worldwide hit, winning first prize in Venice. Audiences in France, Belgium, Norway and the United States applauded not only the film but also Hitler's brief appearances in it.

Hitler and his favorite filmmaker continued to meet and converse, with God and the

Messiah among their topics. But whenever Riefenstahl alluded to Hitler's racist policies, she says, he simply cut her off. Later, during the war, Hitler confided his wish to yield the reins to others after the victory. He himself wanted to make movies with Riefenstahl, a prospect that did not delight her. Her concern apparently was less political, or even ethical, than professional. She feared Hitler would be a nuisance.

Riefenstahl wrote that she lost her faith in Hitler well before war's end. When in 1942 she returned from a trip to Italy and saw Jews forced to wear the yellow star, she was, she says, "indignant and ashamed." That year, at her last meeting with Hitler, she wanted to confront him, she confesses, but "held my tongue."

After the war, Riefenstahl's association with Hitler ruined her career. Her repeated attempts to find financing for a new film always ended in failure. Public screenings of her movies and exhibitions of her photographs invariably prompted protests. As recently as 2002, she was briefly investigated in Germany on accusations of race-hatred crimes, but no charges were brought. At the end of a 1993 documentary, Ray Müller, a German filmmaker, tried to provoke her into admitting guilt for her past.

"What do you mean by that?" Riefenstahl asked, clearly surprised. "Where is my guilt? I can regret. I can regret that I made the party film, *Triumph of the Will*, in 1934. But I cannot regret that I lived in that time. No anti–Semitic word has ever crossed my lips. I was never anti–Semitic. I did not join the party. So where then is my guilt? You tell me. I have thrown no atomic bombs. I have never betrayed anyone. What am I guilty of?"

In an interview with the *New York Times* in 2002, she said: "I didn't do any harm to anyone. What have I ever done? I never intended any harm to anyone."

Hitler Meets Sir John Simon and Anthony Eden

On March 16, 1935, Hitler announced military conscription. He was rearming Germany, defying the Treaty of Versailles. The French were upset. But the British decided to go their own way. Sir John Simon, Britain's foreign secretary, and Anthony Eden, Lord Privy Seal, flew to Berlin to meet with the Führer for two days of talks. On March 24, a gray airplane flying the British flag dropped down out of a lowering gray sky over Tempelhof Air Field just before sunset, and swooped down to a perfect landing.[7] Dr. Otto Meissner, German state secretary, saluted. The British ambassador, Sir Eric Phipps, and a group of silk-hatted German Foreign Office officials, headed by Foreign Minister Constantin von Neurath, greeted Simon, Eden, and other British officials, who emerged in traveling dress. Several thousand people waited expectantly along the edges of the airfield, and a horde of photographers swarmed over the arrivals, all but eclipsing them, until the party sped off to tea at the British Embassy.

The first meeting with Hitler took place the next day in the Reich Chancellery. Hitler was confident and self-assured.[8] Paul Schmidt, meeting Hitler for the first time and acting as his interpreter, remarked on the genial atmosphere at the beginning of the talks. He had expected the raging demagogue he heard on the radio. Instead he was impressed by the skill and intelligence with which Hitler conducted the discussions.

Anthony Eden recognized a change in Hitler since the first time he had met him a year earlier. "Hitler was definitely more authoritative and less anxious to please than a year before," he recalled. "Another twelve months of a dictator's power and growing military force to back it had had its consequence." Hitler handled the talks "without hesitation and without notes, as befitted the man who knew where he wanted to go."

Not surprisingly, the German dictator dominated the proceedings. In the first morning session of almost four hours, Simon and Eden could do no more than pose the occasional question during Hitler's monologues—translated by Schmidt at 20-minute intervals—on the menace of Bolshevism. Simon, with his large brown eyes, looked at Hitler with sympathetic interest as he listened to him. Simon's face expressed a certain paternal benevolence. Perhaps he was pleasantly surprised to find, instead of the wild Nazi of British propaganda, a man who was emotional and emphatic, but not unreasonable or ill natured.

But interpreter Schmidt occasionally noticed a more skeptical expression flit over the face of Eden, who understood enough German to be able to follow Hitler more or less. Some of Eden's questions and observations showed he had considerable doubts about Hitler and what he was saying.

When Eden mentioned Lithuania as a member of a proposed Eastern Pact, projected to include Germany as another partner, Hitler became furious, his eyes blazing, his Rs rolling, his fists bunched. "He suddenly seemed to have become another person," noted Schmidt. "We will under no circumstances take part in a pact with a state that is stamping on the German minority in Memel," he screeched, referring to a trial nearing its end of Germans accused of treason.

Then, suddenly, the tantrum abated as quickly as it had flared. Hitler was once more the skilled negotiator, effectively parrying all efforts to draw Germany into multilateral agreements. When Simon criticized Germany's increase in army strength contrary to the stipulations of the Versailles Treaty, Hitler asked ironically if Wellington had inquired of lawyers in the Foreign Office, as Blücher came to his assistance at Waterloo, whether Prussian army strength was in accord with treaty agreements. This struck Eden as a witty response, the nearest Hitler came to humor.

At the end of the talks, Hitler gave a dinner for his British visitors. At a musicale afterward, the Führer and Eden began talking about World War I, in which both had fought. Hitler had been a corporal in the Sixteenth Bavarian Infantry, composed largely of volunteer students. Eden had been first a lieutenant, then a captain in the King's Royal Rifle Corps from 1915 onward. Hitler and Eden agreed that war was unpleasant to participants in all ranks and that there ought to be no more of it.

"Where were you?" asked Hitler.[9]

Eden said his regiment had been based in Ypres and had served in several nearby sectors. Hitler recalled that his regiment had held a hill south of Wervik, near Ypres. Eden and Hitler drew maps of their respective positions on a tablecloth.

"Then at one time we must have been facing each other," remarked Eden. Hitler thought it was very probable and they laughed over the idea that the corporal using a rifle and the lieutenant an automatic pistol might have taken a few potshots in the direction of one another.

On July 16, 1945, while Eden and the others in his party explored the water-soaked depths of Hitler's abandoned bunker, British Prime Minister Winston Churchill took off his hat, sat down on a battered rock in the shade, and puffed his cigar. Anthony Eden was particularly interested in the Reich Chancellery. Eden pointed to a bomb-shattered room and said, "I had dinner with Hitler right over there in 1935."

"You certainly paid for that dinner, Anthony," Churchill replied.[10]

Hitler receives Sir John Simon (left) and Anthony Eden in the Reich Chancellery, March 25, 1935. Winston Churchill later lamented "how the English-speaking peoples through their unwisdom, carelessness, and good nature allowed the wicked to rearm" (Bayerische Staatsbibliothek).

HITLER MEETS LORD LONDONDERRY

Charles Stewart Henry Vane-Tempest-Stewart, the 7th Marquess of Londonderry, was born to power and command. Scion of one of Britain's most aristocratic families, cousin of Winston Churchill and confidant of the king, owner of vast coal fields and landed estates, married to the doyenne of London's social scene, Londonderry embellished his class, the 0.1 percent of the population who still owned 30 percent of England's wealth as late as 1930. Acknowledging that he had "no great affection for Jews," Londonderry urged friendship with Hitler's Germany. He managed to make Joachim von Ribbentrop look good, snatching back the over-generous half-crown tip that the German Ambassador gave to a golf caddie and replacing it with a shilling. Wags called the pro–Nazi nobleman "The Londonderry Herr." Churchill called him a halfwit.

II. Hitler Named Reich Chancellor

In his book *Making Friends with Hitler: Lord Londonderry and Britain's Road to War*, Ian Kershaw uses the Marquess as a case study in appeasement. Londonderry's story, Kershaw writes, was "a mirror of Britain's struggle to come to grips with the problem of Hitler." It casts light on the mentalities and political structures that shaped British foreign policy during the 1930s. It is also "an elegy on the decline and fall of the British aristocracy."

Prime Minister Ramsay MacDonald damaged his reputation by making Londonderry secretary of state for air in 1931. Although the marquess did his best for the RAF by promoting Hurricanes, Spitfires and radar, he was terribly gaffe-prone and had a penchant for being on the wrong side of every argument. He was denounced as "the bomber's friend" for his defense of air raids as a means of "policing" Iraq and other parts of the empire. And he was condemned, most of all by Churchill, for being complacent about the rise of the Luftwaffe. Londonderry deplored undue alarm over the growth of German air power and was gratified by Hitler's "definite acceptance" of its limitation.

Hitler greets Lord Londonderry (left) in the Reich Chancellery, February 4, 1936, attended by Ambassador Joachim von Ribbentrop. "Very agreeable ... a kindly man, with a receding chin and an impressive face." So reported Lord Londonderry after meeting Hitler. Lady Londonderry, the society hostess, saw "a man with wonderful, far-seeing eyes ... simple, dignified, humble." Later, she wrote to the Führer: "You and Germany remind me of the Book of Genesis in the Bible" (Ullstein Bilderdienst).

After Stanley Baldwin succeeded MacDonald he dismissed Londonderry, who grumbled: "I've been sacked — kicked out — sacked." He was permanently embittered, poisoned by pique, "wounded in my heart." So he sought a cause that would assuage his unbearable humiliation and establish for all time his credentials as a statesman. The cause he chose was European peace, to be won by appeasing the Third Reich. This seemed a reasonable policy in 1935. Hitler had not only restored order, defeated unemployment, destroyed trade unions and crushed the Communist Party, but he had also convincingly presented Germany as the victim of Versailles. Appeasement was not yet a dirty word. But Churchill's judgment of the Nazis was sound, and he warned Londonderry that Hitler would "confront Europe with a series of outrageous events and ever-growing military might."

Londonderry showed good judgment only once. When the organ played "Deutschland Über Alles" during a service at Durham Cathedral and Ribbentrop sprang up to give the Heil Hitler salute, Londonderry pulled down his hand. Otherwise, driven by insatiable vanity, the marquess made every possible blunder. He described Hitler as a "kindly man" who "dreads war." He fostered the Führer's disastrous illusions about Britain. He justified Hitler's Rhineland reoccupation and annexation of Austria. He said that Chamberlain had brought "peace with honor" from Munich. He "would not venture to argue" with Göring over the Kristallnacht pogrom against the German Jews. He thought Hitler's seizure of Prague was "hardly distinguishable from war," but his comments on it in the House of Lords were favorable to Hitler.

When war broke out, Londonderry lobbied privately for a negotiated peace, along with noblemen such as the Duke of Westminster, who was supposedly anxious not to have bombs dropped on central London because he owned so much of it. Still imbued with faith in the power of patronage, Londonderry hoped for office when Churchill came to power. But by now even Londonderry was concluding that he was not a worthy heir of his ancestor Lord Castlereagh, who had represented Britain at the Congress of Vienna in 1814. When the Luftwaffe bombed Londonderry's grand London house, the marquess finally acknowledged that in the Führer, "I backed the wrong horse."

Hitler Meets Max Schmeling

On June 27, 1936, Hitler received the German boxer Max Schmeling, along with Schmeling's wife and mother, in the Reich Chancellery. Schmeling said that his winning match with African-American boxer Joe Louis was the most arduous of his career. Louis had struck Schmeling below the belt, but Schmeling gallantly insisted that the illegal blow was an accident. Louis was a superb boxer, asserted Schmeling, with a perfect eye, and never missed an opening. The 1936 bout with Louis at Yankee Stadium was not for the title, but Schmeling's victory was heard on the radio throughout Germany. The voice of the announcer, Arno Helmis, shouting, "Aus, aus, aus," to echo the referee's announcement of a knockout, is still in the memory of many Germans.

Schmeling got a special cabin on the zeppelin *Hindenburg* and returned to Berlin in triumph a week after the fight. He became "Maxe," a plainspoken national hero for Nazis and non–Nazis alike. *Angriff*, the Nazi party newspaper, saw the match as a fight for white supremacy: "Schmeling, the German, ... succeeded against world opinion. And he says he would not have had the strength if he had not known what support he had in his homeland. He was allowed to speak with the Führer and his Ministers and from that moment his will for victory was boundless."[11]

Max Schmeling and his wife, the movie actress Anny Ondra, meet Hitler in the Chancellery, 1936. Ondra was a star at the UFA studio in Germany before World War II. A noted pro–Nazi in the 1930s, she was not allowed to continue her career after the war. Schmeling remained married to Ondra for 54 years until her death in 1987. They had no children. "I had a happy marriage and a nice wife," Schmeling said in 1985. "I accomplished everything you can. What more can you want?" (Ullstein Bilderdienst).

Schmeling was born Max Siegfried Schmeling in East Prussia on Sept. 28, 1905, the son of a Hamburg sailor. He says that his simple beginnings later made him susceptible to Hitler's mystique. Schmeling began boxing professionally in 1924 and was a sensation, winning the German and European light-heavyweight championships, and then the heavyweight championships, before he was 25. In 1928, he went to the United States, the center of heavyweight boxing. On June 12, 1930, Schmeling won the heavyweight championship from Jack Sharkey, and he became the first foreigner ever to win the heavyweight title.

Before the 1938 Schmeling-Louis rematch, the pickets chanted "Nazi! Nazi!" and marched around the St. Moritz Hotel in New York. "The whole day, they went around the sidewalk," Schmeling remembered. "In the newspapers, they write Max Schmeling is taking the boxing money to buy cannons for Hitler."

"It was not true," Schmeling told *New York Times* reporter Paul Montgomery. "But what could I do about it?"

Louis was better prepared than in 1936. And the fight had taken on international importance. Schmeling says he never made the master-race comments attributed to him then. "The papers wrote bad things; they said Max Schmeling wanted to knock out the black man because Hitler wanted it," Schmeling said. But Louis walloped Schmeling.

An X-ray revealed a cracked vertebra, Schmeling said. "I was paralyzed by that punch. I was an open target. He hit me on the chin and that was it."

Schmeling's reception in Germany after the loss was cool. He went back to New York in early 1939 to talk to the promoter Max Jacobs about a third bout with Louis. They made a plan for a title bout in September 1940. "But then all of a sudden the war broke out," Schmeling said.

By one informed estimate, Schmeling made $1,600,000 in his boxing career, almost all of it in the United States from 1928 to 1938. Schmeling's manager for his American fights was Joe Jacobs, a Jew who insisted on kosher food wherever they went. Schmeling says the Nazis wanted him to get rid of Jacobs and join the Nazi Party. He refused. Schmeling enlisted in the German army as a paratrooper and was wounded in Crete in 1941. He spent much of the war on his estate in Pomerania. From time to time, he gave boxing exhibitions for the troops.

At war's end, Schmeling's property in Pomerania, now in Poland, was confiscated by the Communist regime without compensation. The British military authorities, after a hearing in 1946, cleared him of any complicity in war crimes and he was allowed to continue boxing. But Schmeling was reduced to refereeing wrestling matches, suffering a loss of status much like Louis. After a disastrous trip to the United States in 1954, when he refereed a boxing match in Milwaukee and no one came, Schmeling re-established relations with James G. Farley, who had been the New York State Athletic Commission chairman in Schmeling's prime. Farley had influence at Coca-Cola, and in 1957, Schmeling got the soft-drink company's concession for Hamburg as a co-owner. He later picked up the Black Forest area as well. Max Schmeling & Company became one of Germany's most prosperous soft-drink bottlers.

Schmeling waxed philosophical about his loss to Joe Louis in 1938. "Every defeat has its good side," Schmeling told reporter Montgomery. "A victory over Joe Louis would perhaps have made me into the toast of the Third Reich."

In his final years, Schmeling spent three to four hours a day watching television in his home in Hollenstedt. He died February 4, 2005, aged 99.

Hitler Welcomes German Athletes

To turn the 1936 Berlin Summer Olympic Games into a showcase for other German achievements, Hitler made efforts to play down his regime's notorious anti–Semitism. He allowed a few token Jews to represent the Reich, among them the fencer Helene Meyer and the hockey star Rudi Ball. Another Jew, Wolfgang Fürstner, built and organized the Olympic Village. Anti-Semitic posters along the highways, and notices barring Jews from resorts, were taken down. Julius Streicher's rabidly anti–Semitic newspaper, *Der Stürmer,* vanished from Berlin newsstands. These gestures received international publicity, and foreigners flocked to Berlin, where they were enthusiastically received.

On August 1, under a clear blue sky, Hitler led the parade into his new Olympic Stadium, the world's largest, along the Via Triumphalis. Richard Strauss conducted the orchestra in a brassy thirty-trumpet fanfare, then *Deutschland über Alles* accompanied by a chorus of 3,000, then the *Horst Wessel Lied,* and finally the Olympic Hymn, which Strauss had written specially for the occasion. The crowd of 11,000 cheered wildly as Hitler took his seat in the official stand.

The next day Hitler congratulated Hans Wölke, a German, for breaking the Olympic record for the shot put. He also congratulated three Finns for winning the 10,000-meter run, and two German women who placed first and second in the javelin throw. But he was not present to shake the hands of three American winners, among them two blacks. As a result, the president of the International Olympic Committee informed the Führer that, as guest of honor, he should congratulate all the victors or none at all.

Hitler chose the latter option, and turned his back on Jesse Owens, the magnificent black American athlete who won four gold medals. As Albert Speer recalled, "People whose antecedents came from the jungle were primitive, Hitler said with a shrug; their physiques were stronger than those of civilized whites. They represented unfair competition and hence must be excluded from future games."

Strangely, Owens later claimed that Hitler did pay him a tribute: "When I passed the Chancellor, he arose, waved his hand at me, and I waved back at him. I think the writers showed bad taste in criticizing the man of the hour in Germany."

Olympic Games 1936. Nazi poster.

Hitler attended almost every track and field event. Face contorted, he watched the German athletes with puerile enthusiasm. When the games ended on August 16, Hitler was present for the closing ceremonies, although he had no official role. There were a few isolated cries of *Sieg Heil*! Others took up the cry, and in a moment the entire Olympic Stadium reverberated with the chant, "Sieg Heil! Unser Führer, Adolf Hitler, Sieg Heil!"

The games were almost an unqualified Nazi propaganda triumph. The Germans had won the most gold medals, 33, and many visitors left Berlin impressed by the Reich and flattered by their hosts' cordiality. Leni Riefenstahl's film of the event, *Olympia*, is considered a documentary classic and is available on video today.

On August 16, 1936, the German Olympic team and the German Olympic Committee

Olympic Stadium. Hitler and the international and national Olympic committees have passed through the marathon gate and are descending the marathon steps into the stadium, as the games open, August 1936 (Bayerische Staatsbibliothek).

were Adolf Hitler's guests at a reception in the Chancellery.[12] Hitler cordially thanked his visitors for their achievements. He also discussed the problems confronting German sports in connection with the Olympics in Tokyo in 1940, subsequently cancelled because of the outbreak of war.

Sports, Hitler said, an element in the lives of nations, prevents development of "super-intellectualism." Also, sports were invaluable as a means of strengthening self-consciousness among peoples and nations.

The Nazi newspaper *Angriff* burbled,

> We can scarcely contain ourselves, for it is truly difficult to endure so much joy. If one may be permitted to speak of intoxication from joy, then every German may be said to have reeled with happiness. It was also surprising for we had not reckoned with so many gold medals and so many victories. It is an odd but familiar experience and once again we have discovered after hard struggles what reserves are contained in us.

Reviewing the games' progress, the *Angriff* concluded that although the Germans did not command a monopoly of certain sports categories, as did the Finns in running, the Japanese in swimming, and the Americans, "with their dark-skinned warriors," in running and jumping, the Germans sought to cover a wider range of sports. The result, said the Nazi organ, was the large number of silver and bronze medals the German team captured. The *Angriff* added, "The influence of [Hitler's] personality which has made itself felt in so many other forms of our national life" is also responsible for the regeneration of German

Top: Hitler welcomes Olympic victors in the Reich Chancellery garden ballroom (Ullstein Bilderdienst).
 Bottom: Hitler receives the International Olympic Committee in the Reich Chancellery, August 1, 1936. IOC President Henri Comte Baillet-Latour is speaking to Hitler. Reich Interior Minister Wilhelm Frick is behind Hitler at the far right. Further back are Reichssportführer Hans v. Tschammer und Osten and State Secretaries Walther Funk and Hans Pfundner. Also present are Berlin Police Chief Wolf Heinrich Graf v. Helldorf; Press Chief Alfred Ingemar Berndt; Oberstleutnant Werner Baron von und zu Gilsa, commandant of the Olympic Village; and Captain Wilhelm Fürstner.

sports and gymnastics, and the constant presence of the Führer at the games unquestionably served as an incentive and stimulus to many German contestants.

There was a melancholy Olympic aftermath. Because of his Jewishness, Wolfgang Fürstner was replaced at the last minute as commandant of the Olympic Village. After he attended the banquet for his successor, he shot himself.

HITLER RECEIVES SIR THOMAS BEECHAM

Hitler was a lover of music, especially the operas of Richard Wagner. On November 19, 1936, the Führer attended a performance of the London Philharmonic, conducted by Sir Thomas Beecham.[13] That afternoon, Hitler had received the British conductor in the Chancellery. The Reich was concentrating efforts on impressing the British upper classes, and Chancellery officials thought the reception of Sir Thomas would be a step in this direction. Hitler confided to Sir Thomas that his favorite opera was not Wagner's *Die Meistersinger* (as always reported by Nazi propagandists) but Franz Lehár's *Merry Widow*. Sir Thomas invited Hitler to visit him in England. "[Hitler] said that he was afraid it might

Hitler attends a performance of the London Philharmonic under Sir Thomas Beecham. Hitler is in the honor loge of the Berlin Philharmonic with (left to right, front row) Reich Interior Minister Wilhelm Frick, Joseph Goebbels, Hitler, General Field Marshal Werner von Blomberg, and Reich Traffic Minister Paul Baron von Eltz Rübenach. In the background (from left) are Hitler's doctor Karl Brandt, the Berlin Police President Wolf Heinrich Count von Helldorf, and Hitler's personal adjutants Fritz Wiedemann and Julius Schaub (Ullstein Bilderdienst).

put too much strain on our police force.... Naturally, I made no comment on that" ("Enthusiastic Amateur," *Time* magazine, April 5, 1943).

Even in the absence of British conductors, the musicale was a popular Chancellery event. One musicale, February 18, 1938, collected 1,050,000 reichsmarks from guests, who were wealthy German industrialists.[14] The money went to the Winter Help Campaign.

Hitler Receives Thomas J. Watson

Thomas J. Watson, the chairman of IBM, met with Hitler in the Chancellery on June 28, 1937. Seated in the overstuffed floral armchairs Hitler liked, the two men huddled with members of the International Chamber of Commerce over a small serving table sipping tea. Watson told the *New York Times* that the gist of his conversation with Hitler was that there would be no war because no country wanted or could afford it. Later at the Berlin opera, Hitler walked in to vast applause and Watson raised his arm halfway in a Hitler greeting before stopping himself.

Hitler awarded Watson the Merit Cross of the German Eagle with Star. Watson, since 1933, had furnished IBM's second biggest customer with punch card technology, a com-

The Berlin Opera (Städtische Opera, (1936), which Hitler and Thomas J. Watson visited after their meeting in the Reich Chancellery. When architect Heinrich Seeling designed the building in 1911–1912, it was called the Deutsches Opernhaus and had the largest stage in the world. The building was destroyed during World War II (Bundesarchiv, Bild 146-1998-015-34A/Photographer: A. Frankl/License CC-BY-SA-30).

puter precursor, that enabled the Nazis to keep track of Jews, round them up, and pack them in trains to the death camps. IBM leased Germany their machines and sold the Nazis the punch cards they needed for millions of murders. Edwin Black, the child of Polish Holocaust survivors, asserts that IBM knew full well what Hitler was doing with its technology but sacrificed all morality for the sake of corporate profit.

Hitler's Birthdays in the Chancellery

Hitler's birthday, April 20, was always a big Chancellery event. For example, on his forty-eighth birthday in 1937, gifts poured in from all over Germany. The most unusual

Hitler in the entrance of the Reichskanzlerpalais on his 50th birthday, April 20, 1939, with visiting children.

was a crated pair of giraffes from African Nazi sympathizers. The animals were immediately consigned to the Berlin zoo, reported the *New York Times*.¹⁵ Other presents, placed among heaps of flowers, filled the Chancellery's large reception room. Among them were a concert grand piano, an antique musical clock, a picture of the town of Marienburg done in amber, and a gold box with intricate scrollwork, which was the gift of the city of Berlin. Children of workers in the Ruhr district sent a carving executed in coal.

A Mysterious Intruder

A mysterious intruder made his way undetected into the offices of Hitler's secretary of the Reich Chancellery, Hans Heinrich Lammers, in November 1937, and was examining papers on the desk when he was discovered.¹⁶ The intruder walked into the Chancellery wearing the dark blue suit and black tie customary for government employees. Without arousing suspicion he went to the second floor, where Hitler and Lammers had offices. Both men were at Berchtesgaden, Hitler's Bavarian retreat.

By chance another official entered and found the intruder going through papers on Lammers' desk. The official asked the intruder what he was doing and received in reply a punch on the chin. In response to the official's cries, the London *Daily Telegraph* wrote, members of the Elite Guard hurried in and arrested the intruder. He broke loose after striking one of the guards in the stomach, but was felled by a revolver shot to the knee. According to the *New York Times*, the intruder was taken to an asylum for the insane at Buell, outside Berlin. He refused to make any statement.

Hoover Visits the Chancellery

Former U.S. President Herbert Hoover arrived in Germany on March 7, 1938, for the first time since his postwar relief work in 1919. His car traveled from Carlsbad, Czechoslovakia, through Dresden and on to Berlin. The following afternoon, March 8, Hoover visited the Reich Chancellery.

During Hoover's other visits to heads of state, such as to King Leopold of Belgium and President Eduard Benes of Czechoslovakia, a traveling companion, Paul Smith, general manager of the *San Francisco Chronicle*, had accompanied Hoover. But the German Foreign Office informed Hoover that the Führer would not receive Smith "because he is a newspaper man."¹⁷ Hitler hated foreign reporters.

The noon conversation between Hoover and Hitler lasted 40 minutes. Hoover gave Hitler the unusual experience of hearing doubt cast on the fundamental ideas of National Socialism. Hitler gave Hoover the unusual experience of being yelled at. Hoover told Hitler that National Socialism was not likely to be a successful system of government, and was built on principles that would be wholly impossible for the American people to tolerate in their own country. Americans believed that social progress and personal liberty were inseparable, said Hoover. Hitler responded that personal liberty might be possible in a country with large resources, but not in Germany. As Hitler warmed to the subject, he became quite noisy, irritating the polite, mannerly Hoover. Afterward, Hoover refused to be quoted, asserting that it would be contrary to the rules of international courtesy for him to say anything about the conversation. But reliable reports of the meeting were obtained at a luncheon that Hugh R. Wilson, the U.S. ambassador, gave for Hoover, which was attended by several persons who had been present during the conversation or who were attached to the Chancellery or to Hoover's entourage.

Left to right: Herbert Hoover, Hitler, interpreter Paul Schmidt, and Hugh Wilson, U.S. Ambassador in Berlin, March 1938 (Bayerische Staatsbibliothek).

Hoover lunched at Carinhall March 9 with Hermann Göring and his retinue. Huntsmen played old German hunting horns for Carinhall's lord, who was also Reich Master of the Hunt. The following day Hoover left for Warsaw.

Hitler Announces Germania, the New Berlin

On December 4, 1937, Hitler announced his plans to turn Berlin into a new Rome, not merely a city but a symbol of political power, as Rome was in the ancient world.[18] Hitler was fulfilling an aim that he had expressed in his 1923 book, *Mein Kampf*:

> How pathetic is the comparison today between state and private structures. If Rome's fate were to come upon Berlin, future generations would find as the mighty monuments of our times the ruins of Jewish department stores and a certain number of hotels. We only need to consider the criminal lack of proportion between the buildings of the Reich and those of finance and commerce.

Hitler had appointed Albert Speer as "Inspector General of Buildings for the Renovation of the Federal Capital" on January 30, 1937. Speer would build Hitler's new Rome. "Do a good job," Hitler said to Speer, presenting him with a document certifying the appointment.

Berlin was to be renamed *Germania*. In its center, Hitler wanted a broad central avenue running north and south, with a triumphal arch at its south end and a domed hall at its

Top: Hitler's sketch of triumphal arch. Speer adhered to Hitler's design closely when building an architectural model of the arch (Bayerische Staatsbibliothek).
Bottom: Model of Hitler's triumphal arch (Bayerische Staatsbibliothek).

Large Load Body. Corner General-Papestraße/Loewenhardtdamm. Tempelhof. The large load body, 14 meters high, 21 meters wide, and 12,000 tons, sits near the center of Berlin. In 1941, the regime paid the firm Dyckerhoff & Widmann 400,000 Reichsmarks to build this huge cylindrical concrete hulk, now gray, cracking, and surrounded by weeds. French prisoners of war did the work. A mysterious edifice, it now serves no purpose but would be difficult to remove. The large load body is one of the key structures Hitler left behind. Architect Albert Speer wanted to test the load bearing capacity of the sandy Berlin subsoil for Hitler's triumphal arch. In September, 1941, the German government contracted for shipments of Swedish granite for the arch. But because of reverses on the battlefields, the arch was never built, and only the large load body remains. Until the 1990s the German Research Society for Terrestrial Mechanics used the large load body for many investigations, and published their findings in international journals. But in the past few years, the civil engineers have abandoned the structure, which Berliners call "the mushroom." When homeless people tried to move into the rooms within the large load body, workmen sealed off the entrance. The large load body has been under landmark protection since 1995. But no one knows quite what to do with it.

north. Baron Georges Haussmann's designs for Paris had inspired Hitler, but Hitler would do Haussmann bigger and better. Hitler's central avenue would be two-and-a-half times the length of Haussmann's Champs Elysées, and 70 feet wider. Hitler had first sketched his triumphal arch in 1925. It would be 117 meters high, 170 meters wide, and 119 meters long. Hitler dreamed that the street under the arch would remind every visitor to Berlin that he was in the domain of the "masters of the world" and would "take his breath away." Speer presented Hitler with a model of the arch on April 20, 1939, during the Führer's 50th birthday dinner party:

> At midnight the diners offered Hitler the proper congratulations. But when I told him that to celebrate the day I had set up a thirteen foot model of his triumphal arch in one of the salons, he immediately left the party and hurried to the room. For a long time he stood contemplating with visible emotion the dream of his younger years, realized in this model. Overwhelmed, he gave me his hand without a word, and then, in a euphoric mood, lectured his

Germania (model): Triumphal Arch and Great Domed Hall.

birthday guests on the importance of this structure for the future history of the Reich. That night he returned to look at the model several times.

The domed hall, down the street from Hitler's triumphal arch, would be so huge that it could contain several replications of St. Peter's in Rome. The diameter of the dome was to be 825 feet. Beneath it, in an area of approximately 410 thousand square feet, more than 150 thousand people could assemble standing.

On March 11, 1942, Hitler announced to his inner circle, "As a world capital, Berlin will be the equal of old Egypt, Babylon, or Rome. What is London, what is Paris in comparison?"

Germania didn't impress everyone. Speer's architect father remarked of the designs, "You've all gone completely crazy." Undaunted, Hitler and Speer proceeded to build Germania. The first new building on their agenda was the New Reich Chancellery.

III. The New Reich Chancellery

Myths are a part of history, and the New Reich Chancellery on Voß Straße is one. Hitler propagated the myth that the New Chancellery arose in 12 months, the work of 4,000 men laboring day and night.

In fact, the history of the New Reich Chancellery began four years earlier when the regime began accumulating property on Voß Straße. In 1934 the Reich expropriated the lot at Voß Straße 16 from Reinhold Meyer. A year later, the Reich Minister for Finance, Count Schwerin von Krosigk, wrote to the German Central Credit Corporation: "The Reich is interested in the Berlin lot Voß Straße 2. I would like to know immediately whether you are prepared to sell the land and under what conditions."

In 1937, the Wertheim Department Stores were Aryanized and seven Voß Straße lots Wertheim owned became Reich property. Wertheim had bought many pieces of land near the flagship Leipziger Straße store to prevent other merchants from encroaching on the Wertheim franchise. The Reich obtained this land at fire-sale prices.

Speer finished most of the plans for the new Chancellery in July 1937, working from a sketch Hitler had made in 1935. Hitler's sketch showed the Voß Straße long axis of the building, which Speer built. Hitler included the honor court, the entry from the Chancellery Annex, the elongated gallery leading to a reception hall, and the huge terrace on the garden front. Architectural historian Angela Schönberger discovered Speer's plans in the Bayerisches Hauptstaatsarchiv in Munich, and published them in 1981. She found many floor plans, along with drawings of the cellar and top floor, at a scale of 1:100. Voß Straße between Wilhelmplatz and Hermann Göring Straße is designated as the location of the building, and the honor court, mosaic hall, Hitler's office, cabinet meeting room, and reception rooms are rendered in minute detail. Indeed, even before 1937, Hitler, with his dreams of world dominance, needed an imperial stage on which to act out his role. Neither the Reichskanzlerpalais nor the Chancellery Annex fulfilled his requirements. To acquire land for his perverted theater, the Führer decimated and beggared two prominent German Jewish families, the Meyers and the Wertheims.

The Meyers

Berlin, in June — Dorle Wilke's memory sometimes brings back the smell of silver cleaner and musty, airless rooms; but she associates a pleasant feeling of security with this smell. Dorle Wilke recalls the odor of Sidol silver cleaner when she stands in front of a pretty

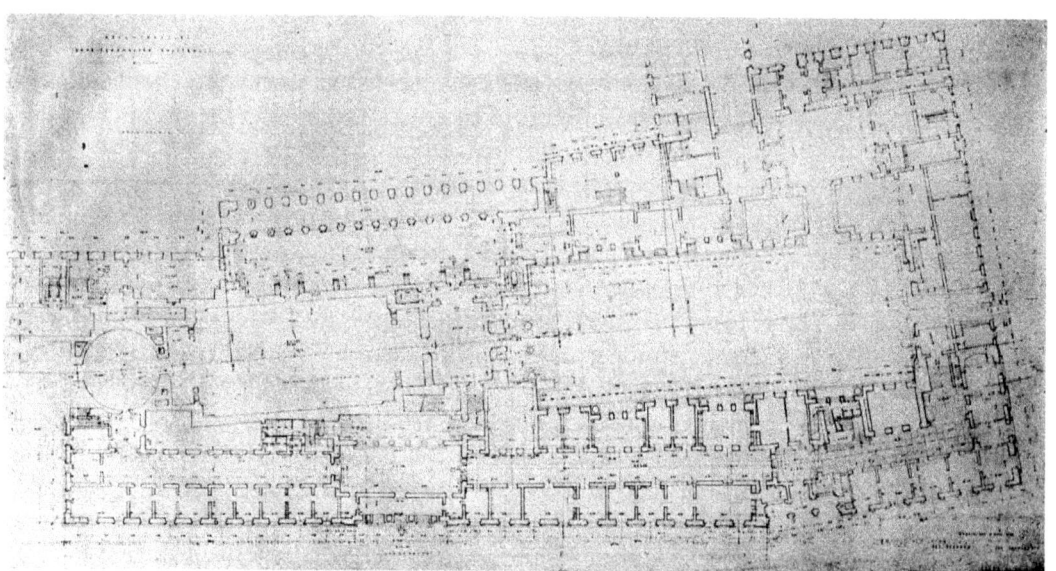

Top: Hitler's sketch of the New Reich Chancellery, 1935. Hitler made a preliminary sketch of the building as land for it was being acquired on Voß Straße. Hitler's plan envisioned Voß Straße 2–7 as the site (half as large as the final site).
Bottom: Speer's plan for ground floor, New Reich Chancellery. Pencil on transparent paper, dated July 20, 1937, modified February 9, 1938, shows the Wilhelmstraße entrance, honor court, fore-hall, mosaic hall, and round hall at a scale of 1:100. Dampness and age have considerably degraded the image.

yellow villa in the Frohnau suburb of Berlin. Dorle once lived in the villa. Dorle also remembers the bittersweet taste of sticky green ice cream on a stick and the memory fills her with dread. She recalls buildings in Berlin-Wedding. Wailing Christian women stood in front, terrified they would never again see their Jewish husbands, including Dorle's father, who were being held inside in "protective custody." Dorle carried a package of food for her father, which she had prepared — semolina pudding and raspberries. "When I think back on this time," says Dorle, now 70, married with two grown sons, "I remember constantly collecting berries because Papa had been arrested again."[1]

Dorle's mother, who was not Jewish, took Dorle by the hand as they went from one prison to another, looking for Dorle's father. Her mother took food with her and pleaded with SS guards for help. That was in the 1940s, when Dorle's name was Dorothea Meyer, though everyone called her *Dorle*. Because her father was Jewish, he was a forced laborer in Berlin factories. There were repeated raids on the family home until finally the SS picked him up. By this time, the family had lost everything: their home, their money, paintings, jewelry, and Dorle's father's health.

Dorle's ordeal is not over, by any means. It is intimately entwined with officials who decide questions of property, federal building officials, and museum officials. The correspondence between these worthies and Dorle Wilke fills many folders. For example, sheaves of letters concern the lot, Voß Straße 16, just around the corner from Potsdamer Platz. A picket fence obscures the view.

Dorle Wilke, who still sports a pageboy hairdo and pleated skirts, recently climbed the fence like a small girl with Christiane Kohl, a reporter for the *Süddeutsche Zeitung*. Dorle stood on a sandy hillock and recounted the time when a magnificent villa had occupied the site. Her grandparents and parents lived in the villa. Dorle's grandfather, Richard Moritz Meyer, was a literary lion, a renowned Goethe expert and Friedrich Nietzsche's biographer. With his wife Estella, a beauty with black flowing locks, Richard Moritz Meyer made Voß Straße 16 a literary salon. The historian Ricarda Huch, Hugo von Hofmannsthal, librettist of *Der Rosenkavalier*, and the poet Stefan George were frequent guests.

The Voß Straße 16 villa was exquisitely appointed. The library had rare first editions, a cream white Meissen tile oven, paintings and tasteful furniture. Meyer commissioned Franz von Lenbach and Reinhold Lepsius to paint portraits of his sons. The sculptor Max Klinger made a bust of Reinhold, the youngest son. Needless to say, the Meyer family was quite rich. The ground floor of the villa originally housed the EJ Meyer Bank, founded in 1816.

The oldest son, Richard, died of meningitis. The second son was killed in the First World War, and Richard Moritz Meyer died in 1915. Estella remained in the villa with her youngest son, Reinhold, born in 1898. Reinhold apprenticed as a bookseller and studied literature. His first published work was a catalogue of his father's library. In 1924 Reinhold, who had been baptized, married Lucie, a lively, vibrant Christian woman. The infertile couple adopted children: in 1929 a non–Jewish child, Klaus, and in 1934, Dorle, who was half–Jewish. The family lived in Voß Straße 16, and their garden adjoined the gardens of the Justice Ministry and Foreign Office. The Meyers often exchanged friendly greetings with the diplomats.

In 1934, one year after Hitler came to power, the Reich wanted Voß Straße 16 and forced the Meyers out. In early 1935, Reinhold Meyer and his family moved to a house in Berlin-Dahlem. A year earlier, Stella entered a mental hospital in Wannsee. The deaths of two of her sons had depressed her severely.

The house in Dahlem was smaller than the Voß Straße 16 villa. Reinhold Meyer was forced to store his Persian carpets, Chinese vases, baroque armoire, and Max Klinger bust in a shed on Voß Straße. He would never see these articles again. In 1936, the German Reich bought the Voß Straße 16 villa from Reinhold Meyer for 480,000 reichsmarks, half its actual value. But Reinhold fared better than his cousin, the banker Adolph Ernst Joachim

Meyer. As Adolph Ernst tried to remove his belongings from a shed, Nazis seized him. Then they Aryanized the Meyer Bank and turned it over to the industrialist Kurt Richter. Adolph Meyer immigrated in early 1939.

The Nazis compelled Reinhold Meyer to give up the Dahlem house, as well as three apartment buildings he owned. The family moved to a rented house in Frohnau. They put into storage, in a cellar on Savigny Platz, furniture, Meissen china, paintings by Franz von Lenbach and crates of valuable books, all of which subsequently vanished. Other paintings also disappeared: an oil by Max Liebermann, works by Ferdinand Hodler, Lovis Corinth, Paula Modersohn-Becker, and a pastel by Adolf von Menzel. A Menzel painting that Reinhold Meyer owned, *Sunday Afternoon in the Tuileries,* ended up in Dresden's Albertinum. In 1935, Meyer sold the painting for 25,000 reichsmarks, a bargain for the museum "under moderately normal circumstances," said the director, Hans Posse. The painting, according to Posse, should have fetched 60,000 to 70,000 reichsmarks. In 1939 Posse became Hitler's chief adviser for the art museum that the Führer planned for his hometown, Linz. By 1945 Posse had accumulated a huge trove of art for Linz, most stolen from Jews.

In the meantime, the Meyer family had moved again, landing in a half-finished bungalow in Hohen Neuendorf, in the northern part of Berlin. Plastered white with a terrace and a brick base, the house is still there. Later occupants changed very little. Dorle Wilke looked enchanted to see the garden, according to reporter Christiane Kohl. In the corner window was the small piano for which the Meyers had traded their Blüthner grand. A nearby door led to the bathroom.

"On Sundays, Papa liked to listen to Zarah Leander singing while he shaved. I sat on the staircase," recalled Dorle.

On March 3, 1939, Dorle's parents wrapped all their silver in newspaper: silver teapots, silver cake plates, silver caviar knives and silver asparagus tongs. "Then Papa put our silverware in a Maedler leather satchel and left in a taxi." Reinhold Meyer also took with him diamond chokers, pearl necklaces, and diadems. His destination was a pawnshop in the Jaegerstraße. The Nazis had demanded that Jews turn in all their gold and silver. Yet Reinhold Meyer did not consider immigrating. He had to take care of his mother, Estella, in Dr. Wiener's mental hospital in Bernau, near Berlin. "When we visited grandmother," said Dorle, "she always asked the nurses to serve us tarts, like in the old days."

In summer 1939, the Meyers decided to immigrate to Brazil. Reinhold had made contact with Pastor Martin Niemoeller of the Confessional Church, who arranged to send the Meyers' son Klaus as a so-called "guaranty-child" to England. Because Klaus was adopted and Aryan, Nazi officials had threatened to take him away. With the outbreak of war, September 1, 1939, all hope of immigration vanished. Reinhold was conscripted into forced labor at a salary of 19 *pfennig* per hour. He shoveled snow, worked in a garden center, and built roads. The work was so arduous that he developed a double hernia and had surgery in a Jewish hospital. When he recovered, the Nazis put Reinhold to work in a plumbing and pipe fitting company. An anti–Semitic supervisor forced him to operate a welding apparatus that almost burned his hands off. The Labor Office transferred Reinhold to a Jewish work group in the Barthelmes Drill Company in Berlin-Wittenau, which manufactured boring tools. Dorle often had to bring her sick, exhausted father home. "That hurt me terribly," she said.

Yet life still held some pleasures. Uncle Karl, an army officer, often visited, along with Gerhard Schnierbel with his violin. Reinhold played his cello, and Uncle Karl played piano. Dorle pressed her ear against the wall next to her bed so as not to miss a single note. It also was nice when Aunt Kunze, the tailor, came. Dorle's Mother sometimes took a curtain from the window, and Dorle got a new dress.

But Dorle herself faced much hardship. The girls in kindergarten called her the Jew-child, withheld her milk, and ostracized her. Later Dorle was excluded from the German Girls' League (BDM), which she ardently wished to join. The BDM leader ridiculed Dorle, calling her a shitty Jew-brat.

In July 1942, Reinhold received a letter from a mental hospital in Poland. Estella and other Jews had been sent there, and the letter said that Estella Meyer had "unfortunately" died of dysentery. By this time, the deportations had begun. Many of the Meyers' friends came to the house in Hohen-Neuendorf to say goodbye. The visitors posed, smiling, for a photo with Dorle, who was well aware what their deportation letters signified. "When they deported you, you were dead." Dorle got graphic proof during a call on her former doctor, Professor Kalischer, who lived on Havelplatz. The house smelled of gas and the old man lay dead, slumped over the kitchen table.

One day, an SS man named Wiesmann appeared at the house in Hohen-Neudorf and ordered the Meyers to clear out immediately. They moved into an arbor on the river Havel. A hay wagon was sufficient to transport their few remaining possessions. A short time later Dorle and her mother used the wagon to bring the unconscious Reinhold to the arbor. He had been hit on the head with a sledgehammer. He was ill for three months. "Papa's head was much bigger than usual and so pink," said Dorle. But Reinhold did not have to return to his job at Barthelmes, because the company was using Ukrainian prisoners.

Reinhold's new job was at a light bulb factory, Osram, in Warschauer Straße. In comparison to Barthelmes, Osram was pleasant and humane. Then the raids began. In February 1943, in the so-called "factory action," Reinhold and thousands of other Berlin Jews married to Christian wives were imprisoned in a building on Rosenstraße, near Alexanderplatz. The Jews were supposed to be deported to death camps. But a spontaneous protest began in front of the Rosenstraße building.[2] "The street was suddenly black with people," recalled Dorle, who was there holding her mother's hand. "Women stood screaming for their husbands." After Reinhold and the other men were released, Reinhold was assigned to sweat as a track worker on the German railways.

There were more raids and arrests. Reinhold was picked up again. Lucie raced around Berlin with her daughter, carrying clean underwear, sandwiches, and porridge, looking for her husband. They started at the Frohnau Villa, with its musty silver-polish odor. Johann Hinrich Luehmann, the current occupant, allowed Lucie to use his phone. Then she began searching the camps. The men were not allowed to show themselves at the windows, but they were allowed to approach the windows for air. The inmates would clamber up to the air vents until the women recognized their husbands. Dorle, meanwhile, sucked her sticky, bittersweet green ice cream.

Once while in custody, Reinhold had to destroy personnel files of murdered Jews. Another time he was ordered into a car for deportation and then, miraculously, was called out again.

Dorle's mother was also conscripted into forced labor. In an electronics firm Lucie assembled carpet bombs for air attacks. She was forced to sell her last jewelry to feed herself and Dorle. Every two weeks she had to report to the Gestapo, who pressed her to divorce Reinhold. But Dorle remembers that her mother always refused. "I'm not crazy," she would say.

After the war, Reinhold was a sick, broken man, and Lucie was exhausted. The fam-

Rosenstraße — middle. Memorial to mass wives' protest against deportation of Jewish husbands. Mixed marriages were a thorny problem for the Nazis. When the final roundup of Berlin Jews began on Saturday, February 27, 1943, some 10,000 Jewish men who were partners in mixed marriages, among them Reinhold Meyer, were taken to the Jewish Sozialverwaltung building, Rosenstraße 2, and the Jewish old age home in Große Hamburgerstraße. Sunday morning, the non–Jewish wives banded together and went out to find their Jewish husbands. They converged on Rosenstrasse 2. There they stood, refusing to leave, shouting and screaming for their men, hour after hour, throughout the day and the night and into the next day. Worried SS leaders assembled in their nearby Burgstrasse headquarters, not knowing what to do. They had never been faced with such a situation. Would they have to machine-gun thousands of German women? All night the arguments raged, until at noon on Monday a decision was reached: all men married to a non–Jewish wife could return home. "Privileged persons," the official announcement said, "are to be incorporated in the national community." The Jewish men remained in an uneasy state of limbo until the end of the war. This monument on Rosenstraße commemorating the wives' protest was dedicated in 1995. Ingeborg Hunzinger, a Jewish sculptress who fled Berlin in 1939, created the memorial from porphyry. But Frau Hunzinger complained that she had been underpaid for her work. The Berlin Senate finally made a supplementary payment to the 82-year-old sculptress in 1997 (Ullstein Bilderdienst).

ily remained for years in refugee camps. In 1945 Reinhold received a compensation payment for his once huge fortune, 347.77 marks. In 1950 he found a job in a bookstore in Hessen, run by a man accused of having been a Nazi, who wanted a token Jew as an employee. After the bookstore owner had been officially de–Nazified, he fired Reinhold, who found work selling soap and shoe polish.

Reinhold received very little reparation for what he had suffered, other than a couple thousand marks for the buildings in West Berlin he had lost. He died in 1965, and afterward Lucie received various payments, among them 15,000 marks for her confiscated gold and silver. There was never any significant reimbursement for Reinhold's forced labor, which almost cost him his life. Barthelmes' liability evaporated when the company was liquidated in 1956. Osram still exists but, with various legal maneuvers, has evaded paying anything to former forced laborers. The German Railroads, part of the federal government, presumably contribute some of the governmental payments to Nazi victims.

The lot at Voß Straße 16, once in East Berlin, has now been returned to the Meyer family. But Dorle and her relatives can sell the property for at most 1.5 million marks, although it was worth one million marks in 1930. Moreover, the city of Berlin wants four million marks reimbursement for the lot, supposedly for development costs. The Meyers never received a penny for the paintings stolen from them. The Meyer Bank, after Aryanization, now exists as the Hamburg Bank Woelbern & Co. In 1945 the bank was suspected of harboring stolen art.

A few years ago, Dorle discovered the family's Klinger bust by chance at an exhibition in the Leipzig Museum of Fine Art. "There's Papa!" she exclaimed. The museum initially rejected her claims on the bust, but recent court rulings may compel the museum to give it back.

Dorle still has trouble understanding all that happened. She is a bookseller, working in the same profession her father had to abandon more than half a century earlier. She wants her father to have the recognition that he shunned.

Dorle Wilke and reporter Christiane Kohl visited the Meyers' former home in Frohnau. They found place settings and coffee, but no trace of the smell of Sidol silver polish. An exceptionally nice man, the grandson of old Johann Hinrich Luehmann, lives in the house.

"Does anyone in the family know about the little kindnesses Johann Hinrich once performed?" asked reporter Kohl.

"Oh yes," responded young Luehmann, "we all know he hid the Jew Meyer."

For a moment Dorle Wilke looked as though she had turned to stone. Outside the house, Dorle said to Kohl, "Isn't there anyone who thought of us as normal people?"

The Meyer family's claims for losses during the Nazi era are not large. Many Jewish families lost more. The largest claim ever filed, for $600 million dollars, came from the other Jewish owner of Voß Straße land, the Wertheims.

The Wertheims

In 1907, the publicist Paul Göhre described his impression of Berlin's Wertheim Department Store in Martin Buber's magazine *Society*: "It is as if the attraction of this store were magnetic for humans. In the future the human stream will not only flood the whole building, but also the overfilled roads on which the store is built. Customers will spurt ceaselessly in a raging torrent over the roof, and gush from the bowels of the earth."

Wertheim, which changed the face of Berlin and other German cities, began inauspiciously in 1875. In the provincial Baltic town of Stralsund, Abraham Wertheim, a Jewish merchant, opened a textile and clothing store. A few years later, his three sons, Georg, Franz, and Wilhelm, joined him.

Before the department store, buying and selling involved a battle of wills. The seller wanted to earn as much as possible without driving the prospective buyer away. The buyer wanted to pay as little as possible. The result? Intense pressure to buy, as well as endless haggling and dickering. And if the buyer succeeded in purchasing an article, *caveat emptor*, that is, no exchanges or refunds.

Georg Wertheim recognized that there was something inherently wrong with this process. He was able to convince his father that *caveat emptor* and haggling over price alienated customers and were bad for business. Abraham, who had not been particularly successful, was willing to try new tactics. Instead of barter, Georg Wertheim established fixed cash prices paid immediately for all articles. A customer could exchange any product he bought or turn it in for a full refund. No one was pressured to buy anything. The good burghers of Stralsund had never seen anything like this before, and they loved it. In fact, *Au Bon Marché* in Paris had been doing the same thing for 20 years with an additional wrinkle. The Paris store was an agglomeration of stores under one roof selling every imaginable product. Georg Wertheim dreamed of doing the same. In 1894, he opened *A. Wertheim* in Berlin's Oranienstraße. Germany's first department store, with high quality goods at low fixed prices, was a resounding success. "Friendliness and politeness were *de rigueur*," wrote Erica Fischer and Simone Ladwig-Winters in their biography of the Wertheims, "no matter how much or how little the customer bought, no matter whether he was rich or poor."[3] German nobility and working people rubbed elbows at the sales counters.

In 1896, Georg Wertheim built a magnificent new store on Leipziger Straße, with "everything under one roof." The building was the *chef d'oeuvre* of the German Jewish architect Alfred Messel. It had a palm court with grottos and waterfalls, a 24-meter high light court, and a gigantic hall with onyx-clad walls adorned with paintings and sculptures. In his diary, Wertheim wrote, "The upsurge in our business has been astounding and sensational."

A customer could easily spend a whole day in the store. He could dine in the restaurant while an orchestra played, visit the barber, borrow books from the lending library, view works of art in the modern gallery, have his photograph taken, and stop at the travel agency to plan a trip.

Wertheim had competitors. Leonhard Tietz in Stralsund, Hermann Tietz in Gera (Hertie), Rudolph Karstadt in Wismar and Adolf Jandorf (Kaufhaus des Westens, KaDeWe) in Berlin. All of these men were German Jews, except for Karstadt. Wertheim's phenomenal success also provoked considerable envy tainted with ugly anti–Semitism. The department store was part of a malicious Jewish plot to bankrupt the German middle class, people said.

Before his wedding to a Christian woman in 1906, Georg Wertheim was baptized in the Kaiser Wilhelm Memorial Church. So were his brothers and many other wealthy Jews. Because the church was near Adolf Jandorf's department store, Kaufhaus des Westens, German Jews began calling the church *Taufhaus des Westens* (Baptismal House of the West).

Kaiser Wilhelm II visited the Wertheim store on Leipziger Straße, January 23, 1910. The All-Highest, the Kaiserin (empress), and their retinue arrived in three automobiles. "Ursula [Wertheim] and I received them in the ante-room of the staircase at the garden entrance," Georg Wertheim wrote in his diary, one of the few times he mentioned his wife. "Ursula gave the Kaiserin a bouquet of lilacs."

The royals and the Wertheims took the elevator to the second floor, to the carpet display. "The display, with its floral decorations, made an excellent impression," wrote Wertheim.

> The Kaiser stared at the great light court with its two bridges and was astounded. I guided the Kaiser through the display, and Ursula followed with the Kaiserin. There was a life size

portrait of the Kaiser with lilies, painted by Heydel. The upright posture, particularly the position of one leg, was impressive. The Kaiser was pleased. He waved to Privy Councilor von Etzdorf and said that he wanted to take the portrait with him.

The group then made a cursory tour of the remainder of the store.

> I accompanied the Kaiser. Ursula again escorted the Kaiserin, followed by the retinue. We passed through the antiquities department to the old light court, down the main stairs to the ground floor. After a peek in the conservatory we passed through the perfume department in the Onyx Hall and from there to the cleaning wares.

The Kaiser looked at the clock. He declared everything to have been most interesting but said he was forced to excuse himself. He had to board his train to Potsdam. Georg Wertheim assured His Majesty that the train would not leave without him. "In the cleaning department the Kaiser looked at our many artificial flowers. We arrived punctually at the exit, where the Kaiser and Kaiserin took their leave in the best of moods. Privy Councilor von Etzdorf was pleased that everything had gone so well."

Alfred Messel. Messel (1853–1909) designed Berlin's Pergamon Museum and the offices of German General Electric (AEG), as well as Wertheim's Leipziger Straße store. One of Messel's students, Paul Baumgarten, built the Haus am Großen Wannsee 56–58, the Wannsee Villa. On January 20, 1942, in the dining room of the Villa, Reinhard Heydrich announced Hitler's decision to murder the Jews of Europe (Ullstein Bilderdienst).

Georg Wertheim became a friend, guest and advisor of the Kaiser, and was a generous donor to the new Kaiser Wilhelm Institute. But the average German was not pleased. On December 16, 1912, the *Staatsbürger Zeitung* wrote: "There are many German people, true supporters of the monarchy, who are pained that His Majesty has visited not only a Jewish department store but a Jewish synagogue, thereby favoring Jews. These Jews, as science has shown, have a racial instinct to trounce German merchants of every sort."

Wilhelm ignored this sort of calumny. He was no fan of Jews himself, but cultivated a small number of very wealthy, successful ones. James Simon, heir to the Simon Brothers textile fortune, was a close associate of the Kaiser, and funded the archeological digs of the Deutsche Orient-Gesellschaft that were Wilhelm's hobby horse. On one of these digs, December 1912, Ludwig Borchardt unearthed the limestone bust of Queen Nefertiti (ca 1350 BC), wife of the Egyptian pharaoh Akhnaton (Amenhotep IV).[4] Another of Wilhelm's Jewish friends was Albert Ballin, owner of the Hapag Steamship Company. Ballin committed suicide in 1918, filled with despair over the lost war. Other Jewish friends were the banker Carl Fürstenberg, as well as Emil and Walther Rathenau, the father and son who controlled German General Electric (AEG). Wilhelm sought the advice of these men in economic matters, and they were generous donors to the charitable causes he favored. Zionist Chaim Weizmann referred to them contemptuously as "Kaiser-Jews."

On January 12, 1913, Wilhelm bestowed the Red Order of the Eagle, 4th Class (bronze), on Georg Wertheim in the Berlin City Palace. Wrote Wertheim,

> There were hundreds of people present. The Kaiser and the Kaiserin, as well as the rest of the court, were all standing. The holders of royal orders were lined up in rows. Everyone was called by name, walked up to the Kaiser and Kaiserin, and bowed. It took two or three hours before the process ended. I have no desire to go through this a second time. Even the Kaiser and Kaiserin must have found it stressful.

The Kaiser's friendship with Georg Wertheim served to mute the poisonous anti–Semitism. But after World War I and the Kaiser's abdication everything changed. In 1930, Georg Wertheim wrote in his diary, "Reichstag opened.... Stones smash our display windows."

When Hitler came to power in January 1933, he decreed a boycott of Jewish stores. *Der Stürmer*, a Nazi newspaper, published this doggerel:

"Ins Judenkaufhaus gehen wir nicht!"	We don't go to Jewish Department Stores!
Die Mutter zu dem Kinde spricht	Said the mother to her child.
"Nur deutsche Waren kaufen wir	We only buy German wares.
Mein liebes Kind, das merke Dir	My dear child, take note.
Nur das, was deutsche Hand geschafft	Only that which German hands make
Durch deutschen Fleiß und deutsche Kraft	With German industry and German strength
Soll'n deutsche Frauen kaufen	Should German women buy.
Nun wollen wir nun laufen	Now we want to run
Ins Haus der deutschen Waren	To the house of German wares
Wo wir auch mehr ersparen	Where we also save more
Weil billig alles ist und echt	Because cheap and genuine are everything
Beim Juden aber kauft man schlecht"	From Jews one buys badly
Drum merke, was die Mutter spricht	So note what mother says
"Bei einem Juden kauft man nicht!"	"Don't buy from a Jew!"

"We understood the situation completely," Albrecht Wertheim, Georg's son, told Simone Ladwig-Winters.

In 1933, Franz Wertheim died. He owned one-third of Wertheim, which that year had total sales of more than 100 million Reichsmarks. The shares passed to Franz's sons, Günther and Fritz. Georg Wertheim was the majority shareholder, but by 1934 he was no longer permitted to go to his office. In order to retain his interest in his company, Georg transferred his shares to his Christian wife, Ursula. On January 1, 1937, Georg wrote in his diary, "The store is declared to be German." A sign in front read, "Jewish customers not wanted." Under intense pressure, Georg divorced Ursula. He died in 1939, a deeply embittered man. Arthur Lindgens, a Wertheim lawyer and trusted family advisor, married Ursula in 1941 and gained control of the company.

Günther Wertheim fled to Cuba in 1939, then the United States. Three other Wertheim family members were murdered in the Nazi death camps. The Wertheim Department Store on Leipziger Straße was destroyed during the war. After 1945, Voß Straße and most of the former Wertheim holdings were in Communist East Berlin. The Communists declared all this land state property.

Fritz and Günther tried to get their wealth back. In 1950, they applied to government authorities to regain their shares in the Wertheim stores. They had lost them in 1937, when Hermann Göring ordered the firm's name changed to the General Department Store Company (AWAG), and all Jewish shareholders and employees ousted. Arthur Lindgens came to New York in 1951 and convinced Fritz and Günther Wertheim that their shares were virtually worthless. The Soviets had seized their property in East Berlin, said Lindgens, and the rest of the company in West Berlin would go belly-up unless it received a new line of credit, which he would not apply for unless he controlled all the shares. Lindgens paid the brothers $5,000 for their shares. Within days of the transaction, he merged the Wertheim Company with Hertie, of which he took control. Karstadt-Quelle acquired Hertie in 1994, and with it a claim to the Wertheim properties in the former East Berlin. But with the fall of the Berlin Wall in 1989, Güther Wertheim's daughter, 68-year-old Barbara Principe (née Bärbel Wertheim), suddenly became aware of her family's former Berlin property.

Barbara is a Lutheran who lives in Newfield, New Jersey. She is the mother of seven children and worked on the Peerless Perl Company assembly line, checking that shirt buttons the company manufactured all had the proper number of holes.

"A simple individual," said Barbara Principe, "a simple life."[5]

Barbara Principe left Germany when she was six years old. The Wertheims had a family mansion, a nanny, mother's Advent calendars, and gifts under a Christmas tree.

Günther Wertheim bought a chicken farm in New Jersey and a hard life. On winter mornings, Barbara broke up ice in the troughs for the hens to drink. After school, she collected and sorted eggs.

Günther Wertheim wasn't a born farmer. He had kidney stones and colitis, and carried a bedpan wherever he went.

"He kept getting sicker and sicker," says his daughter. "It was all nerves. It was not a happy, cheerful household."

Her parents never talked about Germany. Neither did Uncle Fritz, who worked as a cook in a psychiatric hospital after surviving Theresienstadt. In 1951, at age 18, Barbara married a local button-factory owner, Dominick Principe. The couple lived with Barbara's parents and Dominick helped with the farm. Three years later, Günther Wertheim died at age 52 of a heart attack. Barbara knew he had been an angry man but did not know why. She found out one day in 2000. A New Jersey lawyer, Gary Osen, called and told her that her father had been a multimillionaire in Germany. She herself might be worth $80 million. Barbara had retained Osen in 1989. She was seeking restitution for a hunting lodge the Wertheims had owned in East Germany. Her mother had also pursued this claim. In 1998 she was awarded $75,000.

A year later, Osen, whose father had fled pre-war Germany, was able to review records of unclaimed Jewish property in government and corporate files. He discovered that Arthur Lindgens had defrauded the two Wertheim brothers, since he had never told them about his deal to merge with Hertie. In fact, Lindgens had a 12-page handwritten contract with Hertie, signed in New York and dated three days before Günther and Fritz Wertheim sold him their shares. Barbara Principe was distressed.

"It's difficult to explain what my feelings are, because when you have not been a part of something all your life, then all of a sudden you are hit with it, it makes you very angry," she told *Philadelphia Inquirer* reporter John Shiffman. "I'm angry because my father died so young. So for him, I will fight for what's rightfully mine."

Barbara Principe faces an uphill battle. Karstadt-Quelle has already sold off some of the Wertheim's Berlin land. One five-acre plot fetched $150 million. The property is slated for a Canadian Embassy and a Ritz Carlton Hotel. The German Government holds title to other pieces of contested Wertheim property and does not want to give it up. The Jewish Claims Conference, an official body that acts on behalf of Jewish Holocaust survivors and the heirs of victims, awarded 15 acres of disputed property to the Wertheim heirs. But the German Government appealed. On March 4, 2005, a German court awarded Barbara Principe and her nephew, Martin Wortham, $17 million for one former piece of Wertheim property. A spokesman for Kardtadt-Quelle said the company would appeal the court's decision. The Karstadt-Quelle five-acre plot, now at the center of the Potsdamer Platz redevelopment, is still in litigation.

In 2000, Barbara Principe traveled to Berlin for the first time since her family fled in 1939. She visited the Wertheim Department Store on Kurfürstendamm and bought a white scarf with embroidered flowers.

She does not want to return to Germany.

"For what?" she asks.

Barbara Principe says she will remain a self-described non-practicing Lutheran. She agrees with what her father often said, that religion should be based in a person's soul, not his church. What will she do with the fortune she may receive? "It will help to pay restaurant tabs," she says. "Every Thursday my whole family has dinner in an Italian restaurant in Newfield."

Hitler's Chancellery Plans Go Forward

By January 4, 1938, all the lots on Voß Straße needed for the New Chancellery had been assembled. Although the acquisition of property occurred over a four-year period, Hitler was suddenly in a hurry. Albert Speer wrote that Hitler worried about the state of his own health, and this concern was the reason for the rush. More likely, Hitler felt pressed to finish the Chancellery because he was preparing for war. On November 5, 1937, Hitler had called the army chiefs and his ambassador to Great Britain, Joachim von Ribbentrop, to a meeting in the Chancellery, where he revealed his war plans. The written record of this meeting is called the Hoßbach protocol, after Colonel Friedrich Hoßbach, who recorded the statements Hitler made. After delivering a long monologue, as was his wont, the Führer got to the point: "There is only one way to solve the German question: force." Hitler was certain that he was an historical personage, and he defined his fixed goals. He declared that he would annex Austria and take Czechoslovakia militarily.

The surviving records indicate that the Führer was in such a hurry for his New Chancellery that he was totally unconcerned with what the work might cost.[6] On March 11, 1938, the Reich Minister and Chief of the Reich Chancellery wrote to the Finance Minister: "The Führer and Reich Chancellor has decreed that the entire framework of the Voß Straße building be finished by August 1, and that the building itself must be ready for occupancy by January 1939. The Führer has also insisted that any circumstance that might delay completion of the building be circumvented."

The letter held broadly estimated costs for various parts of the building and a total cost estimate of 27,500,000 reichsmarks, but no blueprints. In former years the Finance Ministry would never have accepted so nebulous a spending request, but time pressure and the political significance of the New Chancellery overruled fiscal prudence. Operation Otto,

III. The New Reich Chancellery

the annexation of Austria, began one day later, March 12, 1938. The Chancellor of the Great German Reich needed an imperial stage on which to parade his majesty.

While construction was going on, Hitler and his generals were preparing war plans in the Reichskanzlerpalais, Wilhelmstraße 77, and the Chancellery Annex, Wilhelmstraße 78. There were hardly any published pictures of these meetings. Why? Hitler was formulating tactics for using criminal violence to create a mighty empire in unprepossessing rooms, adjacent to a garden where a century earlier Bettina von Arnim had listened to the singing of the nightingales. The Wilhelmstraße rooms were old, restful, with the contemplative, reserved architecture suited to bureaucrats who served a Kaiser or a republican government.

Hitler wanted something entirely different, as he announced on October 11, 1941: "Whoever enters the Reich Chancellery must feel that he is standing in the domain of the masters of the world. His journey to the Chancellery, through the triumphal arch, along the broad streets, past the Soldier's Hall to the Place of the People, will take his breath away."

Because the length of the assembled Voß Straße properties far exceeded their width, Speer followed Hitler's original concept and designed the New Reich Chancellery as a string of rooms on a long axis that ran the entire length of Voß Straße. The building consisted of three main parts: two huge wings (Blocks A and C), housing administrative offices, and a central section (Block B) which contained Hitler's office at the center of the so-called marble gallery, a vast corridor leading to a reception hall. "On the long walk from the entrance to the reception hall they'll get a taste of the power and grandeur of the German Reich," exclaimed the Führer.

An arriving diplomat saw a block-long (1,400 foot), three-story structure, covered with yellow-tinted stucco, trimmed with brown stone. The diplomat passed into an honor court, which replaced the south wing of the Chancellery Annex. Two muscular Arno Breker nudes, "Party" and "Army," flanked the main entrance to the New Reich Chancellery from the Honor Court. Speer had conceived the honor court as a foyer for the reception rooms. As an "interior room" the honor court was not visible from the street or the Chancellery garden. It could be reached through the massive doors that had been built into the Chancellery Annex. Its isolation dampened the noises from the city outside and prepared the visitor for his journey into Hitler's *sanctum sanctorum.*

Between the honor court and the courtyard of the Reichskanzlerpalais was a smaller courtyard. It was originally conceived as a connection between the old and new chancelleries, but became Hitler's private entrance. Three garages were directly underneath and were only accessible from the small courtyard. Unlike the Honor Court, the small courtyard was covered with a skylight of polished, colored glass. Diplomats usually never saw the small courtyard.

Ascending outside steps of the honor court, the diplomat entered a reception room with 17-foot high double doors, which opened into a cavernous hall clad in mosaic. The diplomat climbed a few more steps, traversed a round room with a domed ceiling, and came into a marble gallery 480 feet long, twice the length of the Hall of Mirrors at Versailles. Deep window niches filtered the light, creating an agreeable effect Speer noticed in the *Salle de Bal* at the Palace of Fontainebleau. In the middle of the marble gallery was the entrance to Hitler's office.

Hitler came from Munich to see his New Reich Chancellery on January 7, 1939, and loved it. He praised the "genius of the architect," although he thought the reception hall

Sal de Bal, Palace of Fontainebleau, near Paris. The author stands in one of the window niches. Albert Speer designed similar niches for the marble gallery of the New Reich Chancellery.

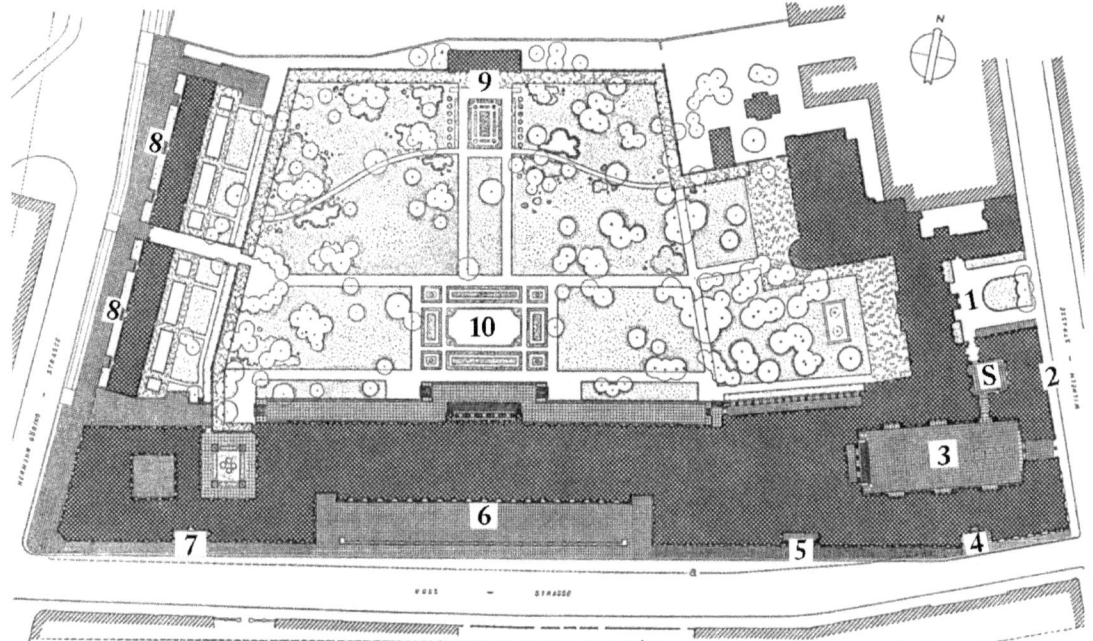

Above: Diagram of Reich Chancellery. (1) Old Reich Chancellery Courtyard, (2) Chancellery Annex, (3) Honor Courtyard, (4) Entrance to the former Borsig Palace, (5) Voßstraße 4 entrance to New Reich Chancellery, (6) Middle portion New Reich Chancellery [block B] (7) Voßstraße 6 entrance to New Reich Chancellery, (8) Leibstandarte SS Adolf Hitler Guard Detachment and Reich Chancellery Staff housing, (9) Greenhouse, (10) Pond, (S) Small Courtyard with Hitler's private entrance to New Reich Chancellery.

Right: Small courtyard, New Reich Chancellery. Originally conceived as a connection between the old and new chancelleries, it became Hitler's private entrance. Three garages were directly underneath. The skylight was of two-colored polished glass plates, giving the small courtyard a more intimate character than the larger honor court.

78　　　The Reich Chancellery and Führerbunker Complex

Above: New Reich Chancellery, Block B. This middle building (Mittelbau, Block B) connected Block A with Block C and was 140 meters long. It was set 16 meters back from the street, the setback forming a plaza in the middle of Voßstraße, directly across the street from the Wertheim Department Store. The limestone façade and the setback from the street proclaimed the importance of this part of the Chancellery, which held the marble gallery and Hitler's office. On the east end of Block B (i.e., the Wilhelmstraße end), was a huge concrete plate-elevator. At the push of a button this plate sank 4.5 meters and was capable of lowering a truck into the cellar of the Chancellery. When closed, the plate-elevator was not visible. In 1944–45, the generals used the plate elevator to lower their cars into the cellar when they attended Hitler's situation conferences. Block B sustained only light bomb damage. The marble that the Russians used in their various building projects came largely from Block B (Bayerische Staatsbibliothek).

Opposite, top: Honor Court. Albert Speer conceived the honor court as a forecourt for the Chancellery reception rooms, a chamber that connected the street with the Chancellery interior. The honor court was not visible from either the street or the Chancellery garden, and replaced the south wing of the Chancellery Annex, which had been razed. The visitor entered the honor court through two massive doors in the annex, which faced Wilhelmplatz. The hermetic construction and the prominent cornice reinforced the sense of isolation from the surrounding city within the honor court, which was meant to prepare the visitor for his journey into Hitler's vast office. Arno Breker's statues, Party and Army, flanked the main entrance. Kurt Schmid Ehmen sculpted the eagle above. The honor court sustained no bomb damage and was a storage point for munitions during the Battle for Berlin in 1945. Breker's statues were removed to a safe storage place in 1944. Schmid Ehmen's eagle is today on display as a war trophy in Moscow's Red Army War Museum.

Bottom: New Reich Chancellery, Block A. This three-story office building was at Hermann Göringstraße and Voßstraße. The simply finished façade emphasized Block A's bureaucratic character. The Nazi Party offices were here. The Chancellery reception hall was the only ceremonial room in Block A. The identical entrances for Block A and Block C emphasized the unity of Party and Wehrmacht. In the middle of Block A was a simple light court. A second open court adjacent to the garden was more elaborate, with fountains and decorated walls. The ornamentation was provided because this courtyard was visible through the windows of the reception hall. Hitler's planned expansion of the reception hall probably would have eliminated the open court. Block A suffered the most severe damage. Two huge bombs destroyed the roof and the entire third floor (Bayerische Staatsbibliothek).

Left: Dining room corridor. The dining room connected the Reichskanzlerpalais to the garden façade of the New Reich Chancellery. The roof structure of the Reichskanzlerpalais was extended over the dining room. This part of the Chancellery was remarkable for its Romanesque-arched corridor, which resembled a medieval cloister. During the war the dining room sustained only very mild damage to the roof.

Below: New Reich Chancellery, Block C. Block C, intended as a transition between Block B and the Borsig Palais, was divided into two parts: the west part, adjacent to Block B (Part I), extended to the main entrance, and the east part extended from the main entrance to the Borsig Palais (Part II). The simply finished façade emphasized the bureaucratic character of Block C. The two story Part II housed the Presidential Chancellery and connected to the two stories of the Borsig Palais and the three story Chancellery. Part II was the same height as the Borsig Palais. Part I shared many architectural characteristics with its two-story neighbor, Block B. Part I had three stories and housed the Wehrmacht offices. Block C sustained practically no bomb damage.

Terrace, garden front. The New Reich Chancellery looked so different from the garden that a visitor might have thought he was seeing a wholly separate building. The terrace ran the entire length of Block B, as well as a quarter of the length of Blocks A and C. The garden façade with its slanting roof symbolized the private section of the Chancellery. The most prominent portion of the façade was the protruding section with its columns, behind which were the windows of Hitler's office. At either end were Austrian sculptor Josef Thorak's horses. The terrace sustained very little bomb damage. Until 1994 Thorak's horses stood at a Soviet military sport site. Their current whereabouts is unknown.

Top: Dining room interior. This was a state dining room used for official functions. A separate restaurant was reserved for chancellery personnel.
Bottom: Barracks, Hitler's guard regiment, Hermann Göring Straße.

Top: Hitler's office.
Bottom: Cabinet meeting room. Hitler never used this wood-paneled room. Sometimes a visitor would walk in to look at it. The Führer used his own office solely for meetings or receptions. He continued to work in the Reichskanzlerpalais. Most of the time the gigantic rooms in the New Reich Chancellery stood empty.

Marble gallery (Walter Frentz).

was too small. He wanted it three times as large. The long trek state guests and diplomats had to make down the gallery was a concern to Speer. He had worried about the polished marble floor, which he did not want to cover with carpet. Hitler had no such qualms. "That's exactly right," said Hitler. "Diplomats should have to practice moving on a slippery surface."

Hitler was delighted with his vast office, which was larger than Benito Mussolini's, and fitted out with five tall windows. He found particularly appealing an inlay on his desk of a sword half drawn from its sheath. "Good, good," he said, "when the diplomats sitting in front of me at this desk see that, they'll learn to shiver and shake."

Speer had incorporated four gilded panels over the four doors of the office, the Four Virtues, who gazed down at Hitler: Wisdom, Prudence, Fortitude, and Justice. The Führer ignored them.

The mammoth marble-topped table by the window was ornamental until 1944. As the Allied armies were closing in on Germany, Hitler held military conferences in his office with maps spread out on the table.

The bureaucrats' office space in the New Reich Chancellery was mainly located in its westernmost section (Block A) and easternmost section, (Block C) at the corner of Voß Straße and Hermann Göring Straße and adjacent to the Borsigpalais, respectively. The plain three-story façades of these two office blocks emphasized their administrative character. The offices of the Nazi Party were situated within the westernmost block (block A), while the easternmost block (block C) held the offices of the Presidential Chancellery.

At the topping out ceremony in the Deutschlandhalle, August 2, 1938, Hitler told the workmen that the building was timeless:

Marble gallery with Gobelin from Vienna's Kunsthistorisches Museum. For centuries, the Austrian emperors collected French and Dutch Gobelins and made the Vienna Gobelin collection the largest in the world. After World War I, the foreign minister of the Austrian Republic proposed to liquidate part of the imperial collection to relieve the utter destitution of the population. But the Gobelins were considered too precious to sell. They remained in Vienna and from time to time were displayed in public. In 1938, the Nazis forced the Kunsthistorisches Museum to lend three series of tapestries, 21 in all, to the Reich Chancellery. They were handed over with borrowing slips dated February 27, 1939. At the end of World War II the Gobelins disappeared. The tapestry series depicted scenes of the life of Alexander the Great (eight tapestries, Dutch, 17th century, following Charles Le Brun's paintings and the cartoons made after them for the Gobelin manufacturing in Paris); scenes of the life of the Roman Consul Decius Mus (five tapestries, Brussels, 17th century, with the city symbol of Brussels, after cartoons by Rubens); and episodes from the life of Dido and Aeneas (eight tapestries, Antwerp, 17th century, by M. Wauters following cartoons by Giovanni Francesco Romanelli). Hermann Göring took other Gobelins from the Kunsthistorisches Museum and hung them in his mansion, Carinhall.

> This is the special, wonderful property of architecture. When the work has been done, a monument remains. That endures. It is something different from a pair of boots, which also can be made, but which the wearer wears out in a year or two and then throws away. This remains, and through the centuries will bear witness to all those who helped to create it.

Forty-five hundred workers toiled in three shifts to complete the New Reich Chancellery, wrote Speer. After they presented their Führer with the keys to the place, Hitler spoke to them, January 9, 1939, in the Sportpalast (the weather was bad and the ceremony could not be held outside the Chancellery):

> As a German racial comrade I am what I have always been and I do not want to be more. My private home is exactly the same as before my accession to power and always will be the

Hitler greets cleaning women at the dedication of the New Reich Chancellery, January 9, 1939. Hitler's salutation to the cleaning women suggests a special irony. His paternal grandmother, Maria Anna Schicklgruber (1795–1847), was also a cleaning woman. Hitler's father, Alois Schicklgruber, may have been half–Jewish. He was Maria Anna's illegitimate son. In Linz, Maria Anna had become pregnant while working in the house of a wealthy Jew named Frankenberger, and Frankenberger's young son might have been the father. In 1842 Maria Anna married Johann Georg Hiedler, who never adopted or legitimized the stepson. Hiedler's brother, Johann Nepomuk Hüttler, executed this legal nicety in 1876, when Alois was 39 years old. The name "Hitler" probably arose through a hearing error of the pastor filling out the document. For a detailed account of the various theories about Hitler's paternal grandfather, see *Explaining Hitler* by Ron Rosenbaum (Random House, 1998) (Ullstein Bilderdienst).

same.... I stand here as a representative of the German people. And whenever I receive anyone in the chancellery, it is not the private individual Adolf Hitler who receives him, but the leader of the German nation—and therefore it is not I who receives him, but Germany through me. For that reason I want these rooms to be in keeping with their high mission. Every individual has contributed to a structure that will outlast the centuries and will speak to posterity of our times. This is the first architectural creation of the new, Great German Reich.[7]

Even as a ruin, Speer hoped, the Chancellery and his other buildings would be eternal monuments. In 1934, Speer proposed "A Theory of Ruin Value." His idea was that buildings of modern construction were poorly suited to form that "bridge of tradition" to future generations that Hitler was calling for. It was hard to imagine that rusting heaps of rubble could communicate the heroic inspirations that Hitler admired in the monuments of the past. Speer's theory was intended to deal with this dilemma. By using special materials and by applying certain principles of statics, Speer wanted to build structures that even in a state of decay, after hundreds or thousands of years, would more or less resemble Roman ruins.

To illustrate his ideas Speer had a romantic drawing prepared. It showed what Hitler's

The author in the Mohrenstraße subway station. Chancellery marble covers the walls, pillars, and benches.

reviewing stand on the Nuremberg Zeppelin Field would look like after generations of neglect, overgrown with ivy, its columns fallen, the walls crumbling, but the outlines still clearly recognizable. Hitler's entourage regarded this drawing as blasphemy. That anyone could even conceive of a period of decline for the newly founded Reich, destined to last a thousand years, seemed outrageous to many loyal Nazis. But the Führer himself accepted Speer's ideas as logical and illuminating. He gave orders that in the future the important buildings of his Reich were to be erected in keeping with the principles of this "law of ruins."

To implement the law of ruins, Speer and his associates planned to avoid, as far as possible, steel girders and reinforced concrete. Despite their height, the walls were intended to withstand the impact of wind even if the roofs and ceilings were so neglected that they no longer braced the walls. The static factors were calculated with this in mind. But Angela Schönberger has written that Speer's theory of ruin value was a euphemism that hid the real reason why this building technique was preferred: the economic necessity to minimize the use of iron, which was urgently needed for armaments. In the event, Speer didn't need to worry about ruin value. The New Reich Chancellery did not endure for centuries. It was badly damaged during the Allied bombing of Berlin, and the Communists razed it. They used the marble for their war memorial in Berlin-Treptow, and in the Mohrenstraße subway station, which is adjacent to the corner of Voß Straße and Wilhelmstraße. Authorities are divided over whether the red marble in the foyer of Humboldt University came from the Chancellery.[8] A Berlin theater, the Volksbühne, destroyed during the war, was rebuilt with Chancellery wood paneling.[9]

Events in the New Reich Chancellery

DEDICATION

On January 12, 1939, Hitler and the diplomats accredited to the Reich exchanged New Year's greetings in a ceremony that incidentally marked the dedication of the palatial new Chancellery. As a popular attraction the dedication left the diplomats a poor second in the day's ceremonies, wrote the *New York Times*' Guido Enderis.* The gigantic building, stamped out of the ground in nine months, was the whole show.

"Although its course ran stormy, the year just ended also bequeathed us a day of cheer and promise, and the memory of it fills us with strength and hope," Msgr. Cesare Orsenigo, the Papal Nuncio, told Hitler at the outset of his greetings.[10]

"The German nation," said Hitler, "recalls with profound gratitude that the year 1938 also brought the German people fulfillment of its incontestable right to self-determination. If this was achieved without disturbing the peace of Europe for one single day it was actually due to the wise discernment of the powers, which found expression in the peace of Munich."

Hilter mingled with the diplomats for half an hour, conversing with Msgr. Orsenigo and the ambassadors, including Alexei T. Merekaloff, the Soviet envoy. Then the Führer went down the line to shake hands with the ministers and chargés d'affaires. The reception took place in the reception room adjoining Hitler's mammoth office. To reach it, according to Guido Enderis, the diplomats had to traverse a stretch of richly marbled, soft-carpeted floor banked with a profusion of orchids for a distance of about 1,000 feet.

Hitler's desk, at the far end of his office, had no push buttons for summoning adjutants. The desk equipment included nine pencils in various colors in two simple, grooved trays, a glass inkwell mounted on a bronze pedestal, an ordinary pair of scissors, an electric lamp with a light yellow shade, a pad of writing paper, an ordinary desk telephone, a large magnifying glass, and a case for eyeglasses. Behind the desk stood a bronze bust of the late Reich President Paul von Hindenburg, while at the other end of the room a spacious divan and several cozy chairs suggested a spot where Hitler could converse with visitors. Franz von Lenbach's portrait of Bismarck adorned the wall above.

The office books included *Mein Kampf* and directories of the Reichstag, directories of all government offices, directories of youth hostels, and a book about British and German lines in World War I. Also among the books was Hans Frank's new compendium of German law, *Rechtsgrundlegung des nationalsozialistischen Führerstaates*. Frank, Hitler's lawyer, became governor-general of Nazi-occupied Poland in 1939, and was hanged at Nuremberg in 1946 for war crimes and crimes against humanity. G.M. Gilbert, an American psychologist, interviewed Frank in prison. Gilbert quoted from Goethe's *Faust*, Part I:

> Zwei Seelen wohnen, ach!, in meiner Brust,
> Die eine will sich von der andern trennen;

---

*Guido Enderis, who had joined the *Times* in 1928, was a Nazi sympathizer with limited journalistic talents. When Germany declared war on the United States after Pearl Harbor, Enderis was the only American journalist not arrested and detained. Instead, the regime allowed Enderis to continue to live in Berlin's Adlon Hotel. Enderis eventually moved to the *Times*' bureau in Berne, where his sympathies continued to unsettle the *Times*' editors. "Disappointed and concerned tone your Goebbels story yesternight," managing editor Edwin James cabled Enderis in October 1944. Enderis had suggested in his report that Germany would be able to hold off the Allied advance. (Laurel Leff, *Buried by the Times*, 279.)

Hitler and Papal Nuncio Cesare Orsenigo. The former Milan priest took up the German assignment in 1930, after serving as Apostolic Nuncio to Hungary and Poland. His predecessor in Berlin was Eugenio Cardinal Pacelli, who later became papal secretary of state and then Pope Pius XII. When Hitler was slaughtering Jews *en masse*, Orsenigo said virtually nothing, since Pius wished to avoid the reprisals that public condemnation of the massacre might have provoked. Orsenigo remained in Berlin until a few weeks before the Russians captured the city in 1945, when he moved to Eichstätt, south of Nuremberg. He died in Eichstätt April 1, 1946, age 73.

> Die eine hält, in derber Liebeslust,
> Sich an die Welt mit klammernden Organen;
> Die andere hebt gewaltsam sich vom Dunst
> Zu den Gefilden hoher Ahnen.
>
> Two souls live, oh!, within my breast,
> The one wants to separate itself from the other;
> Crudely lustful, the one holds to the world with clasping organs;
> The other lifts itself forcefully from the haze
> To high ancestral fields.

"Yes, we do have evil in us," Frank agreed, "but do not forget that there is always a Mephistopheles who brings it out."[11]

First Foreign Visitor

On January 16, 1939, Count Stephen Csaky, the Hungarian foreign minister, became the first official foreign visitor to the New Reich Chancellery, according to the *New York Times*.[12] Foreign Minister von Ribbentrop met Csaky at the railroad station and conferred with him for two hours. Hitler received Csaky at the Chancellery in the afternoon, and expressed considerable irritation at Hungary because the previous foreign minister, Coloman Kanya, showed a "weak" attitude at Munich when the Führer grabbed for the Sudetenland. A dark cloud overshadowed relations between Germany and Hungary, said Hitler, who claimed he always considered Kanya an enemy of Germany. Csaky's Berlin visit lasted two days.

Emil Hacha Yields Czechoslovakia

On March 14, 1939, Emil Hacha, president of Czechoslovakia, was ushered into Hitler's New Reich Chancellery. Hitler had annexed the Sudetenland, on the Czech-German border, in September 1938. Now he intended to press the ailing Hacha to surrender the remainder of his country. Hacha was a small, shy, sickly former lawyer who arrived by train, since he had a heart condition and was unable to fly. His foreign minister Frantisek Chvalkovsky, his secretary, and his daughter accompanied him. To increase the pressure on Hacha, Hitler kept him waiting in the Adlon Hotel until midnight. As Hacha sweated, Hitler watched a movie. ("The old tested method of political tactics," Goebbels wrote in his diary).

At midnight, Hitler summoned Hacha. The Czech president inspected an honor guard, then was led into Hitler's vast office. Göring, called back from a vacation, Foreign Minister Ribbentrop, Otto Meissner, Walter Hewel, General Wilhelm Keitel, Press Chief Otto Dietrich, and interpreter Dr. Paul Schmidt were already there. Accompanying Hacha were Chvalkovsky and Dr. Voytech Mastny, the Czech ambassador in Berlin. Hacha was red faced

Left to right: Two unidentified men, Hitler, and Count Stephen Csaky, the Hungarian Foreign Minister (Bayerische Staatsbibliothek).

III. The New Reich Chancellery

with indignation and anxiety. He listened nervously as Hitler launched into a diatribe against the Czechs and their former president Benes, who had resisted giving up the Sudetenland in 1938, and later fled to London (and whom Winston Churchill called "beans"). It was necessary to impose a protectorate over Czechoslovakia to safeguard the Reich, shouted Hitler. German troops were already on the march. Keitel confirmed that they would cross the Czech border at 6 A.M. The document Hitler wanted signed lay in its final form upon a table, as well as an *aide memoire* relating to the future administrative status of Bohemia and Moravia. Hacha and Chvalkovsky declared they could not sign. If they acquiesced, their people would forever detest them.

The Germans were pitiless. They chased Hacha and Chvalkovsky around the table, bringing them forcibly back to the document and repeating that if they refused to sign half of Prague would be destroyed in the space of two hours by German airplanes—and that would be only the beginning.[13] Hundreds of bombers were awaiting the order to start, said Göring, which they would receive at 6 A.M. if the signatures had not been affixed by that hour. In fact, snow had grounded all the planes. Said Hitler to Albert Speer,

> At last I had so belabored the old man that his nerves gave way completely, and he was on the point of signing; then he had a heart attack. In the adjoining room Dr. [Thedor] Morell gave him an injection, but in this case it was too effective. Hacha regained his strength, revived, and was no longer prepared to sign, until I finally wore him down again.

The Germans tried to phone Prague but initially the call would not go through. Ribbentrop was livid with fury at the German Post Office, which was responsible for the telephone network. Finally, over a very poor connection, Hacha ordered that Czech troops not fire on the invading Germans.

Hitler attributed Hacha's ultimate acquiescence to the intimidating effect of the New Reich Chancellery. But Hacha was convinced that he had no choice. After the British Prime Minister Neville Chamberlain and the French President Edouard Daladier had sold out Czechoslovakia at Munich the previous year, the Czechs lost their powerful border fortifications, and were helpless against a German invasion. The German Army proceeded to roll into Prague, and Czechoslovakia ceased to exist.

The loss of Czechoslovakia was an unmitigated disaster. Britain and France were immediately deprived of 21 regular Czech army divisions, 16 second line divisions already mobilized, and the Czech mountain fortress line. Until September 1938, this fortified barrier alone had tied down 30 German divisions, the main strength of the mobile, fully trained German army. Germany also gained control of the Skoda Works, the second largest armaments maker in Central Europe (Krupp in Essen was the largest). In 1938 Skoda's production was the equivalent of the entire British arms industry.

The situation of the Western Allies vis à vis Hitler had taken a disastrous turn for the worse. The annexation of Austria in March 1938 had brought 6,750,000 Austrians into the Reich, the Munich agreement another 3,500,000 Sudetens, over 10 million workers and soldiers. Germans now acknowledged their Führer as an authentic genius.

Yet in 1945, contemplating suicide in his Berlin bunker, 12 meters underground, Hitler lamented his "lost opportunity," and railed against the dead Chamberlain: "The fellow spoiled my entrance into Prague."[14]

"The war should have been started in 1938," Hitler added. Then it would have been won "easily and quickly." But the Western allies "accepted everything. Like weaklings, they gave in to all my demands."

Hitler and Hacha in the New Reich Chancellery, where Hacha agreed under pressure to make Czechoslovakia a German protectorate. Hacha remained Czech president until 1945. When the country was liberated, the Russians imprisoned him, and he died on June 26, 1945. He is buried in an unmarked grave in Vinohrady Cemetery (Ullstein Bilderdienst).

Rome-Berlin Axis Sealed

On May 22, 1939, amidst gaudy ceremonies, Germany and Italy signed an automatic offensive-defensive alliance for 10 years, the so-called *Pact of Steel*. The pact provided for the closest economic, political, and military collaboration and support in peace and war. The declared objective was the reorganization of Europe and the creation of a "just peace" throughout the world. At 11 A.M., Joachim von Ribbentrop and Count Galeazzo Ciano, Italian foreign minister and Benito Mussolini's son-in-law, signed the pact in a festively decorated hall of the New Reich Chancellery. Hitler witnessed the event in his simple brown uniform. He looked grim and determined, according to *New York Times* correspondent Otto D. Tolischus, as he sat between the two foreign ministers in their elaborately bemedalled uniforms. But when the pact had been signed, the Führer broke into a broad smile, and "grasping Count Ciano's hand with both of his, he nearly lifted the Italian off his feet with the warmth of his congratulations." Hitler then presented Ciano with the Grand Cross of the German Eagle.[15]

Opposite (top and bottom): Hitler inspects Czech border fortifications, 1938. The Czech border defenses astonished the German generals. To their surprise, a test bombardment showed that German weapons would not have prevailed against them. Hitler was impressed. The fortifications were amazingly massive, he said, laid out with extraordinary skill and echeloned, making prime use of the terrain. "Given a resolute defense, taking them would have been very difficult and would have cost us a great many lives. Now we have obtained them without loss of blood."

III. The New Reich Chancellery

The day had not been declared a holiday, and so the crowd that usually witnessed Chancellery events was small. But a thousand boys and girls of the Hitler Youth and some groups of office and factory workers turned out. They cheered loudly outside and their cheers escalated into a roar when Hitler and Ciano appeared on the Chancellery Annex balcony.

(Ciano came to a bad end. Convicted of treason, he was executed in Rome, on Mussolini's orders, with a shot to the back of the head, January 11, 1944.)

Hilter Congratulates Submarine Commander Günther Prien

On October 18, 1939, Lieutenant Commander Günther Prien and the crew of the German submarine U-47, which sank the British battleship *Royal Oak* at Scapa Flow, a British naval base in Scotland, were flown to Berlin. The October 14, 1939, sinking drowned 833 British sailors and severely damaged British morale. Hitler had sent his own four-engine Condor airplane to fetch the heroes. They received a tumultuous reception from the population. Hitler welcomed them in the New Reich Chancellery at noon.[16]

The U-47 crew, looking tired and bewildered after a day of publicity, marched into the Chancellery single file and sat at long tables arranged in horseshoe form. There were some thirty crewmembers in all. Press Chief Otto Dietrich described them as "living proof that Churchill lies and suppresses new German victories." The young men silently listened

Hitler receives Lieutenant Commander Günther Prien in the New Reich Chancellery (Ullstein Bilderdienst).

to their 31-year-old commander tell his story, how he "wormed and twisted his way through the mine barrier." Then he suddenly found himself inside the bay. After sinking the giant battleship, he escaped through the same narrow passage whence he had come and safely reached his homeport.

Hitler presented Prien with the Knight's Order of the Iron Cross. "This great, daring deed has only strengthened the whole German people in their unshakable faith in victory," said the Führer.

Following the presentation, Commander Prien and his crew went to lunch in Hitler's private residence in the Reichskanzlerpalais.

From all parts of the Reich, gifts poured in for the submarine crew. The sailor who fired the torpedoes that sank the *Royal Oak* received furniture for his living room and kitchen. The entire crew was offered free vacations in all parts of the Reich, along with cigarettes, crates of wine, and homemade socks. The mayor of Wiesbaden invited the men to spend two weeks as guests of the city.

Over the next two years Prien is credited with destroying 28 merchant ships. He also published his memoirs, *I Sank the Royal Oak,* which hit the bestseller list in Britain. While leading an attack on an Allied convoy, Prien was drowned when a British destroyer, the *Wolverine,* sank the U-47 on March 6, 1941.

HITLER TELLS HIS GENERALS OF HIS PLANS TO ATTACK THE WEST

At noon, November 23, 1939, 200 of Hitler's generals assembled in the New Reich Chancellery.[17] Hitler announced that he planned to attack the West immediately.

Hitler boasted of his string of successes, and added, "In fighting I see the fate of all creatures. Nobody can avoid fighting if he does not want to go under." Then he reiterated his old canard, the need for *Lebensraum.* Germany needed oil fields, rubber, and mineral wealth. Germany no longer had to fight on two fronts, the *bête noire* of every German military strategist since Carl von Clausewitz. The road to the West was wide open, but no one knew for how long. "Basically, I did not organize the armed forces in order not to strike. The decision to strike was always in me," said Hitler. A few divisions were sufficient to hold the Polish front, Hitler added. "We can oppose Russia only when we are free in the West. Everything is determined by the fact that the moment is favorable now. In six months, it might not be."

Hitler told his generals that he was everything:

> In all modesty I must describe my own person: irreplaceable. Neither a military man nor a civilian could replace me. Attempts at assassination may be repeated. I am convinced of my powers of intellect and decision. Wars are always ended only by the annihilation of the opponent. Anyone who believes differently is irresponsible. Time is working for our adversaries. Now there is a relationship of forces which can never be more propitious for us, but which can only deteriorate. The enemy will not make peace when the relationship of forces is unfavorable for us. No compromise. Hardness towards ourselves. I shall strike and not capitulate. The fate of the Reich depends only on me.

Flattering his generals, Hitler emphasized that the army was much better than it had been in 1914, and was certainly superior to the armies of Britain and France. Furthermore, the Ruhr, the industrial heartland of Germany, had to be protected. If Britain and France advanced through Belgium and Holland, German heavy manufacturing would be crippled.

Germany must occupy Belgium and Holland first, then lay mines off the English coast to achieve a blockade.

"I shall attack France and England at the most favorable and earliest moment. Breach of the neutrality of Belgium and Holland is of no importance. No one will question that when we have won," asserted Hitler. The German people were at a peak of psychological readiness for war, he declared. "I want to annihilate the enemy. Behind me stand the German people, whose morale can only grow worse."

Hitler's final comments were ominous. "If we come through this struggle victoriously—and we shall come through it—our time will go down in the history of our people. I shall stand or fall in this struggle. I shall never survive the defeat of my people. No capitulation to the outside, no revolution from within."

SUMNER WELLES PEACE MISSION

President Franklin D. Roosevelt sent his undersecretary of state, Sumner Welles, to Europe in a last-ditch effort to secure peace. On the platform of Berlin's Anhalter station, March 1, 1940, the staff of the American embassy, which had no ambassador, waited for Welles' train from Zurich. Roosevelt had recalled the U.S. ambassador in response to German violation of the Munich Agreement and the occupation of Czechoslovakia in 1939. Uniformed representatives of the German Foreign Office accompanied American embassy officials. The train was late. At last it puffed into the smoke-stained train shed, and Welles, who wore a brown soft hat instead of the diplomat's traditional top hat, alighted. There were formal introductions, and as the American envoy and his aides drove off to the Hotel Adlon, Berlin's air-alarm sounded, in one of its regular rehearsals.

On March 2, the massive bronze doors of the New Reich Chancellery swung open to admit Welles' car. In the courtyard an honor guard of black-uniformed SS troops was drawn up, their rifles and leather puttees glistening in the sun. A red carpet was down. Welles passed into the study of the Führer.

"In an atmosphere just a trifle less desperate than that prevailing yesterday but without fundamental change in the situation, Chancellor Hitler today received Sumner Welles, United States Under-Secretary of State, and conferred with him for one and a half hours," wrote *New York Times* correspondent Otto D. Tolischus.[18]

Welles showed no cordiality in his conversation. He began by defining his mission, saying that America was interested in the creation of lasting peace in Europe, and not in a temporary truce. The government of the United States had sent him to ascertain the possibilities of such a peace. He could, however, make no proposals, nor could he undertake any commitments on behalf of the United States. Welles reminded interpreter Paul Schmidt of the French ambassador in London, René Massigli, who, on a similar mission during Franco-German negotiations in the 1920s, opened the parley with the words: "I am no more than a pencil with two ears." Even if Hitler had been eager to start peace talks, Welles' icy reserve would hardly have encouraged him.

In fact, Hitler's peace conditions were impossibly onerous. They included: 1) the end of the British "strangle-hold" on the world's economic life, with dismantling of Gibraltar and the Suez Canal defenses; 2) German hegemony over Czechoslovakia, Poland and Hungary; 3) guarantees that Britain and France would not stir the Balkans or Scandinavia against the Reich; 4) freedom of the seas; 5) the return of Germany's former colonies, which the Allies had taken away after World War I.

Hitler told Welles that the German armed forces were only waiting the command to strike, that all was in readiness and that victory was assured. Britain was in a dangerous spot because of a German submarine blockade, while Germany herself was strong enough economically to resist the Allied attempts to starve her into submission. Not surprisingly, Hitler's meeting with Welles accomplished absolutely nothing. Berlin morning newspapers carried only a small paragraph regarding Welles' visit, and some even failed to mention it.

The next day, Welles visited Hermann Göring in his vast hunting lodge, Carinhall. He viewed Göring's art collection, much of it stolen from Jewish collectors. Göring also had a gigantic collection of baroque uniforms in pastel shades of white, blue, and gray, bedecked with medals. He adored jewelry and wore huge diamond and emerald rings on both hands. On his desk was a pot of diamonds, which he would fondle during interviews. At Carinhall he kept a menagerie, including bison, elk, and lion cubs. Occasionally wearing outlandish costumes, such as forester or sultan, Göring received his guests. Not all were impressed. After his visit to Carinhall, Welles said, "It would be difficult to find an uglier building or one more intrinsically vulgar in its ostentatious display."

On April 4, 1940, Hitler decreed that the bronze on the massive doors leading to the honor court, where distinguished guests were received, would be stripped and contributed to Hermann Göring's collection of essential metals for weapons. The bronze dressing on the huge portals was replaced with wooden panels. So it was that Sumner Welles, on his failed peace mission, became one of the last foreign visitors to pass through these doors. Meantime, the Reich was collecting metals and other war materials, including bronze church bells, which were presented to Hitler on his 51st birthday, April 20, 1940.

Bronze main entrance doors, New Reich Chancellery.

(In September 1940, Welles was returning on a train to Washington with Roosevelt and other dignitaries from the Alabama funeral of House Speaker William Bankhead. At 4 A.M., Welles, quite drunk, solicited sex from a Pullman car porter. The immensely wealthy, aristocratic, Groton and Harvard educated Welles had a huge sexual appetite for women and men, black and white, but his money, foreign travel, and cordon of servants had hitherto allowed him to disport himself without public scandal. This time, Welles came a cropper. His advances to the porter were reported to the Secret Service and the president of the railroad. Roosevelt tried to protect Welles, but in 1943 had to cashier him.)

HITLER RETURNS TO THE CHANCELLERY AFTER HIS ARMIES SMASH FRANCE

The reception awaiting Hitler in Berlin when his train pulled into the Anhalter-Bahnhof at three o'clock, July 6, 1940, was astounding.[19] It surpassed even the homecomings after the great pre-war triumphs like the annexation of Austria in 1938. Many people had been standing for six hours, as the dull morning gave way to brilliant sunshine in the afternoon. The streets were strewn with flowers all the way from the station to the Reich Chancellery. Hundreds of thousands cheered themselves hoarse. Field Marshal Wilhelm Keitel (who was hanged at Nuremberg in 1946) praised Hitler as the greatest warlord of all time. The Führer was called out time after time onto the Chancellery Annex balcony to soak up the wild adulation of the throng. This was Hitler's last spectacular victory.

Sumner Welles and Hermann Göring at Carinhall (Library of Congress).

MOLOTOV VISITS THE CHANCELLERY

Vyacheslav Molotov, the Soviet foreign minister, set off late November 10, 1940, from Moscow's Belorussia Station. He carried a pistol in his pocket. A retinue of 60, including

16 secret policemen, three servants and a doctor, accompanied him. Everyone wore identical dark blue suits, grey ties, and cheap felt hats, obviously ordered in bulk.[20]

At 11:05 A.M., November 11, Molotov's train pulled into Berlin's Anhalter Station, which was decorated with flowers and Soviet flags. Molotov wore a dark coat and a grey Homburg hat. Ribbentrop, Heinrich Himmler, and Field Marshal Keitel welcomed him. Molotov conferred with Ribbentrop in Bismarck's old office and was inscrutable. "A rather frosty smile glided over his intelligent, chess-player's face," noticed interpreter Paul Schmidt. Seated nearby in one of Bismarck's massive chairs, the diminutive Soviet ambassador to Berlin, Vladimir Dekanozov, could barely touch the floor with his feet. After lunch at Schloß Bellevue, a Mercedes sedan drove Molotov to the Chancellery. He was led through bronze doors, guarded by heel-clicking SS men, into Hitler's enormous office. The guards threw open the doors and formed an archway with Nazi salutes. Molotov marched stolidly toward Hitler's vast desk at the far end of the room. Hitler hesitated, then walked jerkily to greet Molotov with small, rapid steps. The Führer stopped and made a Nazi salute before shaking hands with a cold, moist palm. Molotov was unimpressed:

> Hitler.... There was nothing remarkable in his appearance. But he was a very smug, and, if I may say so, vain person. He wasn't at all the same as he is portrayed in movies and books. They focus attention on his appearance, depict him as a madman, a maniac, but that's not true. He was very smart, though narrow-minded and obtuse at the same time because of his egotism and the absurdity of his primordial idea. But he didn't behave like a madman with me. During our first conversation he spoke a monologue most of the time while I kept pushing him to go into greater detail.[21]

Hitler led Molotov to a lounge area where Molotov, Dekanozov and the interpreters sat on the sofa, while Hitler occupied his usual armchair. The Führer immediately launched into a speech, claiming he had defeated Britain, been generous to Stalin, and had zero interest in the Balkans, all lies. Molotov responded with sharp questions about the relationship between Germany and Russia.

"You've got to have a warm-water port. Iran, India—that's your future," said Hitler. Molotov replied, "Why that's an interesting idea, how do you see it?" Hitler furnished no answer.

At 2 P.M. the next day, Hitler received Molotov, Vsevolod Merkulov and Dekanozov for a lunch with Goebbels and Ribbentrop. Molotov described the gathering:

> Hitler said, "The war is on, so I don't drink coffee now because my people don't drink coffee. I don't eat meat, only vegetarian food. I don't smoke, don't drink liquor." I looked and it seemed a rabbit was sitting next to me eating grass—an idealistic man. It goes without saying that I was abstaining from nothing. Hitler's team drank and ate, too.

"Hitler clasped me with one hand when our picture was being taken," said Molotov. "I was asked in Canada in 1942 why I was smiling in that picture. Simply because they got nothing from us and never would!"

The second meeting between Hitler and Molotov, after lunch, lasted for a tense three hours. Hitler accused Russia of greed and almost exploded when Molotov pressed him about German troops in Finland and Romania. "Those are trifles," Hitler angrily exclaimed. Hitler came out of his office when Molotov was leaving and walked him to the coat rack. States Molotov, "He told me while I put on my coat, 'I am sure history will remember

German Foreign Minister Joachim von Ribbentrop (right) bids goodbye to Soviet Foreign Minister Vyacheslav Molotov in the Anhalter Bahnhof (Railroad Station) after Molotov's visit to Hitler in the Reich Chancellery, November 14, 1940. Interpreter Gustav Hilger is between Ribbentrop and Molotov. Hilger was born of German parents in Moscow, studied engineering in Germany and lived in Russia from 1908 until 1941. Knowing both countries and languages equally well, he served as the aide to various German ambassadors accredited to the Moscow Government from January 1923 to June 1941. He was present at Foreign Minister Ribbentrop's Kremlin visit in September 1939, and spoke of the signing of the Hitler-Stalin pact as the crowning achievement of his efforts on behalf of a good German-Soviet relationship. Hilger was also on hand at the fateful morning interview on June 22, 1941, when the German ambassador, Friedrich Werner Graf von der Schulenburg, delivered Hitler's war declaration to Molotov. After Hilger returned to Berlin from Moscow, he became the liaison between Ribbentrop's office and the SS Einsatzgruppen, or Special Task Forces, which murdered some 1.4 million Jews on the Eastern Front. Hilger's boss Ribbentrop was hanged for his crimes in 1946, but the CIA took Hilger to the United States and paid his salary for years. "We were very glad he was here because he had a tremendous knowledge about the Soviet Union," said U.S. diplomat George F. Kennan. "We brought him here because we were worried that, if we didn't, the Soviets would get him."[22] Hilger, who died in Munich in 1965, was one of 22 ex-Nazis the CIA brought to the U.S. Among them were Gestapo Officer Klaus Barbie, the "butcher of Lyon," and Walter Schreiber, whom a Polish tribunal convicted in absentia of conducting gruesome medical experiments in the Auschwitz death camp. The U.S. government helped many of these men avoid prosecution (Bundesarchiv, Bild 183–1984–1206–523/Photographer: unknown/License CC-BY-SA-3.0).

Stalin's name forever!' 'I don't doubt it,' I answered. 'But I also hope it will remember me, too,' Hitler said. 'I don't doubt this either.'"

Molotov gave a banquet, attended by Göring, Deputy Führer Rudolf Hess, and Ribbentrop. British bombers attacked Berlin during the meal. Because the Soviet Embassy had no air-raid shelter, Ribbentrop took Molotov to the Foreign Ministry bunker. Ribbentrop was contemptuous of the English. "Britain is finished," he told Molotov. "If that's so, then why are we in this shelter and whose bombs are those falling?" Molotov responded.

On June 22, 1941, Hitler's armies invaded the Soviet Union. The meetings with Molotov had hardened the Führer's resolve to be done with Russia once and for all. When the Soviet diplomats left Berlin, someone hung a sign on their embassy, "Closed for fumigation." But after four years of Hitler's catastrophic military blunders, the Russians did the fumigating.

Franz Gürtner's Chancellery Funeral

Franz Gürtner was Reich Justice Minister under Hitler. Gürtner's first official contact with Hitler was just after the November 1923 Beerhall Putsch. Hitler and his cronies had tried but failed to overthrow the government of Bavaria. As an official in the Bavarian Justice Ministry, Gürtner ruled that the people's court in Munich, rather than the federal court in Leipzig, should try Hitler and his followers, assuring a light sentence. Gürtner also ruled against the repressive measures that had been imposed on the Nazi Party, in particular the ban on Hitler's public speaking.

In 1932, Reich Chancellor Franz von Papen made Gürtner Reich Justice Minister. When Hitler came to power in 1933, he left Gürtner in his post to give his regime legitimacy. The Führer expected that Gürtner would rubber stamp new policies. Gürtner complied. In 1934 Gürtner formulated the Emergency Federal Defense Act, which legalized Hitler's murders of his adversaries, in particular Ernst Röhm, during the Night of the Long Knives. With the introduction of the Nazi People's Court and the Gestapo, Germany became a terror state. Heinrich Himmler and Reinhard Heydrich administered their own brand of justice. Gürtner wrote briefs giving the appearance of legality to what the Nazis were doing.

Gürtner told *Time* ("Psychic Justice," September 2, 1935),

> We have substituted for the outworn maxim *nulla poena sine lege* ("no punishment unless law has been infringed") the more efficacious *nulla crimen sine poena* ("no crime left unpunished"), regardless of whether or not law has been infringed.

In 1937, Gürtner joined the Nazi Party. When World War II began, Nazi persecutions increased, and Gürtner wrote statutes legalizing the tyranny. He died in Berlin, January 29, 1941, and his funeral was held in the New Reich Chancellery. Hitler, Nazi Party leaders, Axis diplomats, government officials, army representatives and friends attended. "Never in its history has Germany faced as serious and far-reaching a fight for justice as at present," said Dr. Wilhelm Frick, interior minister, who delivered the funeral oration. "Germany is now about to raise victoriously the banner of justice in all Europe. It is a tragic fate that Gürtner had to leave us at this time."[23] Wilhelm Frick was hanged at Nuremberg for crimes against humanity, October 1, 1946.

Japanese Foreign Minister Yosuke Matsuoka Visits the Chancellery

All Berlin, it seemed, turned out for the visit of Japanese Foreign Minister Yosuke Matsuoka, March 27, 1941.

Franz Gürtner, Reich Justice Minister under Hitler (Ullstein Bilderdienst).

Flags were flying from most houses. Interpreter Paul Schmidt noticed that the Berliners pronounced Matsuoka's name clearly, without changing it into Berlinese, as they had done at the time of the Kellogg Briand Pact in the 1920s, when President Calvin Coolidge and Secretary of State Frank B. Kellogg were nicknamed Kulicke and Kellerloch. Schmidt drove through Berlin with Matsuoka during his visit, and observed the Berliners' reaction to the little man from Japan. "Look, there's Matsuoka!" people would shout. "Watch out that the little man doesn't slip away under the car!" a portly Berliner called out. Matsuoka took this as a compliment and raised his top hat solemnly.[24]

Accompanied by the Japanese Ambassador, Lieutenant General Hiroshi Oshima, Matsuoka laid a wreath on the German war memorial on Unter den Linden. Then he paid his first official call on Foreign Minister Joachim von Ribbentrop. Matsuoka and Ribbentrop conferred for three hours.

"If the Soviet Union should one day adopt an attitude which Germany regards as a threat, the Fuhrer will destroy Russia," Ribbentrop proclaimed. "Germany is absolutely convinced that a war against the Soviet Union would result in a complete victory for German arms and the total destruction of the Russian army and the Russian state." Ribbentrop sensed from the alarmed expression on Matsuoka's face that he had gone too far in his revelations. He therefore quickly added: "I do not, however, believe that Stalin will pursue a foolish policy."

In the afternoon, Matsuoka paid his first visit to Hitler. More than 100,000 people crowded the Wilhelmplatz to watch his arrival and departure. Hitler received Matsuoka in his gigantic office in the New Reich Chancellery. The visit lasted two and a half hours.

"I advise you," he told Matsuoka, "to take a look, while you're in Berlin, at the negligible damage done by British air attacks, and compare it with the devastation we have wrought in London; that will give you an idea of our supremacy in the air." Hitler insisted that England had already lost the war. "It's now only a question of England being sensible enough to admit her defeat. Then we shall see the collapse of the persons in the British Gov-

Junkers advertisement showing their planes over the Thames attacking London.

III. The New Reich Chancellery

Hitler and Yosuke Matsuoka on the Speer Balcony of the Chancellery Annex. Matsuoka died in prison in 1946, after having been arrested for war crimes.

ernment who are responsible for Great Britain's senseless policy." To keep the United States out of the conflict, Hitler suggested that the Japanese attack Britain by way of Singapore.

Matsuoka sat quietly opposite Hitler. Like many others who "conversed" with the Führer, he had not been able to get in a word. At last, however, Hitler stopped talking. The English words came slowly and deliberately from Matsuoka, who had mastered the language during his long sojourn in the United States. With regard to Singapore, Matsuoka replied, he could give "no firm promise on behalf of Japan at the moment." Hitler's expression plainly showed his disappointment. Matsuoka did say that an attack on Singapore had been the subject of detailed examination by the Service Departments, who regarded three months as the necessary time in which to complete the operation. Being cautious, Matsuoka preferred to reckon on six months. These long delays Japan put forward were a severe frustration for the impetuous Hitler. The next day, Matsuoka went to Carinhall, Hermann Göring's hunting lodge near Berlin.

Carinhall had been further enlarged, wrote interpreter Paul Schmidt. Among its rambling passages Schmidt sometimes got the impression of being in a small museum. In Göring's study, with its vast seats and mighty writing table, and especially, of course, in the huge hall with its heavy beams, the little man from Japan seemed even more diminutive than he had in Berlin. When everyone sat down in the magnificent dining room, one whole wall of which was a window, Schmidt was almost surprised that Matsuoka, sinking into his seat, could see over the edge of the vast table, with its heavy silver and floral decorations.

Japanese Foreign Minister Yosuke Matsuoka and Hermann Göring inspect the treasures of Carinhall.

The surroundings seemed rather to oppress Matsuoka. He gazed meditatively at the snowy landscape outside the enormous window. Looking at the snow-covered pine trees of the Schorfheide, which stood out like filigree work against the gray March sky, he said to Schmidt: "That reminds me of the pictures we love in Japan. The marvelously delicate drawing makes me feel quite homesick...."

Göring naturally took Matsuoka on a tour of the house. The master of the house, like a big boy showing his possessions to a younger playmate, displayed with pride the treasures he had collected, the pictures, Gobelin tapestries, art, antiques, sculptures, and valuable old furniture. Göring took Matsuoka through the whole house, starting at the cellar, where once he had shown the Duchess of Windsor how Elizabeth Arden's massage apparatus worked, and which now contained in addition an excellent swimming pool. "I hope that one of these gentlemen in their beautiful uniforms doesn't slip on the tiles and fall in!" Matsuoka whispered to Schmidt with a grin. Then Matsuoka came to the large room on the ground floor, where a model railway had been set up. "There's three hundred square yards here," said Göring, and he went to the control station and released a Flying Dutchman, a perfect model of a German express. The train seemed to run as steadily as a main line train. The Duke of Windsor would not now have had to stand on tiptoe to pick up the trains that had run off the line. "The track is 1,000 yards long and there are 40 electric points and signals," the big boy told the small boy, who was shyly admiring this splendid toy.

A Day in the Chancellery

Erich Peter Neumann (pseudonym: Hubert Neun), a writer for the weekly newspaper *Das Reich*, visited the Chancellery and recorded his impressions in issue number 14, April 6, 1941.

> The front of the New Reich Chancellery measures four hundred meters, and no one can walk by without wondering what goes on inside....
>
> The officials in their brown uniforms behind the massive swinging doors know the government executives well. They recognize their faces and the way they move, whether they are taciturn or friendly.... On many days three generals' coats hang on coat hooks in the waiting room. On other days, the checkroom is filled with the coats of Reichsleiter, Gauleiter, SA officials, or armament inspectors. Sometimes civilians also check their coats.
>
> The elevators are completely automatic, the doors opening and closing noiselessly. Unerringly the guards appear and demand passes. Slowly the eye accustoms itself to the unusual dimensions of Speer's building, which are constantly surprising the visitor. Anxiety generated by the long corridors gradually dissipates. One begins effortlessly to orient oneself, and what one hardly noticed on first pass becomes clear: the relationship between location and way.
>
> The visitor walks over thick carpets that muffle all sounds. Here and there, yellow signs point to the air-raid shelter.
>
> There are more than 400 rooms.... In contrast to the size of the chancellery, the number of officials, employees, and workers is small. Only about seventy people are actually performing the tasks of government. The entire staff consists of 250 people, but most are engaged in maintaining the building.
>
> Employees stride up and down the steps with gray folders under their arms. Cleaning women with innumerable whirring vacuum cleaners fill the long marble halls. A workman is bent over repairing a damaged spot in the floor...
>
> Like every other corporate office, the mailroom is the first stop for much of the day's business. Early in the morning the letter carrier brings sacks of mail from the Leipzigerstraße post office to the third floor chancellery mailroom. Many letters and packages are immediately forwarded to their ultimate destination, while others must be evaluated. In 1932, 51,500 pieces of mail arrived. In 1933, the volume increased to 375,000. As unemployment decreased, the flood of letters diminished to 200,000 annually and has stabilized at that number.... Every letter, no matter how important, is logged in. If the Chancellery cannot answer it, the letter is forwarded to the appropriate agency. In all cases the sender receives an acknowledgment with a file number so that he may at any time inquire regarding the status of his correspondence.
>
> Along with official communications, every day brings a mountain of letters from individuals. People from every corner of the Reich, and foreigners as well, write about personal concerns. A glance at today's pile reveals the peculiar address designations: "To the Führer's cabinet," "to the Reich government and revered Führer," "To his Excellency the noble, highborn Führer," "To the Obersalzberg in Berlin." The huge outpouring of opinion provides a glimpse of the trust accorded Adolf Hitler by a broad swath of the German population. The volume of letters from foreign countries is substantial, and the foreigners' letters, by and large, have the highly reverent addresses...
>
> An ordinary chancellery day passes swiftly. Couriers come and go. The grand rooms are often empty, but the offices are constantly busy, even more so since the war began.... One little office holds a cot for the night concierge. The telephone switchboard is in operation twenty-four hours. A chancellery official is always on call. The chancellery never closes.

Propaganda Minister Joseph Goebbels published the first issue of *Das Reich* May 26, 1940. Goebbels himself wrote many of the front-page articles in an attempt to reach the educated classes, both inside and outside of Germany. Erich Peter Neumann's best-known

Top: The Chancellery mailroom (Ullstein Bilderdienst).
   Bottom: The Chancellery restaurant. The third floor room where bureaucrats met to eat. A large cafeteria in Block A's basement was connected to the first floor by escalator (Ullstein Bilderdienst).

III. The New Reich Chancellery 107

Chancellery cleaning women at work. In this photograph they clean the cabinet room, which no one ever used (Ullstein Bilderdienst).

article for *Das Reich* was a March 1941 report on the Warsaw Ghetto, in which he described "the horribly repulsive variety of all Jewish types in the East." Neumann wrote Nazi propaganda for other publications, including the *Berliner Tageblatt* and the *Deutsche Allgemeine Zeitung*. After the war, Neumann continued to prosper by churning out anti-communist propaganda for the West German government. With his wife, Elisabeth Noelle-Neumann, who also wrote for *Das Reich*, Erich Neumann compiled opinion surveys for Konrad Adenauer and founded the *Deutsche Korrespondenz,* a compendium of foreign press clippings that was very popular among government officials.

THE ANTI-COMINTERN PACT

The Anti-Comintern Pact was concluded between Nazi Germany and Japan on November 25, 1936. The pact was ostensibly directed against the Communist International (Comintern) but was specifically directed against the Soviet Union. In case of an unprovoked attack by the Soviet Union against Germany or Japan, the two nations agreed to consult on what measures to take "to safeguard their common interests" and agreed that neither nation would make any political treaties with the Soviet Union. Germany also agreed to recognize the Japanese puppet regime in Manchuria. In 1937 Italy joined the pact, thereby forming the group that would later be known as the Axis Powers.

Hitler broke the terms of the pact when he signed the Molotov-Ribbentrop Pact with the Soviet Union in August 1939, before attacking Poland; he was attempting to avoid a war on two fronts. By 1940 Hitler once again began to consider invading the Soviet Union, and he dispatched the German foreign minister, Joachim von Ribbentrop, to negotiate a new treaty with Japan.

On September 25, 1940, Ribbentrop sent a telegram to Vyacheslav Molotov, the Soviet foreign minister, informing him that Germany, Italy and Japan were about to sign a military

Chancellery corridor; arrow points to the air raid shelter (Ullstein Bilderdienst).

alliance. Ribbentrop pointed out that the alliance was to be directed toward the United States and not the Soviet Union. "Its exclusive purpose is to bring the elements pressing for America's entry into the war to their senses by conclusively demonstrating to them that if they enter the present struggle they will automatically have to deal with the three great powers as adversaries."

The Anti-Comintern Pact was broadened with great pomp in 1941, after Germany's assault on the Soviet Union, and on November 25th its renewal for another five years was celebrated. In a ceremony at the New Reich Chancellery lasting an hour-and-a-half, representatives of 12 European and Asian governments affixed their signatures to the pact, technically directed not against Russia but against the activities of the Moscow Communist International. The signatories were Germany, Japan, Italy, Hungary, Spain, Manchukuo, Bulgaria, Croatia, Denmark, Finland, Rumania, and Slovakia. The Japanese-sponsored Nanking regime announced its participation by cable. Six of the signatories had not declared war on Soviet Russia, among them Japan, which also had a neutrality agreement with the Soviet Union.

General Hiroshi Oshima, whose speech had been awaited with much interest, delivered his endorsement only in general terms, saying that Japan was as ever firmly determined

Hitler and General Hiroshi Oshima. On December 13, 1941, Hitler awarded Oshima the Great Cross of the Order of the Eagle in Gold for meritorious service in creation of the Three Power Pact (i.e., the Axis). Foreign Minister Ribbentrop is at left and State Secretary Otto Meissner is in the background. In 1948, Oshima was condemned to life in prison as a war criminal, but was released in 1955. He died in 1975 (Ullstein Bilderdienst).

to establish the new order in the East in the spirit of the pact. He pledged that his country would never swerve from that path and would cooperate until the common goal had been reached. As General Oshima spoke, a Japanese task force in mid–Pacific was preparing to attack Pearl Harbor.

Count Ciano, speaking for Italy, admitted that the way to peace was rough and full of difficulties. "Not only must we fight bolshevism," he said, "but we must also fight its allies and supporters, particularly England who, forgetting its duties as a member of the cultural commonwealth, has set itself up as a protector of what the British themselves once upon a time branded as the most barbarous tyranny."[25]

Britain had allied itself with the Soviet Union after the German attack, June 22, 1941, to defeat the common enemy. The British may once have called the Soviets a most barbarous tyranny, but as the old Arab proverb has it, my enemy's enemy is my friend.

The ceremonies in connection with the conference were exclusively Ribbentrop's, with dignitaries of other ministries remaining away or discreetly in the background. Hitler played host to the foreign delegations before their departure.

Hitler Confers with Haj Amin al-Husseini

Appointed Mufti of Jerusalem by the British in 1921, Haj Amin al-Husseini was for 15 years the most prominent Arab figure in Palestine. Fearful that increased Jewish immigration would damage Arab standing in the area, the mufti engineered the bloody riots against Jewish settlement in 1929 and 1936. The mufti was dismissed from his position following the riots of 1936. No longer able to stay in Palestine, he continued his extremist activities from abroad. In 1941, Haj Amin al-Husseini fled to Germany and met with Adolf Hitler, Heinrich Himmler, Joachim Von Ribbentrop and other Nazi leaders. He wanted to persuade them to extend the Nazis' anti–Jewish program to the Arab world. The mufti sent Hitler 15 drafts of declarations he wanted Germany and Italy to make concerning the Middle East. One called on the two countries to declare the illegality of the Jewish home in Palestine. On December 9, 1941, the mufti met with Hitler in the Reich Chancellery. Hitler told the mufti that the Jews were the foremost enemy, but rebuffed the mufti's requests for a declaration in support of the Arabs, telling him the time was not right. The mufti offered Hitler his thanks for the sympathy that he had always shown for the Arab and especially Palestinian cause, and to which he had given clear expression in his public speeches. The Arabs were Germany's natural friends, said the mufti, because they had the same enemies as had Germany, namely the Jews. Hitler replied that Germany stood for uncompromising war against the Jews, which naturally included active opposition to the Jewish national home in Palestine. Germany would furnish positive and practical aid to the Arabs involved in the struggle, said the Führer, since Germany's objective was solely the destruction of the Jewish element residing in the Arab sphere. In that hour the mufti would be the most authoritative spokesman for the Arab world. The mufti thanked Hitler profusely.

Fritz Todt's Chancellery Funeral

Dr. Fritz Todt was the engineer who built the Autobahn and was Hitler's armaments minister. Todt died in a mysterious plane crash at Hitler's East Prussian headquarters, February 8, 1942. Hitler immediately appointed Albert Speer as Todt's successor. Some histo-

Grand Mufti Haj Amin al-Husseini confers with Hitler in the Reich Chancellery, December 9, 1941. Although he continued to be involved in politics, al-Husseini lost influence after the defeat of the Arab armies in 1948, and the creation of the State of Israel. Amin al-Husseini died in 1974 (Ullstein Bilderdienst).

rians believe that Hitler had Todt killed on account of his opposition to the war and that Speer might have had a role in Todt's elimination. On February 12, 1942, Todt's funeral was held in the New Reich Chancellery. Hitler recalled how Todt had participated in the early struggles of the Nazi Party. With his death, said Hitler, the Reich had lost a faithful and unforgettable comrade of incomparable creative genius:

> At a moment when war clouds were gathering in Europe [referring to the period prior to the Munich crisis of 1938], the security of the Reich was in danger, and at that time Todt alone was the only man capable of building before the Maginot Line a series of fortifications which could — even with a major part of German forces engaged in the east — protect the vital German regions of the west. To realize this protection it was necessary to construct, at the latest by September 1938, a total of 5,000 armored fortification works [the Westwall]. But when the job was finished a total of 12,000 works attested to a job well done.[26]

Hitler recalled that when the Todt organization had finished the work of "protecting the vital regions" in the western part of the Reich, it had delivered "a total of 23,000 armored positions in less than a year and a half." With the conquest of Norway, Hitler continued,

Fritz Todt

still further tasks were presented to Todt. Referring to Todt's achievements on the Russian front, Hitler said "the greater part of his task in this field will not be known until after the war," at which moment the German people would be allowed to see and admire Todt's accomplishments.

Todt's daughter, Ilsebill, suspects that Speer was responsible for her father's death, according to journalist Gitta Sereny. "I think he is capable of anything," Ilsebill said. "[Ilsebill] visited the Federal Archives a few times," a former archivist in Koblenz related to Sereny, "and she spit poison about Speer."

Todt was buried in Berlin's Invalidenfriedhof. His tombstone disappeared after 1945. His daughter tried to have a new marker placed upon his grave, but the city government refused, fearful of creating a magnet for neo-Nazis. Todt's daughter has now taken the matter to court.[27]

Reinhard Heydrich's Chancellery Funeral

During the Third Reich, Heydrich was Heinrich Himmler's chief lieutenant in the SS, who instituted mass executions in occupied territories during the opening years of World War II. Blond, handsome, vain and fiercely ambitious, Heydrich was also a fine violinist, a champion skier and fencer, a fearless pilot and an outstanding organizer. A virtually friendless loner, he was pitiless in dealing with "enemies of the state," so hated and feared by anti-Nazi elements throughout Europe that he was called "the Hangman." In 1941, Himmler, eager to put some distance between his ambitious subordinate and the center of power in Berlin, got Hitler to name Heydrich Reich Protector of Bohemia-Moravia (Czechoslovakia), replacing the ineffectual diplomat Konstantin von Neurath (later, after his Nuremberg trial, the oldest prisoner at Spandau).

Heydrich's brief governorship, during which he managed to persuade a surprisingly large number of Czechs to cooperate with him, was triumphantly successful. He highlighted his rising status by an act of homage to his composer father, a suspected Jew, who was never quite accepted by polite old-German society. On the evening of May 26, 1942, Reinhard Heydrich inaugurated the Prague music festival with a concert of Bruno Heydrich's chamber works, performed by a quartet of Bruno's former pupils from the Halle conservatory. Heydrich himself wrote the program notes. The following day, Heydrich was to depart Prague for a bigger job in Germany. But two young Czechs, Jan Kubiš and Josef Gabčík, sent from London, attacked him from ambush as he rode in his open Mercedes the 20 kilometers from his residence, the castle of Jungfern-Breschan, to his Prague office in the Hradcin Palace. He died of sepsis from his wounds on June 4th.

On June 9th, Heydrich's Berlin funeral was held in the Mosaic Hall of the New Reich Chancellery. Himmler and Hitler eulogized Heydrich. Hitler said:

> I have only a few words to dedicate to this dead man. He was one of the best National Socialists, one of the strongest defenders of German Reich thought, one of the biggest opponents of all the enemies of the Reich. He fell as a martyr for the preservation and safeguarding of the Reich. As leader of the party and as leader of the German Reich, I give you, my dear comrade Heydrich, the highest recognition I have to bestow: the uppermost level of the German Order. After party comrade [Fritz] Todt, you are the second person to receive this award.

III. The New Reich Chancellery 113

Ich habe diesem Toten nur noch wenige Worte zu widmen. Er war einer der besten Nationalsozialisten, einer der stärksten Verteidiger des deutschen Reichsgedankens, einer der größten Gegner aller Feinde dieses Reiches. Er ist als Blutzeuge gefallen für die Erhaltung und Sicherung des Reiches. Als Führer der Partei und als Führer des Deutschen Reiches gebe ich *dir*, mein lieber Kamerad Heydrich, nach dem Parteigenossen Todt, als zweitem Deutschen die höchste Auszeichnung, die ich zu verleihen habe: die oberste Stufe des Deutschen Ordens.

The German Order was the highest award of the Third Reich, instituted February 11, 1942, and had no clear requirements. (Saying he was awarding Heydrich the uppermost level of the German Order, Hitler seemed to be confusing the order, which had only one level, with another decoration, perhaps the Iron Cross, which had multiple levels—second class, first class, Knights Cross of the Iron Cross, etc.) Note that Hitler employed the familiar form (*dir* = you) rather than the polite form (*Ihnen* = you) when addressing his "dear comrade Heydrich." He undoubtedly had used the polite form when speaking to the living Heydrich.

Heydrich's grave is in Section A of the Invalidenfriedhof, Scharnhorststraße, Berlin. Heydrich was buried with full military honors next to General of Infantry Count Tauentzien von Wittenberg, who fought against Napoleon in the wars of liberation (1813). Heydrich was to have had a monumental tomb, designed by the architect Wilhelm Kreis and the sculptor Arno Breker. Because of the downhill course of the war, the tomb was never built. Heydrich's wooden grave marker disappeared in 1945. His grave is now unmarked. His

Reinhard Heydrich's funeral. Heinrich Himmler eulogizes the fallen Heydrich in the Mosaic Hall of the New Reich Chancellery, June 9, 1942 (Ullstein Bilderdienst).

death mask survives on postage stamps the Nazis issued to commemorate him. The British press called Heydrich's obsequies a gangster funeral in the pompous Chicago style.

GERHARD BOLDT VISITS THE NEW REICH CHANCELLERY

Captain Gerhard Boldt was an army adjutant and saw much of what went on in the Chancellery and Führerbunker in 1945. Escaping from the bunker at the last moment, he wrote down the details.

During the final months of the war, Hitler held some of his *Führerlage*, military briefings, in the New Reich Chancellery. All three armed services took part in these conferences. In February 1945, Boldt was taken to one and introduced to Hitler for the first time. The Mercedes of the Chief of the General Staff pulled up in front of the massive square pillars of the New Reich Chancellery on the easternmost side (block C), the armed-forces entrance. The other entrance, on the west (block A), was kept strictly separate for party members. Colonel General Heinz Guderian, Chief of the German General Staff, stepped out of the car, followed by his adjutant, Major Bernd von Freytag-Loringhoven, and Boldt. The sentries presented arms and the three officers walked past them through the heavy oak doors into the Chancellery.

The high entrance hall was dreary in the sparse light from the few remaining lamps. All the pictures, carpets and tapestries that had hung there had long since been removed because of the increasingly frequent air raids on Berlin. Huge cracks stretched across the ceiling and one of the walls. Many of the windowpanes had been replaced with cardboard or wood. On the side facing the Reichskanzlerpalais, a wooden partition had been constructed to conceal the bomb damage.

An orderly asked for Boldt's official pass. He had neither this nor an equivalent warrant, so his name had to be checked off the authorized list. Finally he was allowed to pass through. Freytag-Loringhoven took him to the Army Adjutancy room and introduced him to Army Adjutant Lieutenant-Colonel I. G. Borgmann, asking him at the same time whether the briefing was to be in Hitler's office or in the bunker. Since there was no danger of an air raid at the time, the briefing was arranged for Hitler's office.

Guderian, Freytag-Loringhoven and Boldt continued through corridors and anterooms. At the head of each corridor SS sentries inspected their passes. Their route was more roundabout than usual because of the heavy bomb damage that parts of the Chancellery had sustained. By contrast, the wing that housed Hitler's office (block B) was largely undamaged. Here the floor was still highly polished, the walls covered with paintings and the windows hung with sumptuous curtains.

Immediately outside the anteroom in the conference area, Guderian, Freytag-Loringhoven and Boldt were subjected to yet another, even more rigorous check by several SS officers and SS guards armed with machine guns. Guderian, Freytag-Loringhoven and Boldt surrendered their pistols, and guards took away and examined their briefcases. Since the attempted assassination of Hitler, 20th July 1944, briefcases had been particularly suspect. Guderian, Freytag-Loringhoven and Boldt were not physically searched but the SS officers ran well-trained eyes over their tight-fitting uniforms. Inevitably their passes were scrutinized yet again, and then, at last, they were allowed to proceed to the anteroom.

The officers were early. The anteroom was deserted except for three orderlies standing next to tables of refreshments and three more armed SS officers on the other side of the room, in front of the door leading to Hitler's office. Guderian took advantage of the delay to make a last-minute telephone call to Army High Command Zossen to get the latest news of the eastern front. Hitler's personal adjutant, SS Sturmbannführer Otto Günsche, arrived and invited Guderian, Freytag-Loringhoven, and Boldt to enter Hitler's office as soon as Hitler had finished his consultation with Martin Bormann.

A few minutes later Bormann appeared at the door of the operations room. He looked about 45 or 50, average height, squat and stocky, bullnecked. His face was round with prominent cheekbones and broad nostrils and wore an expression close to brutality. His eyes and the set of his features suggested cunning; his thinning hair was combed smoothly back. Boldt gazed in fascination at the man who was said to exert such influence on Hitler, to be the evil genius behind the Führer's commands. After a brief greeting, Guderian, Freytag-Loringhoven, and Boldt followed Günsche past Bormann into Hitler's office.

The room was long and very high, and contained very little furniture, though its floor was richly carpeted. Hitler's desk stood out prominently at the opposite end of the room, surrounded by a few upholstered chairs. The narrow, ceiling-high windows, hung with heavy grey curtains, broke up one wall, through which Boldt glimpsed the Chancellery garden. The elaborate marble map table stood halfway along the wall, its black upholstered chair so placed that Hitler could look out onto the garden. On the map-table stood a telephone, an electric bell, two unusually heavy paperweights, a desk set and a few colored pencils. The only other objects in the room were a heavy round table, massive leather armchairs and a couch, arranged along the left and right walls.

Freytag-Loringhoven and Boldt laid out the large General Staff maps in the prearranged order on the map-table, on top the maps of the Hungarian Front, at the bottom those of the Curland Front. Günsche stood behind watching closely. It took only a few minutes, and by four o'clock Freytag-Loringhoven and Boldt were back in the anteroom, where most of the participants in the conference had now gathered. They were standing around or sitting in small groups, talking earnestly over their coffee or schnapps and sandwiches. General Wilhelm Burgdorf, Hitler's chief adjutant, walked across the anteroom and into Hitler's office, reappearing in the doorway shortly afterwards. "The Führer would like you to come in," he said. The officers lined up, in order of rank, and followed him. Hitler was standing alone in the middle of his vast office, facing the doorway. His officers approached him and he greeted almost everyone individually with a silent handshake. Occasionally he asked a question of someone, which was answered with a brief "Yes, Führer" or "No, Führer." Boldt stood near the door, nervously awaiting the approaching ordeal. General Guderian must have mentioned Boldt to Hitler, because the Führer glanced at Boldt and then Guderian signaled Boldt to join them. Boldt walked across to Hitler and the Führer shuffled slowly to meet him, bowed and feeble. He stretched out his right hand and Boldt felt a loose, flabby handshake, quite devoid of strength or feeling.

Hitler's head shook slightly, and the shaking increased as the conference proceeded. His left arm hung limply by his side and his left hand trembled perceptibly. All his movements were those of a sick, almost senile man. His face, especially around the eyes, was weary and exhausted. This was not the vigorous, energetic Hitler the Germans knew, the Hitler that Goebbels still depicted. Only the eyes themselves had an indescribable, flickering brightness, an alarming, totally unnatural effect, and the glance Hitler gave Boldt was strangely penetrating.

The Führer turned and shuffled slowly over to his table, accompanied by Bormann, and sat down facing the pile of maps. He seemed satisfied with the first situation report, presented by Generals Alfred Jodl and Wilhelm Keitel, though Keitel had actually not uttered a single word throughout. (Other generals called Keitel *Lackeitel,* lackey). Hitler raised himself up a little in his chair and turned to Keitel's adjutant, Lieutenant-Colonel Hasso von John. "John, see to it that these two old gentlemen get into the bunker in good time during air-raids."

The rest of the conference was stormy. But Hitler closed the meeting politely. "I thank you gentlemen. Bormann, please stay here." The officers saluted and picked up their documents. Everyone except Bormann trooped out of Hitler's office.

As soon as the gigantic doors had closed, there was a scurry of activity in the anteroom. The adjutants were busy on the telephone, but everyone else sat down for some refreshments and to talk over the situation. An orderly approached General Keitel and offered him a box of cigars. He picked one out with meticulous care and, smiling contentedly, prepared ceremoniously to smoke it. A second cigar disappeared into his right-hand breast pocket. Boldt, Freytag-Loringhoven, and Guderian stayed for about half an hour in the anteroom and then retraced their steps through the long corridors, past the warren of rooms, the sentries and security checks, until at last, they found themselves back in the fresh air.

IV. Bunkers and Führerbunker

The first Führerbunker arose with Hitler's 1933 plans to expand the Reichskanzlerpalais, which he had always considered far too small for his needs. Hitler played with the idea of constructing a large office building in the garden behind the Wilhelmstraße 77 Palais, but finally settled on renovation of the original buildings and the addition of a new garden ballroom. On July 21, 1935, Leonhard Gall submitted his completed plans for a ballroom with a capacity of 200 persons. The structure had two floors, with apartments for Chancellery employees upstairs. The building inspectors approved Gall's blueprints July 29, for what was an unremarkable building.

The cellar was the unusual feature. Gall placed it under the reception hall, and it was composed of ordinary-looking basement rooms. But one-and-a-half meters lower, Gall had situated a huge bunker. This bunker was called the Reich Chancellery Air Raid Shelter, then the Vorbunker, after the Führerbunker had been completed in 1943. Gall's plans for the Vorbunker specified 1.2-meter thick outer walls, an inner length of 15.5 meters, an inner width of 18.5 meters, and an inner height of 3.08 meters. The east-west inner walls were 40 centimeters thick, the north-south inner walls 50 centimeters thick. There were 19 rooms, including the largest, a corridor room measuring 12 by 3.6 meters. One of the rooms housed ventilation machinery, another was a kitchen, and a third was a lavatory. On the east side of the corridor room stood two massive concrete pillars, attached to which was a heavy steel entrance door. The Vorbunker was accessible through three entries, to the west, north, and south.

The Vorbunker roof was 1.6 meters thick, twice as thick as the bunker under the Air Ministry Building, which was built around the same time. Indeed, the Vorbunker was so massive that its walls supported the entire weight of the ballroom above. Sven Felix Kellerhof, a German journalist who has studied the bunkers, writes that Hitler was probably much more interested in an impregnable air-raid shelter than another ballroom.

When the plans were submitted to the Finance Ministry, the cost of the Vorbunker was separated from the cost of the new ballroom. "Regarding the ballroom, Reich funds will not be used. But Reich funds will pay for the air raid shelter," wrote Hans Heinrich Lammers, chief of the Reich Chancellery, on May 7, 1936, to the Reich Building Office. In fact, no private money paid for any of the construction. Much of the cash came from "cultural funds," a black box of discretionary money. Of the 1.4 million reichsmark total, the Vorbunker probably accounted for 250,000 reichsmarks.

By early 1937, the Reich Chancellery had its own air-raid shelter, big enough to hold 200 people because of its electro-mechanical ventilation. But who was permitted to use it?

Top: Hitler with Leonhard Gall (left) and Albert Speer at the House of German Art in Munich. Gall was the architect for the ballroom built in the ministry garden, July 1935–January 1936, and the massive bunker underneath.

Bottom: Ministry garden ballroom. The ballroom (left) was connected to the Reichskanzlerpalais conservatory (right). The central wing had an arched mirrored ceiling.

Interior of ballroom, central section. The interior was made up of three wings with marble pillars.

The first Reich Chancellery air raid drills were planned for September 1937. On August 21, 1937, one of the bureaucrats submitted the following query:

> The Herr Reichsminister for Air Transport [Hermann Göring] has requested all offices and officials, in particular Reich offices, to take part in air raid drills in available shelters. To be able to use the shelter under the new ballroom, we need clarification as to whether this shelter is for all Reich Chancellery employees, or only for the Führer and Reich Chancellor and his aides. We ask the Herr State Secretary to please inform us of the decision of the Führer and Reich Chancellor in this matter.

On September 11, 1937, the reply arrived:

> To carry out the air raid drills, a precise regulation is required for the three office buildings, Wilhelmstraße 77, Wilhelmstraße 78, and Voß Straße 1. The regulation is attached. In case of an air raid, which could take place at night, the officials and residents of Wilhelmstraße 78 and Voß Straße 1 can go to the substitute shelters in Wilhelmstraße 78 and Voß Straße 1. The inhabitants of the Reich Chancellor House, Wilhelmstraße 77, will use the shelter under the ballroom.

The significance of the reply was exquisitely clear. Only the residents of Wilhelmstraße 77 could use the ballroom shelter. Besides the guards, servants, and orderlies, one person lived in Wilhelmstraße 77: Adolf Hitler. The ballroom shelter, cleverly concealed under a non-descript building and 1.6 meters of concrete, had become the first Führerbunker. No one knows how often Hitler visited his new bunker. None of his associates or aides made any comment in their voluminous memoirs. Sven Felix Kellerhof speculates that during

Interior of ballroom, side wing. Note the swastika-patterned mosaic ceiling decoration.

the first years of the war, there was minimal need for an air raid shelter. Hitler probably did make use of his bunker during the British air raids on Berlin, August until December 1940, since he was in the capital during this time. But the dramatic events of early 1945 eclipsed anything that had occurred before.

Bunkers Under the New Reich Chancellery

According to *Time* ("Führer as Father," October 7, 1940), beneath the "sidewalks outside Adolf Hitler's gadget-ridden Chancellery are a number of vast covered pits. From four of them slabs of cement rise and part, and out push anti-aircraft guns." In addition, two bunkers were built into the Chancellery foundation, one in the middle under Hitler's office, the other under the entry adjacent to Voß Straße and Wilhelmstraße.

The biggest bunker was under Hitler's office. The bunker roof was 1.7 meters thick and the floor lay six meters beneath the earth. The bunker was 106 meters long and 29 meters wide. It was divided into 53 rooms and could open onto the Voß Straße sidewalk by means of an hydraulically operated, granite-covered plate. The plate functioned as an elevator that could accommodate trucks. In its closed position it could not be distinguished from the adjacent sidewalk. During 1944–45, when generals came to the Chancellery for situation conferences, the hydraulic plate and bunker below served as their entrance and bombproof garage.

The large bunker was intended as a public air raid shelter and a shelter for Reich Chancellery personnel. At the beginning of the war, September 1, 1939, the bunker was officially declared a public shelter. In 1940, its use was broadened, as a mother-child bunker and obstetric ward. Mothers with young children could use it if they were unable to get a good night's sleep at home, irrespective of whether there had been an air raid or not.

The large bunker was divided into spacious, air-conditioned dormitories with neat rows of white beds, electric kitchens, and an operating room with the latest obstetrical equipment. Night and day nurses of the Nazi Welfare Organization stood by under the orders of five physicians. Before birth occurred, Berlin women were permitted a 24-hour lying-in period in the bunker. In October 1940, while bombs thumped and flak roared during the Royal Air Force's longest attack of the war to date, "two little future soldiers were brought squalling into the world. Next morning Adolf Hitler tenderly blessed the infants, and declared that for every baby born in his underground hospital during a raid he would be godfather," stated the *Time* article.

In 1945, SS Brigadeführer (major general) Wilhelm Mohnke, last commander of the thousand-man Chancellery guard regiment, used some of the vaulted rooms for his headquarters.

Next to the large bunker was the so-called small bunker, which was situated directly under the Borsig Palace, at the corner of Wilhelmstraße and Voß Straße. The small bunker, 20 by 60 meters, with a 1.7 meter thick steel and concrete roof, had 26 rooms. In early 1945 Hitler's personal staff occupied it and used it to store provisions. A passageway connected the small bunker to the large bunker.

Other Nearby Bunkers

In 1990, archeologists found undamaged bunker rooms, along with rotted furniture decorated with swastikas, a few light weapons, abandoned gas masks, and brightly painted murals depicting eagles, SS soldiers in heroic poses, and blonde Rhine maidens. These rooms probably housed SS guards and drivers.

The Foreign Office bunker, behind Wilhelmstraße 76, a dozen meters from the Führerbunker, was relatively small, six rooms and a vault. The bunker was seven meters wide and 13 meters long.

In January 1998, construction workers near the proposed site of the Berlin Holocaust Memorial unearthed Goebbels' bunker. In the bunker, 3,200 square feet, workers found rusted helmets, munitions, two empty safes, collapsed airshafts with torn cables, thick steel doors, and a floor covered with mud. The thick telephone cables and many plugs indicate that the place belonged to a high Nazi official.

"The bunker is completely decayed," construction engineer Dietmar Arnold told Jola Merten, a reporter for the *Berliner Morgenpost*. "For years it was filled with water, to a depth of 1.7 meters. It contains five rooms, approximately the same size, and one larger room missing a separating wall. Although the bunker is burned out, remains of wall covering are recognizable, and there is probably a parquet floor under the mud."

On account of the 1.8-meter thick ceiling, Arnold believes that building of the bunker began in 1941. "The roofs of the first bunkers, such as the one built under the Air Ministry in 1935, were only 80 centimeters thick. But the roof of the Führerbunker was 4.5 meters thick. At the time, bombs were falling, and concrete was the defense."

Arnold says that the *Torfklo* in Goebbels' bunker was standard equipment, "without a whiff of luxury." A *Torfklo* is a toilet bowl connected to a chest filled with peat. The user pulls a lever on the chest, causing peat to plop into the bottom of the bowl, thus guaranteeing a certain standard of hygiene.

Six feet underground, the bunker had been connected to Goebbels' Berlin villa on Potsdamer Platz, the former palace of the Royal Prussian Chamberlain. The villa, in the ministry garden located between the present-day Ebertstraße and Behrenstraße, no longer exists.

Goebbels' bunker was not connected to the Führerbunker, which was several hundred yards away. Workmen have closed up Goebbels' bunker. Its fate is uncertain. Wilfried Menghin, a Berlin archeologist who has examined the bunker, feels that it should be preserved as an historic artifact.

The Führerbunker

On January 16 and 17, 1943, the Royal Air Force, after a long hiatus, bombed Berlin. The two raids, conducted with a hundred airplanes, were minor in comparison to the poundings that other German cities had taken. The residual damage was minimal. But Adolf Hitler noticed. On January 18, 1943, during a conference with Albert Speer in his Wolf's Lair East Prussian Headquarters, Hitler issued an explicit order: "Because the air raid bunker in the Reich Chancellery garden has a roof thickness of only 1.6 meters, a new bunker must be built. The ceiling will be 3.5 meters thick, and the walls will be 3.5–4.5 meters thick. The new bunker will have identical measurements to the existing Führerbunker [i.e. the Vorbunker]. Piepenburg will supervise construction."

Speer, now Armaments Minister, wasted no time. During the night of February 6–7, he showed Hitler the specifications for the new bunker. The Führer approved them with minor modifications. All steel beams were to span the full length of the inner bunker, increasing the resistance of the structure to a direct hit without widening the interior walls. Other air raid rooms in the Chancellery were to be reinforced, without regard to their height or encroachment on usable space. Steel railroad tracks would be laid over the Vorbunker ceiling and encased in concrete, increasing the thickness of the original roof to two meters from 1.6 meters. The construction work began in April 1943. Carl Piepenburg ordered highly rationed building material to be sent to Hochtief, the giant German construction company, c/o Reich Chancellery, Hermann Göring Straße. Thousands of tons of steel and cement ended up beneath the Chancellery garden.

Original plans for the Führerbunker have never been found, either in the building records of the Reich Chancellery or in Hochtief's archives. Sven Felix Kellerhof theorizes that regular plans didn't exist. Indeed, Kellerhof came upon this note in the Chancellery files, now in the Bundesarchiv in Berlin:

> Before construction has begun, the Building Authority cannot accurately compute the total cost (without drawings and individual calculations), as a result of war conditions. The auditor is of the opinion that a retrospective calculation can be made from plans, individual calculations, etc, once the work has been completed. The total cost estimate seems correct, given current material prices.

In 1938, Piepenburg probably built the bunkers under the New Reich Chancellery from sketches. Kellerhof writes that Piepenburg most likely used Leonhard Gall's Vorbunker plans with minor modifications to construct the Führerbunker. Piepenburg may have turned in these plans to the building authorities for cost estimates.

The Führerbunker was built directly to the west of the Vorbunker and 2.5 meters deeper, that is, 8.5 meters beneath the ground. A staircase with two right angle turns and 10 steps led from the Vorbunker to the Führerbunker. The circular staircase shown in many drawings of the two bunkers never existed. No doubt the right angle turns made some visitors think of a circular staircase. Massive airtight steel doors were mounted at the staircase entrance and the Führerbunker entrance. The interior width of the Führerbunker was 20 meters, the interior length 15.6 meters. Assuming the walls were four meters thick, the exterior dimensions would have been 28 meters long by 26.5 meters wide. The floor plates were 2.5 meters thick. The useable interior space, however, would have been even less than these dimensions suggest, because the interior walls were 50 centimeters thick, in order to support the roof in the event of a direct bomb hit.

The thickness of the Führerbunker walls was a prudent precaution. During 1944 and 1945 allied bombs with special detonators damaged German submarine bunkers on the French Atlantic coast with roofs six to seven meters thick. But the submarine bunkers covered a 10- to 20-meter-wide water surface, and the roofs were supported by steel pilings rather than by closely positioned concrete interior walls. Nevertheless, to make assurance doubly sure, Piepenburg reinforced the Führerbunker roof with a second ceiling of steel beams, 20 meters long and 20 centimeters high, sunk 25 centimeters deep in the bunker walls. All this reinforcement of steel and concrete left 250 square meters of useable space, divided into twenty rooms with 3.05-meter high ceilings. The Führerbunker was not roomy, by any means, but it was more spacious than many other Berlin air raid shelters.

One of the enduring mysteries of the Führerbunker is its most salient feature, a cylindrical concrete tower with a conical roof. What was the function of this structure? According to Kellerhof, it was not a watchtower, ventilation tower, or emergency exit. Because the Soviets dynamited the tower in 1947, very little about its actual structure is known. Perhaps the architect felt that a castle, even one underground, must have a tower. Carl Piepenburg was adequately compensated for his work on the Führerbunker. On April 29, 1943, Albert Speer wrote to Hans Heinrich Lammers, chief of the Reich Chancellery:

> Dear Herr Reichsminister,
> For the design and supervision of the construction of the new bunker in the garden of the Reich Chancellery, I direct that the following compensation be paid to Architect Piepenburg: 2.3 percent of the full building costs for the design, 1.5 percent for building supervision. I ask that Architect Piepenburg be paid 20,000 reichsmarks before completion of the work.

On September 30, 1944, Piepenburg submitted a bill for 51,296 reichsmarks, 3.8 percent of the total construction costs of 1,349,899.29 reichsmarks. For unknown reasons, Piepenburg had shaved 17 *pfennig* off his fee.

Führerbunker Details

Because the Führerbunker was buried in Berlin groundwater, the interior was disagreeably damp. Electric pumps ran continuously to evacuate the water that seeped in. When the pumps were finally shut off in May 1945, the water level on the floor rose to a height of 15 centimeters in two months. Later the water in the rooms was 2.35 meters deep.

A 60-kilowatt diesel generator provided uninterrupted power for heat and ventilation.

Führerbunker 1945. Cylindrical concrete tower is at right. Its purpose is unknown. Garden entrance is in concrete block at left. Damaged garden ballroom is directly behind tower. Damaged multistory building in background is foreign ministry (Ullstein Bilderdienst).

Hitler was terrified of dying from Russian poison gas and regularly saw to the changing of the intake and exhaust filters. A pump and an underground well furnished water. A microphone hidden in an external ventilator brought in the sounds of the surrounding area.

On the right of the Führerbunker passageway stood a generator room and a little telephone switchboard, near two cupboards with doors. Further down were a guardroom, secretary's desk, and four-room medical office. The medical office ultimately became home to the Reich Minister for Enlightenment of the People and Propaganda, Joseph Goebbels, his wife and six children.

To the left were Hitler's bedroom, living room, and work room, each measuring about three by four meters, a conference room, and the apartment of Führer-mistress Eva Braun. A room for Hitler's dogs and three bathrooms were nearby. Hitler's office had a desk, a table, three chairs, and a blue-white upholstered linen sofa that had been a bench. A little stand to the right of the sofa held a radio. Anton Graf's portrait of Frederick the Great hung over the desk. Hitler's bedroom had a simple bed, a cabinet, a safe, and a tea table with two chairs. He had an oxygen tank moved into his rooms because of his fear of suffocating. Eva Braun's bedroom was less Spartan than Hitler's, in fact, something of a hodgepodge. A large commode, the doors inlaid with Eva's initials in the form of a four-leaf–clover, stood near the bed and a cane chair. A brightly patterned carpet did little to cheer up the gloomy room.

Chief of the Party Chancellery and Reich Leader Martin Bormann had ordered red carpet, which covered the floor of the corridor. An emergency exit with 37 steps led to the

Position of Vorbunker and Führerbunker. No part of the bunkers remains aboveground, although some of the foundation may still exist (photograph Paul Langrock, Zenit, information from Kellerhof).

The Reich Chancellery and Führerbunker Complex

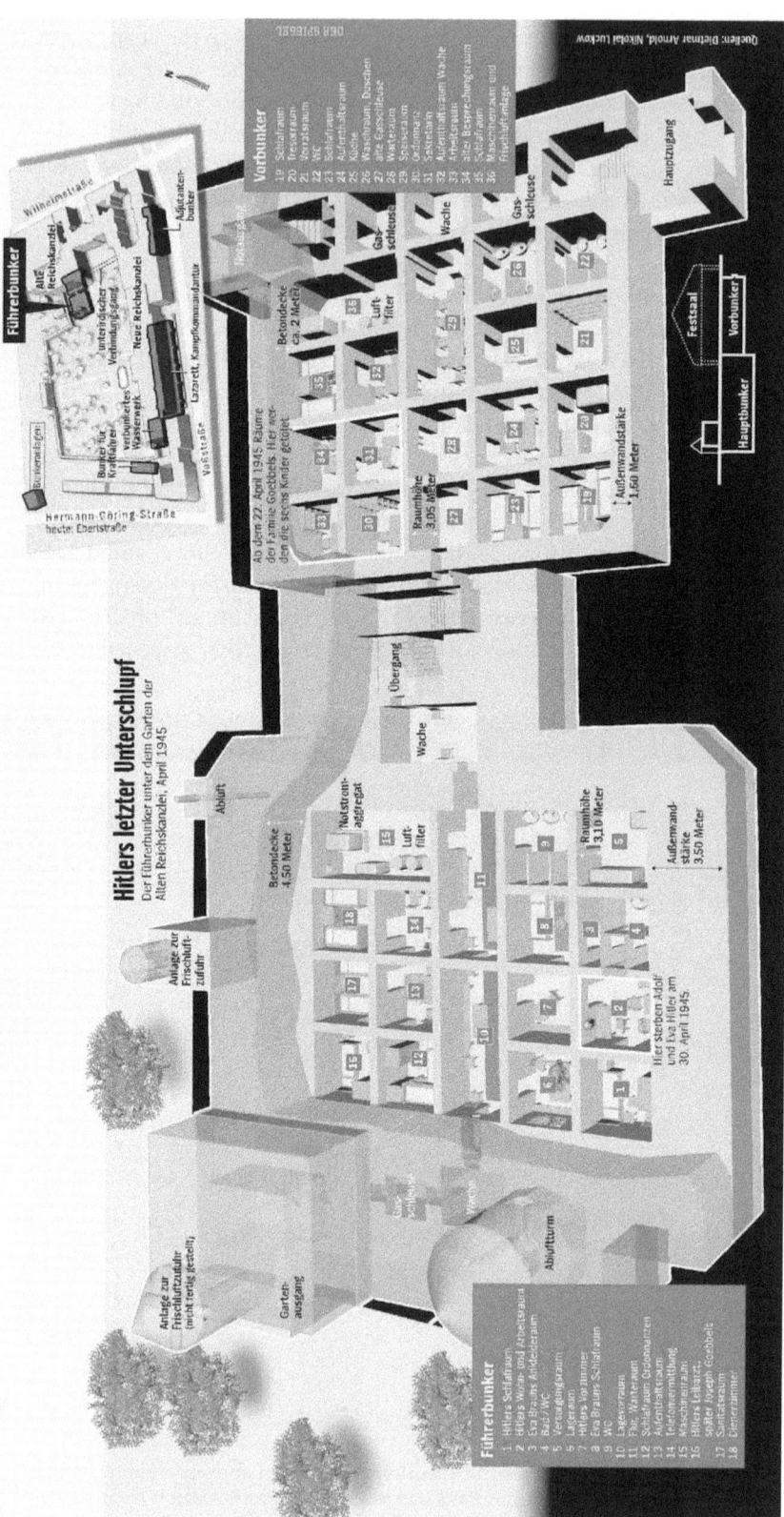

Diagram of Vorbunker and Führerbunker. Built 1935–36, the Vorbunker was called the Reich Chancellery Air Raid Shelter, then the Vorbunker, after the Führerbunker had been completed in 1943. Führerbunker: 1. Hitler's bedroom. 2. Hitler's living room and office. Hitler and Eva Braun died in this room, April 30, 1945. 3. Eva Braun's dressing room. 4. bath and toilet. 5. accommodations room. 6. storeroom. 7. Hitler's antechamber. 8. Eva Braun's bedroom. 9. toilet. 10. storeroom antechamber. 11. corridor, waiting room. 12. orderly's bedroom. 13. conference room. 14. telephone switchboard. 15. machine room. 16. room for Hitler's doctor, later Joseph Goebbels. 17. hospital room. 18. servants' room. Vorbunker: 19. bedroom. 20. safes. 21. provisions room. 22. toilet. 23. bedroom. 24. conference room. 25. kitchen. 26. washroom, shower. 27. old gas lock. 28. waiting room. 29. dining room. 30. orderly. 31. secretary. 32. guards' meeting room. 33. office. 34. old conference room. 35. bedroom. In this block of rooms Goebbels' family lived after April 22, 1945, and his six children were killed here. 36. machine room and ventilation room (*Der Spiegel*)

IV. Bunkers and Führerbunker

New Reich Chancellery bunker entrance. August 8, 1990. The last look at the bunker under Potsdamer Platz which lay directly under the reception rooms of the chancellery (Bundesarchiv, Bild 183-1990-0809-021/Photographer: Hubert Link/License CC-BY-SA-3.0).

garden. A second exit led to the tower, left unfinished. The garden exit was covered with white tile, and some of the stairways were clad with marble remaining from the New Reich Chancellery.

The bunker reminded Albert Speer of "the thick walls and ceilings of a prison. Iron doors and hatches closed off the few openings, and the narrow walkways between the barbed wire brought [Hitler] no more air and nature than the walkway around a penitentiary brings a convict." In fact, in size and design, the bunker was quite similar to the storage cellars for corpses in the crematoria at Auschwitz. Some generals called the Führerbunker a concrete submarine. The absence of windows satisfied Hitler's need to make night into day (Josef Stalin liked to do this also).

Hitler Moves In

On January 16, 1945, a cold winter Tuesday, Hitler's special train rolled into Berlin for the last time. It stopped at the Grunewald Station, an unobtrusive terminal in the leafy

Flooded bunker under the Reich Chancellery. The last look at the bunker under Potsdamer Platz, August 9, 1990. The magistrate in East Berlin allowed journalists to photograph the interior. Because it destabilized the street above, the bunker was closed and filled with concrete. This bunker is not to be confused with the nearby Führerbunker (Bundesarchiv, Bild 183-1990-0809-024/Photographer: Hubert Link/License: CC-BY-SA-3.0).

suburbs. Since 1941, the Gestapo had herded tens of thousands of Berlin Jews through this station on their way to the death camps in the East.

Hitler climbed into his limousine and was driven to the New Reich Chancellery. The building had been bombed and many windows blown out. The honor court and galleries were filled with debris. Leonhard Gall's 1935–36 garden ballroom was heavily damaged, as was the Reichskanzlerpalais, except for its right wing, which had not been hit. Hitler moved into the undamaged Reichskanzlerpalais wing. In the following weeks, he used Bismarck's old rooms for conferences. Except for military situation conferences, he seldom visited the New Reich Chancellery because the place was freezing cold and could not be heated. The bunkers under Speer's immense building had become a hospital. The Vorbunker and Führerbunker served as air raid shelters.

As Allied bombing became more intense, water, power, telephones, and heating became more problematic. "I ask myself how Berlin will look when I see it again," wrote Martin Bormann. At the end of February or beginning of March, Hitler moved out of the Reichskanzlerpalais and into the Führerbunker.

IV. Bunkers and Führerbunker 129

Steel airtight door which closed off the radio broadcast room (Reichsrundfunk) of the new Reich Chancellery bunker (Bundesarchiv, Bild 183-1990-0809-023/Photographer: Hubert Link/License CC-BY-SA-3.0).

LIFE IN THE FÜHRERBUNKER

Two dozen people were continually in the Führerbunker. Among them were the telephone operator Rochus Misch, the diesel generator and ventilation mechanic Johannes Hentschel, and Eva Braun. Hitler had only his closest associates with him in the bunker: Martin Bormann, Hitler's valet and SS Sturmbannführer (major) Heinz Linge, SS Adjutant Sturmbannführer Otto Günsche; SS-Brigadeführer (major general) and bodyguard Johann Rattenhuber with his adjutant, SS-Standartenführer (colonel) and procurator Peter Högl. Along with these men were secretaries Johanna Wolf, Traudl Junge, Gerda Christian, Christa Schröder, and Else Krüger; diet cook Constanze Manziarly; personal physician Dr. Ludwig Stumpfegger; SS Standartenführer and Chauffeur Erich Kempka, Lieutenant General and chief pilot Hans Baur.

Grunewald Station. Dedication of memorial to deported and murdered Berlin Jews, July 5, 2001. Prime Minister Ariel Sharon of Israel (at podium) and German Chancellor Gerhard Schroeder (second from right) lay a wreath at the memorial, consisting of 186 steel plates, each plate bearing the transport date, destination, and number of Jews deported (Ullstein Bilderdienst).

High officials came to see Hitler in the Chancellery or the bunker. Army chief of staff Hans Krebs was a frequent visitor, along with liaison people from the crumbling power organs of the Reich, now in liquidation:

- for Hermann Göring's Luftwaffe, Colonel Nikolaus von Below;
- for the Navy and Großadmiral Karl Dönitz, Vice Admiral Erich Voss;
- for Foreign Minister Joachim von Ribbentrop, the old Nazi ambassador Walter Hewel.
- for Heinrich Himmler's SS, Eva Braun's brother-in-law, SS Gruppenführer (lieutenant general) Hermann Fegelein. But Fegelein did not last long. Intending to escape Berlin by plane, Fegelein slipped out of the bunker April 26, 1945. An SS search party found him, quite drunk, in his apartment (10–11 Bleibtreustraße) in civilian clothes. With him was his mistress, who may have been an English spy, and who escaped through an open window. Fegelein was brought back to the bunker, and a furious Hitler ordered him shot on April 28.

Hitler's day began when he awakened in late morning and did not end until the wee hours, when he went to bed. His military conferences started after midnight and lasted two to three hours. Then he had tea in his living room, and delivered a boring monologue to anyone still awake. At five or six A.M. he would go to bed. The air raid sirens awakened him at eleven A.M. Supper was at nine or 10 P.M.

From his bunker in 1945, Hitler could make war only with difficulty, and finally not at all. Hair graying, hands trembling, back bent, gait shuffling, saliva dripping from the corners of his mouth, the Führer appeared much older than his 55 years. He wandered aimlessly through the corridors and rooms like a ghost who could not find peace. Formerly meticulous about personal hygiene, he now did not bother to shave properly and wore a soiled, stained uniform. "You must not try to look just like old Fritz [Frederick the Great]," remonstrated Eva Braun. (The 18th century Prussian king was indifferent to personal hygiene in his last years.)

Hitler was determined to defend his bunker to the end. He himself was commandant of the government quarter, where the bunker

Top: Hitler greets Hermann Fegelein as Heinrich Himmler looks on.
Bottom: Führerbunker interior, 1945. Left to right: Hitler's doctor, Theodor Morrell; four unidentified men (one almost completely obscured); Hitler's naval adjutant, Admiral Karl-Jesko von Puttkamer (1900–1981); another unidentified man; and Peter Högl, Reich Security Service. Högl committed suicide May 2, 1945 (Bayerische Staatsbibliothek).

Hitler in the Führerbunker, 1945. A painting from Hitler's art collection is hanging on the concrete wall. Hitler is receiving the commander in chief of the navy, Grand Admiral Karl Dönitz. Shortly before the political and military collapse of the Third Reich, and his own suicide, Hitler transferred his own leadership and named Dönitz head of the German state (Bundesarchiv, Bild 183-V00538-3/Photographer: unknown/License CC-BY-SA-3.0).

was located. He named the military district "Citadel," after his final failed Russian offensive at Kursk.

At Hitler's order, holes were made in the concrete walls for gun barrels; grenade throwers were built in, and anti-tank cannon emplacements were spread throughout the garden. SS-Brigadeführer Mohnke's bunker-defenders included members of Hitler's Scandinavian SS bodyguards from the Northland division, 90 French SS men from the Charlemagne division, a few Latvians and some Spaniards.

To protect the Chancellery building itself, navy cadets from the North Sea island of Fehmarn were hastily flown in. These men were being trained for the signal corps and had no other military experience. Their post was the great hall and Hitler's workroom. They were ordered to use Hitler's card table as a shield. Unlike the cadets, Mohnke survived the war and received a fat pension from the German government, despite his alleged involvement in the massacres of British prisoners during the evacuation of Dunkirk in 1940 and American POWs during the Battle of the Bulge in 1944.

Hitler with model of Linz, 1945. In a cellar room of his subterranean labyrinth, under Voßstraße, was a model of Hitler's favorite city. Hitler had intended to retire to Linz, with "Fräulein Braun" and his German shepherd Blondi. Even as Berlin exploded, burned and crumbled around him, Hitler and architect Albert Speer discussed new building plans for Linz (photograph by Walter Frentz).

The Emergency Field Hospital Under the Reich Chancellery

While a befuddled Hitler maundered aimlessly in the Führerbunker, Dr. Ernst Günther Schenk struggled in bunker rooms under the New Reich Chancellery to save the lives of wounded German soldiers.

"Most of my working hours had been spent over the emergency field-surgery operating table," Schenck recalled.

> Casualties were tumbling in from the fierce street fighting just three blocks away at the Potsdamer Platz, and from the larger battle raging for the Reichstag. This was only four or five blocks from us. From time to time, soldiers who were still conscious and could talk told me of their hopeless battle. The younger ones, many under sixteen, were terrified, bawling.... Many a wounded soldier died, in horrible anguish, on the blood-smeared table as I operated.... I was up to my elbows in entrails, arteries, gore.

On April 25, the Russians captured Tempelhof Airport and turned the deadly German 88 twin-purpose guns on the Chancellery. The nearby thump of the heavy shells made Schenck think he was standing in a shot-put pit. Schenck's biggest problem was the shortage of medical supplies: bandages, splints, iodine, morphine, and plasma. With one commandeered Wehrmacht truck driven by his adjutant, Captain Max Müller, Schenck went careening along the battlefront, searching hospitals and supply depots. Toward the end, the last two or three days, Schenck's hospital ran out of bandages. The staff had to rip blood-soaked rags and casts off the unburied dead. Schenck described the human tragedy he witnessed:

> In one abandoned hospital in Berlin-Steglitz, in the basement where I was prowling about with a flashlight in search of supplies, I suddenly came on some dozen very elderly, moaning women. When this hospital was evacuated, two days before, they had been left behind. Apparently there was just no transport. When I entered their basement ward at midnight, they thought I was the first Russian. They began screaming like Valkyries. I made the familiar bedside rounds, gave each patient a few placebo pills. Then I, too, had to abandon them to their fate — hungry, distraught, forlorn. It was ghastly. I simply had to leave them alone in the midnight dark.

Schenck was not a surgeon. He was an internist and a nutrition expert. He would have been useless except for the help of the dying professor of surgery, Dr. Werner Haase. In 1933, Haase had been Hitler's first personal physician in the Reich Chancellery. At Haase's own request his student, Dr. Karl Brandt, replaced him in 1936. (Brandt was hanged in 1947 for performing gruesome medical experiments on concentration camp inmates.) Haase, who wanted to continue his career in surgery, went back to his clinic in the Ziegelstrasse, only a few blocks from the Charité Hospital and not far from the Reich Chancellery.

Haase remained on good terms with Hitler and always attended such formal ceremonies as the Führer's birthday party. In fact, Haase was present at the last one, April 20, 1945. By that time he was a patient in his own clinic, dying of tuberculosis. Haase had only part of one lung left. In the fetid air of the bunker hospital, Haase on most days could not stand on his own feet for more than 30 minutes. Lying on a cot, gasping for breath, he would describe to Schenck how to perform stomach, heart, and spinal incisions, even how to treat delicate head wounds.

On April 29th, Hitler asked to see the doctors and nurses from the bunker hospital, and Haase took Schenck to meet Hitler. Schenck, the last physician to see the Führer, recorded his impressions:

> [Hitler] was wearing the familiar, once spotless, natty pearl gray tunic with green shirt and long black trousers, the simple uniform he had donned on the first day of the war. He wore his golden party badge and his World War One Iron Cross on his left breast pocket. But the human being buried in these sloppy, food-stained clothes had completely withdrawn into himself. I was standing erect, on a kind of concrete step above him. As I glanced down, I could see Hitler's hunched spine, the curved shoulders that seemed to twitch and suddenly to tremble. Somehow his head seemed withdrawn into his shoulders, turtle-like. He struck me as an agonizing Atlas with a mountain on his back.... He seemed hardly able to shuffle the two paces forward to greet us.

The human ruin that stood in front of him shocked Schenck:

> [Hitler's] eyes, although he was looking directly at me, said nothing. They did not seem to be focusing. They were like wet pale-blue porcelain, glazed, actually more gray than blue. They were filmy, like the skin of a soft, ripe grape. The whites were bloodshot. I could detect no expression on his vapid, immobile face. Drooping black sacks under his eyelids betrayed loss of sleep.... Deep folds ran down his large, pulpy nose to the corners of his mouth. This mouth was set firmly, his lips nervously pressing each other. The cold-fish, flapping gesture with which he shook my hand was listless. It was really only a jerky reflex, although it was meant to be amiable enough.... The Führer was a palsied, physical wreck, his face wrinkled like a mask, all yellow and gray. The man, I am sure, was senile, without the dignity of silver hairs.

A little later, Schenck saw Hitler sitting at a table and recognized the unmistakable signs of Parkinson's disease:

> His flabby left hand, in which he was clasping his steel-rimmed spectacles, was also clutching the table. His whole left arm, up to the shoulder, was trembling and, now and then, shuddering. This arm kept tapping the table rhythmically. To brace himself, he had wrapped both his left calf and foot around one leg of the table. This leg was throbbing, shaking. He could not control it.

Hitler's Last Days

"Unfortunately, not exactly a birthday atmosphere," wrote Martin Bormann in his calendar, April 20, 1945. Hitler's birthdays had always been occasions for gaudy celebration, but not this one, his 56th.

Traudl Junge, Hitler's secretary, wrote, "The first Russian tanks were outside Berlin. The thunder of the guns was audible in the Reich Chancellery. The Führer received the best wishes of his faithful followers. All of them came, shook his hand, pledged their loyalty, and tried to get him to leave town.... In vain. Hitler wanted to stay and await events." Christa Schröder, another Hitler secretary, wrote, "The chorus of well-wishers from the personal staff and the military was, in comparison to previous years, quite muted. Not so the Allies' congratulatory din, the deafening air attacks on Berlin that continued from morning till night." After the perfunctory celebration had ended, Hitler withdrew to his bedroom and the exodus began.

Party chiefs and cabinet ministers took to their heels. A perspiring Hermann Göring bade a hurried goodbye, mentioning that he had urgent tasks in South Germany. Everyone knew that the Russians were completing their encirclement, and Göring had sent an aide to get an estimate of how much time was left to skedaddle. Otto Meissner, head of the Presidential Chancellery, had not even come to the birthday party. He telephoned his congratulations, excusing himself by saying he had gone to Mecklenburg to perform his official duties there. Goebbels remarked that he was sorry that now he couldn't do what he had wanted to do for 12 years—spit in Meissner's face.

Eva Braun invited what remained of the inner circle to the damaged living quarters of the Reichskanzlerpalais for one last revel. "She wanted to banish the fear that was gnawing at her heart," wrote Traudl Junge. "She wanted another celebration, even though there was nothing to celebrate. She wanted to dance, drink, forget."

On April 22, after paroxysms of maniacal screaming rage at his remaining generals, Hitler acknowledged that the war was lost and began sending away his most

Otto Meissner. Meissner served as state secretary under three Reich Chancellors. Hitler was the last. After the war, Meissner was acquitted of Nazi collaboration because he had helped many opponents of the regime. He died in Munich in 1953, age 73. Note the dueling scar on Meissner's left cheek.

trusted aides. First he bid goodbye to his secretaries Johanna Wolf and Christa Schröder, then to his diet cook Constanze Manziarly. The other two secretaries, Gerda Christian and Traudl Junge, refused to go.

Hitler got a bad shock on April 28. Partisans had captured Benito Mussolini as the Duce tried to flee through northern Italy. They executed Mussolini and his mistress, Clara Petacci, and hung the bodies upside down from the roof of a filling station. Hitler reacted by confirming what everyone knew: He was determined to commit suicide. "I will not fall into the hands of my enemies, dead or alive. After I'm dead my corpse will be burned and remain forever unidentified."

Calling in his two remaining secretaries, Hitler announced that he would dictate his political and private last will and testament. As Traudl Junge recalled,

> Now we would finally hear what we had waited days for: the explanation for everything that had happened, an acknowledgment, even a declaration, of guilt, perhaps an apology. This last official document of the Thousand Year Reich must contain the truth, told by a man who had nothing more to lose. But my expectations were dashed. Lethargically, almost mechanically, the Führer recited the details, accusations, and demands that I, the German Volk, and the whole world had already heard.

In his private last will, Hitler referred to his marriage to Eva Braun, the disposition of his art collection, and the appointment of Martin Bormann as executor to see that relatives and faithful staff members received a legacy.

By April 29, 1945, conditions in the bunker reflected the destruction of the city outside. Exhaust ducts plugged, the overheated rooms stank of soldiers' sweat and chlorine. The air intake sucked in dust from artillery shelling, as well as the odor of fire and rot. In these disagreeable surroundings, Hitler married Eva Braun. In his private will, he explained why: "In the war years I believed I would not be able to marry. Now, at the end of my earthly existence I have decided to take as my wife the woman who over long years has given me true friendship. Of her own free will she has come to this besieged city to share my fate. She wishes to die with me as my wife."

Goebbels hurriedly rounded up a civilian magistrate, Walter Wagner, for the perfunctory ceremony. Goebbels and Bormann were the witnesses. Eva Braun wore a long black silk taffeta dress. At 1:30 A.M., April 29, the unlucky few aides remaining in the bunker congratulated the newlyweds, as Soviet troops approached to within a hundred meters of the Reich Chancellery. Walter Wagner was shot in the head while rejoining his company and died a few days later.[1]

After Hitler and Eva had retired for the night, the wedding guests went upstairs to the Chancellery to celebrate. Traudl Junge wrote, "An erotic fever seemed to have taken possession of everybody. Everywhere, even on the dentist's chair, I saw bodies locked in lascivious embraces. The women had discarded all modesty and were freely exposing their private parts."

Hitler committed suicide April 30, with a bullet in the head from his 7.65 mm Walther semi-automatic pistol. In *Hitler's War,* David Irving wrote:

> "Blood was dripping from his right temple, a pool of blood was already on the carpet," [Otto] Günsche [Hitler's last adjutant] testified to the Soviets, "It was immediately apparent that he had shot himself from his own pistol, a PPK 7.65mm which eight days previously after an emotional conference [on April 22, 1945] he had taken out of his bedside table and carried with him constantly, loaded."

Eva Braun swallowed poison. Hitler's last meal, one and a half hours before his suicide, was spaghetti with a light tomato sauce.[2] Josef Stalin never stopped complaining that Hitler had not fallen into his hands alive.

SS adjutants doused the bodies of Hitler and Eva Braun with gasoline and burned them. A day later they did the same to the remains of Goebbels, his wife, and their six young children. Goebbels had the children killed, then he and his wife poisoned themselves.

When the Soviets located Hitler's charred remains, "they stank horribly." Dr. Faust Jossifowitsch Schkarawski performed the autopsy on Hitler: "The corpse is strongly blackened and smells of burnt flesh. A piece of

Walther 7.65 mm pistol. Hitler dispatched himself with this popular weapon. Although his last gunshot did not require much marksmanship, Hitler was a crack pistol shot. International News Service correspondent Pierre J. Huss described Hitler asking him during a stroll in the snow near Berchtesgaden to throw a snowball into the air. Huss complied and Hitler drilled the snowball in midair with one bullet from his gun. To prove that the first shot was not a lucky hit, Hitler repeated the feat. "It is generally conceded in the S.S. and the army," Huss quoted Hitler as telling him, "that I am a better pistol shot than most of their best ones. I believe I can say with justification that I am one of the few all-round ballistic experts in the world today." Arthur Axmann, a Hitler Youth leader, picked up Hitler's Walther pistol from the bunker floor and buried it under the Sandkrug Bridge in Berlin. The pistol has never been found.

Site of immolation of the bodies of Hitler and Eva Braun. The author stands in front of a children's sandbox on the site of the pit in which the bodies of Hitler and Eva Braun were drenched with gasoline and burned.

the calvarium is missing.... The lower jaw lies free in the singed oral cavity." Dental records confirmed that the jaw was Hitler's.

Russian troops lost no time plundering the Chancellery and Führerbunker. Eva Braun's dressing room furnished a bonanza for the lady soldiers, since Eva changed her clothes five times a day. Fashion was her obsession. Magda Goebbels, in contrast, had brought along very little to wear.

"Dear Adi": Love Letters to the Führer

Besides millinery, the Soviets carried off furniture, clothing and everything else that wasn't welded down. They could not resist the sturdy metal card files and file cabinets in the New Reich Chancellery. They dumped mountains of cards, folders, and documents onto the floor and carted the cabinets away.

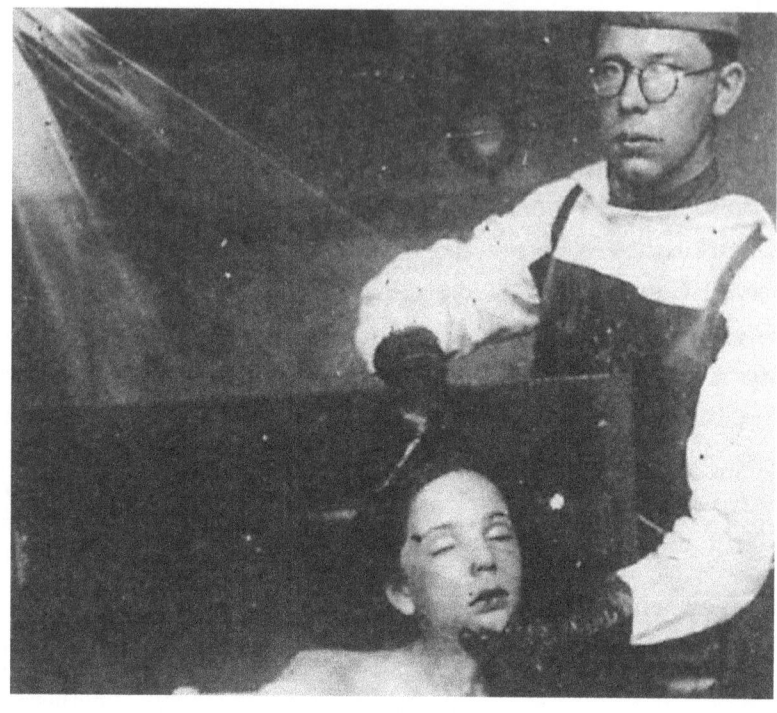

Russian pathologist with the corpse of Helga Goebbels, the oldest daughter. "In the mouth, shards of a crushed glass ampoule were found. During autopsy one could smell a distinct odor of bitter almonds. Chemical analysis of the internal organs confirmed the presence of cyanide."

In 1946, an American intelligence officer, W.C Emker, was stationed in Berlin. Like everyone else, he toured the New Reich Chancellery, its ceiling riddled with gigantic bomb holes open to the sky. Emker picked up a few pieces of paper from the heaps on the floor. They were addressed to "Our beloved Führer." He stuffed the letters into his pocket. A few days later, Emker returned to the Chancellery. He had read the letters and wondered if there were more. It had rained and the piles of paper were turning to mulch. But there were still many legible letters that Emker was able to salvage. Emker became a frequent visitor to the building. He found an unguarded entrance in a side street, and was able to come and go with his briefcase. He rummaged freely through the discarded mounds of letters.

Because the Chancellery was in the Russian sector of Berlin, Emker had to exercise caution. If he heard the voices or footsteps of Russian visitors, he would conceal himself in a nearby room. As a U.S. soldier in U.S. uniform with U.S. identification, he had the right to go where he pleased (Germans were not permitted in the Chancellery). But he did not want the Russians to discover his interest in the discarded documents. Emker returned to the Chancellery 20 to 25 times. He filled his Berlin apartment with eight thousand love letters. He had no time to read through them, so he mailed everything to a girlfriend in New York.

Of course, no one should be surprised that the all-powerful Führer attracted the attention of women throughout Germany and Austria. Hitler himself recognized his hold on the *Frauen*. "Power is the ultimate aphrodisiac," said Henry Kissinger.

The ladies sent their letters to "Dear Adi," telling him they wanted to bear his child. "You'll long for me, you sweet rascal. I send you intimate kisses!" wrote one woman, July 9, 1941. Other letters from foreign women asked Hitler to avoid war or to end it. The lovelorn sent poems and absurd drawings, as well as anti–Semitic and anti–Roosevelt screeds. German and Austrian letters from 1945 demanded total war until the final victory. Only a few letters from 1939 asked Hitler to avoid war, senseless death and slaughter. The pacifist letters were unsigned, while the anti–Semitic and bellicose letters had the writers' names and addresses. Some letters were childishly simple-minded, written in mangled, ungrammatical German. They arrived in packets with socks and scarves the writers had made. Sometimes a woman would send her apartment key with explicit instructions how to avoid the concierge.

Hitler probably saw very little of this material, even items addressed to him personally. Most of the letters have the comment "set aside" penciled at the top. Clerks answered them with form replies. For example, happy birthday letters got something like "The Führer thanks..." Hitler's engraved, personally signed responses were a rarity. Letters asking for assistance were referred to an appropriate agency. Letters with suggestions for war strategy, or redrawing of the map of Europe or Asia, received the reply, "The Führer thanks you, but is too busy running the war to reply personally."

A German playwright, Heike Frank, made the letters into a play, presented in Berlin in 2001. "Some of the women were only sending Hitler affectionate greetings. They thought he was not getting enough love, " she said. "But there were others who believed he was a god." The Chancellery never answered the love letters. But the pathetic women who laid their souls at the Führer's feet often would not give up. They wrote again and again until the bureaucrats sent the letters to the police. A policeman would pick up the offending woman and take her to the health department, where she was declared to be mentally ill. She was then committed to a psychiatric hospital. What happened afterward is anyone's guess. In 1939, Hitler had declared the mentally ill to be "useless eaters" and murdered them by lethal injection.

Ironically, one of Hitler's own relatives was killed for this reason. The woman, Aloisia Veit, was 49 when she was gassed on December 6, 1940, in Hartheim castle near the northern Austrian city of Linz, according to Timothy Ryback.[3] Mental illness flourished in Hitler's extended family. A 1944 Gestapo report described Aloisia's line of the family as "idiotic progeny." Recently released medical files on her say she had schizophrenia, depression, delusions and other mental problems. Her treatment included confinement in cage beds, a practice that was widespread even before the Nazis.

Aloisia was the great-grandchild of the sister of Hitler's paternal grandmother, meaning she was part of the Schicklgruber side of the family. Her family was close to Hitler's, and Adolf's father, Alois Hitler, helped her father get a job as a civil servant in Vienna. The Schicklgrubers were especially hard hit by insanity and "crashed into suicide and mental illness," according to Ryback.

Hitler's Library

In the Reichskanzlerpalais, Hitler had a suite of rooms: a lounge, bedroom, bathroom, a small room for Eva Braun, and a library. In this library, January 26, 1938, in Hitler's presence, a male prostitute named Hans Schmidt confronted Werner von Fritsch, commander

Hitler, Werner von Fritsch and Werner von Blomberg. Fritsch (left) was recalled to duty for the invasion of Poland, September 1939. He was killed in action September 22nd. Reinhard Heydrich sneered that Fritsch had actually committed suicide. The Americans captured Blomberg, who died in his Nuremberg prison cell, March 14, 1946.

in chief of the armed forces, and falsely claimed that he had had sexual relations with Fritsch. Using these charges, Hitler forced Fritsch into retirement. He then dismissed War Minister Werner von Blomberg on February 4, 1938, the pretext being Blomberg's marriage to a prostitute, and took control of the army.

In the spring of 1945, soldiers of the 101st Airborne Division searching a salt mine near

Berchtesgaden discovered 3,000 books from Hitler's library, packed in crates with the Reich Chancellery address. After evaluation at a collecting point in Munich, officials shipped the books to the Library of Congress. An intern was assigned to evaluate the collection. "The intern did what we call 'duping out,'" David Moore, a German-acquisition assistant at the Library of Congress, told Timothy W. Ryback. "If a book was not one hundred percent sure, if there was no bookplate, no inscription to the Führer, he didn't keep it." The 1,200 books that survived this process were sent to the Rare Book Collection. They were originally called the Hitler Library but are now called the Third Reich Collection.

Very few scholars have examined Hitler's books. "Spot-checks revealed little in the way of marginal notes, autographs, or other similar features of interest," an internal Library of Congress review stated in January of 1952. "Indeed, it seems that most of the books have never been perused by their owner."

Ryback discovered that the most important aspect of the books was their marginalia. For example, the Third Reich Collection contains two identical copies of Paul de Lagarde's German Essays. In one volume, 58 pages have pencil marks, the first on page 16, the last on page 370. Given that Lagarde belongs to a circle of nineteenth-century German nationalist writers who are believed to have had a formative influence on Hitler's anti–Semitism, Ryback emphasizes that the marked passages are definitely worth noting. In an essay called "The Current Tasks of German Politics," Lagarde anticipates the emergence of a "singular man with the abilities and energy" to unite the German peoples, and calls for the "relocation of the Polish and Austrian Jews to Palestine." The latter phrase has been underlined and flagged, presumably by Hitler himself, with two bold lines in the margin.

Sometimes Ryback could identify Hitler's jagged cursive hand. For the most part, though, the marginalia are restricted to simple markings whose common "authorship" is suggested by an intense vertical line in the margin and double or triple underlining in the text, always in pencil. Ryback found these markings repeatedly both in the Library of Congress collection and in a cache of 80 Hitler books at Brown University. Hitler's handwritten speeches, preserved in the Federal German Archives, show an identical pattern of markings. In one anti–Semitic rant Hitler drew three lines under the words Klassenkampf ("class struggle"), Weltherrschaft ("world domination"), and Der Jude als Diktator ("the Jew as dictator"). Hitler's habit of underlining key concepts and passages fits with his theory on the "art of reading." In Chapter Two of *Mein Kampf* he wrote,

> A man who possesses the art of correct reading will, in studying any book, magazine, or pamphlet, instinctively and immediately perceive everything which in his opinion is worth permanently remembering, either because it is suited to his purpose or generally worth knowing.... Then, if life suddenly sets some question before us for examination or answer, the memory, if this method of reading is observed ... will derive all the individual items regarding these questions, assembled in the course of decades, [and] submit them to the mind for examination and reconsideration, until the question is clarified or answered.

August Kubizek, Hitler's friend from his teenage years and roommate in Vienna, recalled after the war that Hitler had been registered with three libraries in Linz, where he attended school, and had spent many days in the Hofbibliothek, the former court library of the Hapsburgs, during his time in Vienna. "Books were his world," wrote Kubizek. Hitler had Albert Speer design a vast library that occupied the entire west wing of the New Reich Chancellery. Timothy Ryback found inventory records of the Reich Chancellery at the Hoover Institution at Stanford, which suggest that by the early 1940s Hitler was receiving as many as 4,000 books annually.

New Reich Chancellery Library and ceiling frescoes. The ceiling art was never completed because the war intervened.

Hitler loved the Wild West stories of Karl May. Hitler's first contact with May was in 1912, when May gave a lecture in Vienna's Sophiensäle titled "To the forefront of the ranks of noblemen." In the audience of 3,000 sat Hitler, wearing borrowed shoes.[4]

The 70-year-old writer was quite a scandalous character. Journalists had discovered that the youthful May had been imprisoned for fraud and theft. Worse, he had never seen the foreign lands he described in his wildly popular books.

May was famous for his stories of cowboys, Indians, and the American West that are still best sellers in German-speaking countries. The historian Gordon Craig has called May "a one-man dream factory in an age that did not yet know cinema, radio, or television." Men as diverse as Hitler and Albert Einstein were ardent fans. But May's talk on that March night was devoted to praising the peace movement, to which he had dedicated his book *And Peace on Earth.*

The 68-year-old pacifist Bertha von Suttner, whom May venerated, attended the lecture as an honored guest in the first row. She had called May a "spiritual comrade in matters of peace," defended him against all criticism, and said of him, "We spiritual workers hold the ladder which humanity must climb to attain nobility."

Bertha von Suttner had clearly inspired the title of May's lecture. As a convinced Darwinist, she believed in the upward march of human progress, toward the good and noble, toward peace and the abolition of war.

Although the audience expected to hear another thrilling tale of May's celebrated Indian hero, Winnetou, May's unexpected topic nevertheless delighted them. Afterward, many people congratulated May on the street outside. Suttner remarked that there was "a demonstration of reverence for May and a protest against the slander campaign to which May had been subjected."

The newspaper reporters who attended were far less enthusiastic. According to the *Neue Freie Presse*, the talk "for those listeners who were not enthusiastic May readers was a severe test of patience." The *Fremdenblatt* was more blunt and wrote that May's lecture was a "deadly bore."

Hitler was completely enchanted, both by the talk and by Karl May himself. In discussions at the men's shelter where he lived, Hitler called May a "splendid, complete human being, who accurately describes the most distant parts of the earth." May's writings were "immensely appealing to young people," said Hitler. In answer to the criticism that May had never seen the places he described in his novels, Hitler said that the descriptions "speak for May's genius, since they were far more realistic than those of other researchers and travelers."

When May died 10 days after his talk in the Sophiensäle, the controversy he generated only grew. May's death devastated the young Hitler, who elevated the author to a cult figure. Even as Reich Chancellor, Hitler found time to reread the 60 volumes of May's writings. In 1943, despite the paper shortage, Hitler had 300,000 copies of May's novel *Winnetou* distributed to his soldiers, although May's hero was non–Aryan, i.e., a "redskinned" Indian. Hitler also recommended the stories to his generals, whom he faulted for lack of imagination.

May's books, wrote Albert Speer in his *Spandau Diaries*, "stirred Hitler the way a philosophic text or the Bible moved others." May served as "proof that everything is possible," that it was not necessary "to know the desert to direct troops on North African battlefields." A person with "imagination and sensitivity can know more of a foreign people's psychology than someone who has studied the same people in the flesh," just as May could "understand the soul, customs, and living conditions of Bedouins and Indians." Karl May proved that it was "not necessary to travel in order to know the world," a reassuring thought to Hitler, who had never set foot outside of Europe.

Speer advised historians, when attempting to portray Hitler the supreme commander, to take into account Karl May's influence, especially in the character of Winnetou. Hitler considered Winnetou the model company commander and an exemplary man. From this "heroic figure," young people could learn truly what "noble courage" was. Sadly, Hitler absorbed every aspect of May except his pacifism. Hitler also read closely the works of another German writer, Johann Gottlieb Fichte. Leni Riefenstahl, Hitler's filmmaker (*Triumph of the Will*), had given Hitler the volumes of Fichte.

Ryback found "a veritable blizzard of underlines, question marks, exclamation points, and marginal strikes" in a hundred printed pages of Fichte. In the Holy Trinity, Fichte posited the Father as "a natural universal force," the Son as the "physical embodiment of this force," and the Holy Ghost as an expression of the "light of reason." "Hitler not only underlined the entire passage but placed a thick vertical line in the margin, and added an exclamation point for good measure," wrote Ryback.

Frederick the Great: The King and His Portraits

Frederick the Great (1712–1786), considered the premier military genius of the eighteenth century, annexed Silesia and made Prussia a world power after the Seven Years' War. The Prussian King also detested Jews and enacted anti–Jewish statutes. In doing so, he nullified the actions of his wise and tolerant ancestor, Friedrich Wilhelm, the Great Elector, who in the seventeenth century had welcomed persecuted Jews to Prussia. Hitler frequently compared himself to Frederick. "Prussia owes its rise to the heroism of one man," Hitler told his army leaders. "Everything depended on Frederick the Great."[5] When the German Army drive into Russia stalled before Moscow in December 1941, General Heinz Guderian counseled retreat, or the loss of life would be enormous. Hitler countered, "Do you think Frederick the Great's grenadiers were anxious to die? They wanted to live, too, but the King was right in asking them to sacrifice themselves. I believe that I also am entitled to ask any German soldier to lay down his life." President Franklin D. Roosevelt died April 12, 1945. Hearing the news, Hitler proclaimed that Germany's catastrophic military position would improve. Goebbels, who had recently reread Thomas Carlyle's biography of Frederick the Great, had reminded Hitler that the death of the Czarina Elizabeth brought a reversal of fortune for the Prussian King in the Seven Years' War. The coalition allied against Germany would now be rent asunder, just as in Frederick's time. History would repeat itself. "Here, read this," an excited Hitler told Albert Speer. "Here we have the great miracle I always foretold. Who's right now? The war is not lost. Roosevelt is dead."

Given Hitler's identification with his hero, Frederick the Great, it is not surprising that a portrait of the King accompanied the Führer everywhere. The artist Anton Graff painted the monarch from life. Hitler hung Graff's portrait in his Wolf's Lair East Prussian military headquarters, and in the Führerbunker. One of the bunker telephone operators saw Hitler sitting in his living room, with a candle flickering in the draft from a ventilator, staring at the picture in a sort of trance. Just before his suicide, Hitler gave the painting to Hans Bauer, his pilot.[6]

A second Graff portrait of Frederick the Great hung in the Reichskanzlerpalais. In this portrait, Frederick looks much less like a conqueror and more like a philosopher. Graff painted the portrait in 1781. By this time, "Old Fritz" would no longer pose for artists. Friedrich Nicolai, Graff's contemporary, wrote that the artist daily watched the king at the bivouac of his troops, then "went home to his lodgings to paint." The oval portrait disappeared at the end of the war. Art scholars believe that it was probably a copy made by one of Graff's students.[7]

Hitler's Other Paintings

Hitler intended to build an art museum in Linz, which would be the most splendid in the world. By the end of the war he had accumulated 8,000 works, many of them masterpieces stolen from Jewish collectors, for his museum. In his will, he designated that his paintings should go to a gallery in Linz.

The art Hitler hung on his own walls was considerably more banal than that which his advisors had accumulated for Linz. And he was quite attached to his paintings. When he moved from his apartments in the Reichskanzler-

Frederick the Great. This oval portrait disappeared in 1945. With Hitler is Viktor Lutze, who succeeded Ernst Roehm as head of the SA, after Roehm was murdered during the Night of the Long Knives. Lutze was killed in a crash on the Autobahn, May 2, 1943.

palais to the bunker, he converted the corridor leading to the Führerbunker into a waiting room, and hung the walls with art that had been in his study.

On May 8, 1999, Hitler's personal art went on display in Weimar.[8] The paintings are full of female nudes, for example in Johann Schult's pastoral "Springtime of Life" or in Sepp Hilz's quasi-pornographic "Eva." The unclothed women appear submissive, with their poses suggesting a charged association of power and sex in the Nazi mind. Arthur Kampf's "Venus and Adonis" is ersatz Rubens with pubic hair.

The worker, a revered personage in National Socialism, also figures prominently in Hitler's art collection, muscular, devoted, and generous. The Nazis tried to deify the common man that Hitler put back to work after the hyperinflation and other economic difficulties of the Weimar Republic. The adulation is clear in Rudolf Werner's "Asphalt Workers,"

Venus and Adonis by Arthur Kampf (1864–1950). Venus tries to hold back her lover Adonis from going to the hunt. Oil on canvas, 183 × 158 cm. Once part of Hitler's collection, now property of the German State (AKG Images).

in Waldemar Coste's "Builders," and in Carl Theodor Protzen's "Roads of the Fuhrer" (1940) portraying the Nazi worker constructing the autobahn.

"Hitler's is by far the worst collection of paintings I have ever put on show," Achim Preiss, the organizer of the Weimar exhibit, told the *New York Times*' Roger Cohen. "They are really shockingly boring. But of the 120 works, perhaps 90 have not been seen in Germany since 1945, and they are critical to our understanding of Nazi rule."

Wagner Manuscripts Lost

Were irreplaceable original scores by Richard Wagner lost shortly after Adolf Hitler died in Berlin in 1945? That seems a strong possibility on the basis of a story from the Wagner family. Wagner's descendants still hope that the missing scores will be found. But they have waited vainly since the end of World War II, and they feel now that the priceless documents were either destroyed or stolen from Hitler's bunker.[9]

Hitler's connection with Wagner is complex. Wagner's first great operatic success, *Rienzi*, provides one example of this complexity. The opera tells the story of Cola Rienzi, an idealized historical personality, who wrests authority from a corrupt Roman oligarchy. A performance in Linz of *Rienzi* electrified the 15-year-old Hitler, as his friend August Kubizek wrote:

> My friend, his hands thrust into his coat pockets, silent and withdrawn, strode through the streets and out of the city.... Never before and never again have I heard Adolf Hitler speak as he did in that hour, and we stood there alone under the stars.... It was a state of complete ecstasy and rapture, in which he transferred the character of Rienzi ... with visionary power to the plan of his own ambitions.

Rienzi is imbued with a mission to lead his people out of servitude, a conquering hero overthrown by a mob in the opera's finale. Hitler used the *Rienzi* overture as the musical theme for all Nazi party rallies.

From the beginning, Hitler made use of Wagner to present the Third Reich as the culmination of centuries of German culture and history. The operas stirred him to restore Germany to greatness.

One route was racial purification, an obsession of Wagner's. In the first act of *Die Walküre*, Siegmund and Sieglinde's intense sexual desire derives from sameness. Wagner has made them brother and sister, and their incestuous inbreeding leads to the birth of a true hero, Siegfried. Hitler first codified racial purification in the 1935 Nuremberg Laws, and later carried it to murderous extremes.

As Leon Botstein has remarked, Wagner's *Die Walküre*, in fact the entire *Ring* cycle of which it is a part, can inspire a mix of ambition and frustration with the world as it is, and certainly did so in Adolf Hitler. Swept along by the intensity of his experience in the theater of Wagner, the disaffected, resentful young Hitler fantasized about becoming the fearless hero of the future, whom Wotan, the ruler of the gods, describes in the closing scene of *Die Walküre*. The desire to escape the petty limitations of middle-class life became irresistible all too easily with the help of Wagner's music, and inspired in Hitler grandiosely malevolent schemes.

Wagner's English-born daughter in law, Winifred (1897–1980), was Hitler's early supporter during the 1920s. Gottfried Wagner, the composer's great grandson, says that Hitler proposed marriage to Winifred, and she supplied him with the paper on which he wrote *Mein Kampf* in Landsberg Prison.

As Führer, Hitler was a frequent visitor to Villa Wahnfried, Wagner's Bayreuth home. He tucked in Winifred's two children, Wieland and Wolfgang, who called him "Uncle Wolf." He attended the annual Wagner festivals in Bayreuth, and enshrined the town as a temple of Nazi culture. Because of this odious association, the Allies closed down the Bayreuth Festival from 1945 to 1950 for "decontamination." Villa Wahnfried was heavily damaged during the war, but was rebuilt and is now a museum.

The Wagner scores lost from the Führerbunker:

- The full original manuscript scores in Wagner's hand of his earliest operas—*Die Feen*, *Das Liebesverbot* and *Rienzi*
- The orchestral sketches for *The Flying Dutchman*
- The original fair copy made by Wagner of the whole score of *Das Rheingold* and *Die Walküre*
- The original fair copy of the orchestral sketches for *Siegfried*
- The orchestral sketches for the prelude and first act of *Götterdämmerung*, copied by Hans Richter, one of the celebrated conductors of the nineteenth century and a close associate of Wagner
- The orchestral sketches for the second and third acts of *Götterdämmerung*, copied by another hand, with several pages in the second act probably by Wagner.

All these scores had been in the possession of King Ludwig II of Bavaria, the young monarch who adored Wagner and his music and who helped him to bring his dream of his own theatre and festival to fruition in Bayreuth. The king's heirs, the Wittelsbach family, retained the material until April 18, 1939. On that date they sold the collection to the chief of the German Chamber of Commerce for 800,000 marks (about $200,000). The purchase price was raised by subscription of leading members of the chamber. Two days later the chamber presented the scores to Hitler as a tribute on his 50th birthday. Hitler kept the treasured gift in the Chancellery.

In December 1944, when the war was going badly, two of Wagner's grandchildren, Wieland, the eldest, and Frau Verena Lafferentz, the youngest, traveled to Berlin. They were anxious to take the scores to Bayreuth for safekeeping. They got in to see Hitler but did not dare to tell him what they really wanted. They feared the Führer would accuse them of defeatism if they suggested that Germany was losing and that the scores were in danger. They knew that Hitler had shot some of his close supporters on the charge of defeatism. Wieland and Verena asked to borrow the scores to make facsimiles. In a hoarse whisper, the decrepit-appearing Hitler refused to part with the scores. The securest place for them, he said, was with him in the Chancellery.

Early in April 1945, when the end was near, Wieland Wagner made a last desperate trip to Berlin in an effort to recover the scores. This time Bodo Lafferentz, Verena's husband, who was a leading figure in the "Strength Through Joy" movement, accompanied him. When they telephoned for an appointment with Hitler, they were not permitted to speak to him. Martin Bormann answered the phone, saying he would see if he could reach Hitler. He came back with the message that the scores were in Hitler's bunker with all his cherished possessions and that this was the best place in Germany for them. The Wagner scores were never seen again.

Wieland Wagner died in Munich, October 16, 1966, age 49. He had been a co-director of the Bayreuth Festival. Verena Lafferentz, now age 84, lives in Uberlingen, Germany.

Hitler's Money

Hitler had accumulated a huge fortune by the time of his death, but despite the terms of his private last will and testament, which he dictated in the Führerbunker, his relatives and faithful staff members collected almost nothing. Some of Hitler's money came from royalties he earned on *Mein Kampf*, his best-selling autobiography and political harangue. Every couple who married during the Third Reich were given a copy of *Mein Kampf* by their local community, which had to buy the book from the publisher.

According to Ingo Helm, who made a TV documentary on Hitler's wealth, the Führer earned some 7.8 million reichsmarks from the book alone. This could be as much as $8 million in today's money. In addition, Hitler's friend and photographer Heinrich Hoffmann, in whose shop Hitler first met Eva Braun, held the copyright on official portraits of Hitler, which were used in government offices and on postage stamps. "Hitler probably had a share in that income," Helm told *New York Times* correspondent Steven Erlanger.

Hitler also got part of the contributions made by individual businessmen and corporations to the Nazi Party, which increased after he came to power. "He wasn't simply created by big business," Helm said. "Once he was in power, big business was opportunistic," and gave eye-popping sums. From 1933 until his death in 1945, Hitler received some 700 million reichsmarks in corporate payments, Helm said. In return, the businessmen collected millions more on their investments and military contracts.

There were also special funds from the state budget to which only Hitler and his close associates had access. Of this money, Hitler invested at least two million reichsmarks to covertly rebuild a palace in what is now Poznan, in Poland, for another Führer residence. Kaiser Wilhelm II had originally built the palace, and by 1945 at least 20 million reichsmarks had been poured into the place.

After the war, the Allied Control Commission gave Hitler's property and assets, including a house in Munich he had built for Eva Braun, to the state of Bavaria. The copyright to *Mein Kampf* also belongs to Bavaria, which will not permit the book to be issued. But the American publisher Houghton Mifflin obtained the English language rights before the war, and the English translation is still a brisk seller in American bookstores. In England, *Mein Kampf* regularly sells 3,000 copies a year. The royalties go to a charity, but the publishers will not identify it.[10]

Heinrich Hoffmann paid for the Munich house from the huge sums of money he had received as Hitler's photographer. Hitler rarely visited Eva at the house, even though the villa was thought to be a love nest. But Eva loved the house, since it gave

Delpstrasse 12. Eva Braun in front of her Munich villa. Eva and younger sister Gretl moved into this villa, which Hitler had acquired for them, on March 30, 1936 (Bayerische Staatsbibliothek).

her independence from her parents. Bushes she planted still grow in the garden. Before the war, the street was called Wasserburgstrasse. Afterward it was renamed in honor of Alfred Delp, a priest the Nazis murdered in 1945.

Hitler had no children, although his half-sister, Angela Raubal, did, and his mother had other descendants, who live in the Waldviertel region of Austria. The heirs asked Werner Maser, a Hitler biographer, to investigate their rights to the *Mein Kampf* copyright. But the relatives feuded among themselves, Helm said, and no lawsuit to obtain the copyright was filed. Maser himself tried to make a quick *deutschmark* by claiming Hitler had fathered an illegitimate son in France during World War I, an assertion that turned out to be bogus.

Hitler's sister Paula, who called herself Paula Wolf, became penniless in 1945 except for public assistance and small sums sent occasionally by friends. Until the end of the war, she had lived in seclusion in Vienna on an allowance from her brother. She then spent much of her time trying to get the Bavarian courts to recognize her claim to a share of her brother's fortune and personal effects but failed. One reason was the squabble between Bavaria's courts and West Berlin's courts as to definite proof of Hitler's death. Without a certificate to this effect Paula could not establish her claim. She died June 1, 1960, and is buried in the Bergfriedhof in Berchtesgaden.

The only payment Hitler's heirs have ever received was for Hitler's second book. Writing during the 1920s, Hitler dwelt at length on foreign policy, and outlined a strategy of alliance with Fascist Italy and Great Britain. He believed that Britain would accept a German-dominated European continent so long as Germany did not challenge the overseas British Empire. He also foresaw an inevitable clash with the United States. Hitler did not want this work in print. In 1961 the Institut für Zeitgeschichte in Munich wanted to publish the book. In order to avoid lawsuits, the institute paid Hitler's heirs 2,250 marks. The book appeared the same year.[11]

An American in the Bunker

In July 1945, an American intelligence officer and journalist, James P. O'Donnell, received an assignment to write an article for *Newsweek* on the Führerbunker. To O'Donnell, the Chancellery garden looked like an obscene junkyard, pitted with bomb craters. The bunker entrance was in a rectangular, unsurfaced tawny-colored cement block, 20 feet high, with a narrow oblong entrance and indented vestibule. A single Soviet soldier was on guard.

A second Russian sentry had set up quarters in a room where the walls and ceiling were charred, the floor smeared with gray ash, and the blue Frisian-tile wall paneling covered with soot. This was Hitler's study. The sentry was armed with a submachine gun, but this lay on the table. He held a long-barreled .22 caliber German target pistol.

Huge rats were gnawing the red carpet. But worse than the rats, the darkness, and the humidity was the odor. Although O'Donnell saw, in a separate power room, a quite modern ventilation machine, it had long since been closed down. So had the untended lavatories. These were clogged but obviously still in use.

O'Donnell sloshed through a shallow, stagnant pool at the far end of the central corridor, some three or four inches of water, muck, and slime. He came to a massive steel door that opened into a staircase leading to the Vorbunker. He kicked up by accident what appeared to be a large map. The document was an architect's sketch for the postwar remodeling and enlarging of the Austrian city of Greater Linz.

Russian soldiers had already ransacked the Führerbunker. The floors, corridors, and duckboards were littered with glass shards, bottles, rusty picture frames, German Army cheesecake photos, warped gramophone records, scattered sheet music, dented air-raid-warden helmets, empty first aid kits, bloodied bandages, old knapsacks, tin cans, ammunition drums, empty pistol clips, scattered playing cards, film magazines, cigar and cigarette butts, and slimy condoms.

O'Donnell saw a great deal of printed and written material — military telephone books and telephone-number pads, loose-leaf notebooks, business office files and dossiers, diaries, military manuals, scratch pads, letters. Obviously, the bunker had been not only an air-raid shelter; it had also served as a military headquarters.

Truman and Churchill Visit Wilhelmstraße

On July 16, 1945, both President Harry S Truman and Prime Minister Winston Churchill toured Berlin on their way to confer at Potsdam with Josef Stalin. As David McCullough wrote in his biography of Truman:

> Despite all they had read, all they had been told in advance, the photographs and newsreels they had seen, the visiting Americans were unprepared for the reality of conquered Berlin. "I never saw such destruction," recorded Truman, who had seen his share in 1918. It was "absolute ruin." To Admiral Leahy, whose military career had begun with the famous voyage of the old Oregon around the Horn to Cuba in 1898, it was a calamity against the civilized laws of war. At a notably subdued dinner that night they talked quietly among themselves of the horrible destructiveness of modern war, "now brought home," as Leahy said, "to those of us who fought the war from Washington." Truman was as low as he had felt in a long time.
> "I thought of Carthage, Baalbek, Jerusalem, Rome, Atlantis, Peking ... [of] Scipio, Rameses II ... Sherman, Jenghiz Khan [he wrote that night in his diary].... I hope for some sort of peace — but I fear that machines are ahead of morals by some centuries and when morals catch up there'll be no reason for any of it."
> He kept thinking of the devastated people he had seen wandering in the debris. But they had brought it on themselves. They did it, he would write to [his wife] Bess.
> Churchill, on a tour of Berlin of his own that afternoon, had spent half an hour exploring the Chancellery, the site of Hitler's bunker. ("This is what would have happened to us if they had won the war," Churchill was heard to say. "We would have been the bunker.") Truman had not wished to walk among the ruins, he said, because he would never want those unfortunate people to think he was gloating over them.

But as Charles IX remarked in 1572, when he saw the rotting corpse of Admiral Gaspard de Coligny hanging by its feet from a gallows, "The smell of a dead enemy is always sweet." Churchill added details:

> The city was nothing but a chaos of ruins. No notice had of course been given of our visit and the streets had only the ordinary passers-by. In the square in front of the Chancellery there was however a considerable crowd. When I got out of the car and walked about among them, except for one old man who shook his head disapprovingly, they all began to cheer. My hate had died with their surrender, and I was much moved by their demonstrations, and also by their haggard looks and threadbare clothes. Then we entered the Chancellery, and for quite a long time walked through its shattered galleries and halls. Our Russian guides took us to Hitler's air-raid shelter. I went down to the bottom and saw the room in which he and his mistress had committed suicide, and when we came up again they showed us the place where his body had been burned.[12]

Winston Churchill visits the destroyed Chancellery and Führerbunker, July 16, 1945. Churchill's daughter Mary (in military dress) is behind him at left (Ullstein Bilderdienst).

John F. Kennedy Visits Wilhelmstraße

John F. Kennedy first visited Germany in 1937, and toured Munich, Nuremberg, and Cologne with his friend Lem Billings. Kennedy and Billings stayed in hostels "full of arrogant, evil smelling Germans. The self-declared master race..." wrote Kennedy.[13] On August 1, 1945, the 28-year-old Kennedy returned to Germany. He accompanied Secretary of the Navy James Forrestal to the Berghof, Hitler's Bavarian Alpine Home, and the Eagle's Nest, the aerie Martin Bormann built for Hitler. (Kennedy seems to be concatenating *Wolf's Lair*, Hitler's East Prussian field headquarters, with *Eagle's Nest* to form the term he uses, *Eagle's Lair*):

> In the morning we went up to Hitler's mountain home. It was completely gutted, the result of an air attack from 12,000 pound bombs by the R.A.F. in an attempt on Hitler's life. Leaving the chalet, we drove to the very top of the mountains (about 7,000 feet) where the famed Eagle's lair was located. The road up was covered with solid rock in many places and was cleverly camouflaged. On arrival at the top, we entered a long tunnel carved through the rocks and came to an elevator which took us up through solid rock for the last 600 feet. The elevator was a double-decker — a space being left on the lower deck for the SS guard. The lair itself had been stripped of its rugs, pictures, and tapestries, but the view was beautiful — the living room being round and facing out on every side on the valley below.

This and other Kennedy travel diary entries appear in *Prelude to Leadership: The Post-War Diary of John F. Kennedy* (1995). The book raised a few eyebrows because of Kennedy's comments about Hitler:

After visiting these two places, you can easily understand how within a few years Hitler will emerge from the hatred that surrounds him now as one of the most significant figures who ever lived. He had boundless ambition for his country which rendered him a menace to the peace of the world, but he had a mystery about him in the way that he lived and in the manner of his death that will live and grow after him. He had in him the stuff of which legends are made.

"Bizarre," commented Hugh Sidey, *Time* White House correspondent, who knew Kennedy well. In his introduction to *Prelude to Leadership*, Sidey wrote, "Hadn't he heard of the gas chambers? It's hard to believe."

In Berlin, Kennedy noted upon his arrival, July 28, 1945:

> The devastation is complete. Unter den Linden and the streets are relatively clear, but there is not a single building which is not gutted. On some of the streets the stench — sweet and sickish from dead bodies — is overwhelming. The people all have completely colorless faces — a yellow tinge with pale tan lips. They are all carrying bundles. Where they are going, no one seems to know. I wonder whether they do. They sleep in cellars. The women will do anything for food. One or two of the women wore lipstick, but most seem to be trying to make themselves as unobtrusive as possible to escape the notice of the Russians. The Russians were short, stocky, and dour looking. Their features were heavy and their uniforms dirty. Hitler's Reich Chancellery was a shell. The walls were chipped and scarred by bullets, showing the terrific fight which took place at the time of its fall. Hitler's air-raid shelter was about 120 feet down into the ground — well furnished but completely devastated. The room where Hitler was supposed to have met his death showed scorched walls and traces of fire. There is no complete evidence, however, that the body that was found was Hitler's body. The Russians doubt that he is dead.

Kennedy made several diary references to the cruelty of the Soviet occupation of Germany.

He recorded the impact of the devastating British-American air attacks: "According to our naval experts, the bombing of Germany was not effective in stopping their production, and production increased three-fold during 1942–1944." Right until the end, Kennedy reported, an adequate food distribution was maintained in the German capital: "The feeding in Berlin was extremely well organized, even in the most severe blitz." Ordinary Germans, Kennedy opined, "did not realize what was going on in the concentration camps."

Kennedy and Forrestal toured Bremen, an important north German industrial and commercial center, and a major port city. As Kennedy wrote, the Russians were not the only occupation forces to carry out wide-scale plundering in Germany: "The British had gone into Bremen ahead of us — and everyone was unanimous in their description of British looting and destruction, which had been very heavy. They had taken everything which at all related to the sea — ships, small boats, lubricants, machinery, etc." He noted crimes of U.S. troops. "Americans looted town [Bremen] heavily on arrival," he wrote. "People do not seem to realize," he added, "how fortunate they have been in escaping the Russians. As far as looting the homes and the towns, however, the British and Americans have been very guilty."

In Bremen, Kennedy wrote, the Germans' diet "is about 1,200 calories — ours being 4,000."

In spite of everything, "none of the [American] officers and men here seem to have any particular hate for the Germans."

Less than a year after his European tour, Kennedy was elected to Congress in Massachusetts, beginning a political career that took him to the White House, and which ended suddenly with his assassination, November 22, 1963.

Opposite: John F. Kennedy in Berlin, June 26, 1963. Kennedy, standing on the rostrum, addresses a crowd in the main square in front of Schöneberg City Hall in West Berlin. Kennedy declared "Ich bin ein Berliner," which drew sniggers from the crowd, because what he had said could well be translated "I am a jelly doughnut" (Ein Berliner was a popular local pastry.) The U.S. President was on a 10-day European tour (Photograph by Robert Knudsen. White House Photographs, John F. Kennedy Presidential Library and Museum, Boston).

The New York Times *Visits Wilhelmstraße*

Each year the great hulk of Hitler's New Reich Chancellery was sinking deeper into ruin, wrote Anne O'Hare McCormick in 1948.

> The walls and ceilings left sagging by bombs and shellfire have fallen in. A hill of rubble, the remains of the rotunda, prevents the visitor from walking from the vast entrance hall into the vaster hall beyond. Rain, wind and frost lash through the roofless galleries and gaping windows to eat away what is left of the floors and paneling. The cold mosaic crisscrossing the marble pavement has been picked out. Of the colossus built to the scale of Hitler's ambition, built to be the capital of conquered Europe, only this moldering corpse remains.

Demolition of the Bunker

In late autumn 1947, Russian soldiers packed the Führerbunker with captured munitions and high explosives. On December 11, they set them off. The deafening explosion collapsed the concrete block over the garden entrance and toppled the concrete tower. But Architect Carl Piepenburg had used too much steel and concrete to destroy with a single blast. The bunker rooms, eight-and-a-half meters below the earth, had been damaged but were still accessible. The Soviets decided to fill all the entrances with dirt and leave the aboveground concrete hulks as they were. In 1949 the Red Army razed the New Reich Chancellery ruins along with the smashed Reichskanzlerpalais and Chancellery Annex. Nothing, they decreed, would be left of what the megalomaniac Hitler had built. But the Führerbunker remnants were too expensive to eradicate.

A decade later, the East Germans tried to get rid of the bunker. In June 1959, West Berlin newspapers reported, "Führerbunker to be blown up," and "Compressed air to be used on Bunker remains." The area was to be turned into a park, said the newspapers, and the bunker done away with forever. Workmen bored holes for explosive charges in the roofs of the Vorbunker and probably the Führerbunker as well. On June 18, they set off their dynamite. After an earth-shaking blast, the bunkers still stood. "Capitulation before the Hitler Bunker," reported *Die Welt* in October. The Communists had spent a large sum but had accomplished virtually nothing. Since the bunkers could not be eliminated, the alternative was to create an earthen mound over them to cover them entirely. This same strategy had already been used for two dynamited Flak towers in Friedrichshain. But the Berlin Wall intervened.

When the wall was built in 1961, the East German Secret Police moved to identify and seal off any subterranean escape hatches. Since the Führerbunker lay in no-man's land, adjacent to the wall, it was a logical place to search.

The East Germans located Albert Speer's original plans for Hitler's Reich Chancellery, along with precise drawings of some of the bunkers and tunnels. In the summer of 1973 they explored the maze of underground passageways, made many photographs, and even found pages from Goebbels' diary.

"In one of the lower rooms, torturously, fearfully hemmed in, I give a speech in my best form," Goebbels wrote about his appearance before a course for a group of adjutants. "The young officers are enchanted and give me a great ovation." The searchers also found the double deck beds in which the Goebbels children had been murdered.

From 1986 to 1989, the East Germans dynamited the Vorbunker and parts of the Führerbunker. They carted away the fragments, even the four-and-a-half meter thick steel and concrete slabs that made up the floor.

More of the Führerbunker turned up in October 1999. Construction workers near Wilhelmstraße came upon a concrete slab, which may have formed part of the roof or floor. After archeologists in the Berlin Monument Service made a cursory inspection, the excavation was filled with dirt and closed.

An Italian economist, Guido Pietro, has made geophysical measurements of the ministry garden. Pietro determined that the floor plates of the Führerbunker and the exterior walls, to at least half their original height (1.4 to 1.6 meters), are still *in situ*, though the thick concrete roof is gone. None of the rooms survive. They are entirely filled with debris. The Vorbunker is gone. Although the site is of historical interest, the Berlin Monument Service and the Berlin Senate have absolutely no desire to place any sort of marker over the Führerbunker.

Speer After Hitler

At the Nuremberg trials in 1946, Albert Speer was sentenced to 20 years in prison for his use of slave labor. He served his time in Berlin's Spandau Prison, which had been built during the rule of the Kaisers, and which was razed after Rudolf Heß, its last prisoner, committed suicide, August 17, 1987.

Speer's release from Spandau at midnight, October 1, 1966, was an international media event. Speer went on to become an acclaimed author with two memoirs, *Inside the Third Reich* and *Spandau: The Secret Diaries*. Speer's third book, *The Slave State*, was "very bad, a mélange of bitter accusations against himself and a furious attack on Himmler and his methods of creating a slave state by infiltrating every state organization, 'doubling,' or duplicating, the officials with his own people," wrote Speer's biographer Gitta Sereny. When Speer asked Sereny's opinion of the book, she told him she was not crazy about it. "Well, I'm not either," Speer said. "I think I've done myself a lot of harm with it." In fact, Speer had other things on his mind. Having finally admitted to Sereny his "tacit acceptance of the persecution and murder of millions of Jews" (which, as Sereny concludes, would have gotten him hanged at Nuremberg), he telephoned her a few months later, quite drunk.

"Who was I talking to?" Sereny wrote. "Not the Albert I know? What's happened?" she asked.

"Ah, well," he said, his voice inexpressibly joyful, "I have after all had another Erlebnis [experience, adventure]...."

"Experience?" Sereny asked, "What sort of experience?"

"Ah ... one day soon, we will sit down together over a glass of wine," he promised, "and I'll tell you. Goo-o-od-bye."

In fact, the septuagenarian Speer, married with six grown children, had taken up with a young, blond German woman. Speer's wife Margret was devastated by this late invasion

Opposite, top: Concrete steps between Vorbunker and Führerbunker. In 1988, a German artist, Erhard Schreier, made drawings of the interior of the Führerbunker. The drawing above is of the concrete steps leading from the Vorbunker. These steps are incorrectly referred to as a circular stairway in many descriptions.
Bottom: Blasted safes in the bunker.

of her life. "I was heartbroken for her," said their daughter Hilde. "After everything she had gone through, everything she had done for us, for him. This too, now," she told Sereny. "Did this really have to be?"

"How had Margret found out about it?" asked Sereny.

Hilde shrugged. "Found out?" she repeated, her tone of voice unusually bitter. "He used to 'report absent' [*er meldete sich ab*] when he went to meet her."

On September 1, 1981, Speer and his paramour were in London for a BBC interview. At 4:30 in the afternoon, Wally Dunnage, the chief of security in Speer's hotel, was called to Speer's room.

> When I got to Room 516, the door was opened by a lady — she was about thirty-five to forty, with long fair hair, about five feet eight inches tall, of medium build. She wore a thin cardigan over a dress, or perhaps a skirt and blouse. She looked very pale, very distressed.
>
> An elderly man was lying on his back on the bed; he didn't appear to be breathing, and his skin was clammy cold. The lady said she thought he might have had a stroke. I pressed the center of his chest. There was a sound and he seemed to start breathing. I turned him sideways into the recovery position and worked on him until, only minutes later, the paramedics arrived. I went outside then, as one does, and the lady did, too.

"Do you know who this is?" the lady said to Dunnage. "This is Albert Speer."

Speer was brought in a coma to St. Mary's Hospital, where Alexander Fleming discovered penicillin in 1928. The paramour telephoned Mrs. Speer late that afternoon, said Hilde.

Hitler holds Hilde Speer's hand on his birthday, April 20, 1943. "I had to hand him a bouquet.... I hated it," Hilde told Gitta Sereny in a tense voice. But surely Hilde could not have hated the revered Führer, Sereny said; all children loved him. "What did small children know?" Hilde responded despairingly (Bayerische Staatsbibliothek).

Her mother "had known about the relationship all along, but to learn from [the paramour] that he was dying — it really was too much, you know, almost grotesque." In the end, Hilde's feelings about her father's affair were less critical. "What an extraordinary thing to happen to him — I can't help feeling glad for him."

Speer is interred in the Bergfriedhof in Heidelberg. He is one of the few high officials of the Third Reich with a marked burial plot. Speer's predecessor as armaments minister, Fritz Todt, was buried in Berlin's Invalidenfriedhof, but there is no longer a marker on his grave. The location of Hitler's remains is unknown, except for his skull and jawbone, which reside in a cardboard box in Moscow. Heinrich Himmler was buried in an unmarked grave on the Lüneberg Heath after his suicide (or murder by his British captors). Joseph Goebbels' ashes are said to have been scattered somewhere in Russia. The ashes of Hermann Göring were flushed into an unnamed German river.

Hilde Schramm, 69 in 2005, has devoted her life to public service and good works. She was twice a Berlin city councilor but is now retired from politics. Hilde recently raised £67,000 and used the money to set up a fund to give financial assistance to Jewish women wanting to undertake artistic or scientific projects. The money came from the sale of her father's art collection, most acquired between 1933 and 1943. Albert Speer had bought the art from Jewish owners forced to sell at knockdown prices.[14] Hilde's other projects include one that helps former slave workers and other Nazi victims in the former Soviet Union, where aid is not available.

The Berlin senate had planned to present a £6,700 prize in memory of Moses Mendelssohn, considered to be the father of Jewish enlightenment, to Hilde in a synagogue at the opening of the annual Jewish Culture Festival in November 2004. But Albert Meyer, the chairman of the city's Jewish community, withdrew the invitation after hearing that Hilde was the recipient. Albert Speer had made some of his members slave workers, he said, and, despite his respect for Hilde, it would be an affront to honor a Speer descendant in a synagogue. Hilde said she supported the decision, telling the German magazine *Der Spiegel*: "I am now in the funny role of defending Mr. Meyer."

Albert Speer (photograph by Walter Frentz) and Speer's grave.

She said the Berlin authorities were trying to pretend that relations between Germans and Jews were normal "but it is not so."

Hilde Speer's brother, Albert, became a highly successful architect. He designed Expo 2000, the World Exposition that took place in Hanover, as well as the Beijing Olympic Complex and the Shanghai International Automobile City. After studying architecture in Munich, young Albert, the eldest of six children, began entering architectural competitions. Aged 29, he had his first success. "With my first competition win they opened the envelopes and somebody said 'Albert Speer.' A voice said 'that's not possible — he's in prison.' Luckily some people knew he had a son. That was my start." Of his father's architectural designs Speer said, "I think it was good architecture in the style of the times because classical architecture in the Thirties was done in Germany and Britain and the USA."[15]

Self-assured and affable, Speer talked to *Daily Telegraph* correspondent Toby Helm of the many "master plans" he and his company, Albert Speer and Partners of Frankfurt, drew up over several years for the Hanover Expo, Germany's largest international showpiece since the 1972 Munich Olympics. "This was a new form of planning. We had a new master plan every six months," he said.

Appendix A: King Friedrich Wilhelm I presents Wilhelmstraße 77 to Graf von der Schulenburg

We, Friedrich Wilhelm, by God's grace King in Prussia, Margrave of Brandenburg, Elector of the Holy Roman Empire, Sovereign Prince of Orannien, Neufchatel, and Valengin, in Geldern at Magdeburg, Cleve, Jülich, Berge, Stettin, Pomerania, Mecklenburg, Count in Silesia at Crossen, Burggraf of Nuremberg, Prince of Halberstadt, Minden, Cammin, Wenden, Schwerin, Ratzeburg, East Friedland and Meurs, Count of Hohenzollern, Ruppin, the Marck, Ravensberg, Hohenstein, Tecklenburg, Lingen, Schwerin, Bühren and Leerdam, ruler of Ravenstein, the country of Rostock, Stargard, Lauenburg, Bütow, Arlan and Breda, make known and attest herewith that it is our intention, sparing no expense, to construct new buildings on our property in Friedrichstadt to attract foreigners to our country and provide food and trade for our citizens.

We now declare that Our Major General of Cavalry and Regimental Grenadier Colonel Count von Schulenburg, a devoted subject, is in our special favor. We present him with a lot in Friedrichstadt, on Wilhelmstraße, as well as building materials and diagrams, so that he may construct an elegant, gracious home, between the homes of Privy Counsel and War Minister von Marschall and Regimental Major Pannewitz. According to the diagrams, the front will be nineteen *Ruthen* eight feet, and the depth will be one-hundred-twelve *Ruthen* six feet, to Stadt Mauer Straße. After we have bought the property from the former owner with cash, Graf von Schulenburg will own it free and clear, and may will it to his heirs, who will also own it free and clear and can dispose of it as they see fit. We give Graf von Schulenburg and his heirs our royal word that we will never exercise any claim on this property. Furthermore, the house on the property will never be taxed, nor may anyone else ever file a claim against it.

We have signed this document below and affixed our royal seal.

Executed in Berlin, 21 September 1736.
(signed) Friedrich Wilhelm.

Appendix B:
Reich Chancellors 1871–1945

Otto von Bismarck, 1871–1890, was one of the outstanding leaders of the 19th century. As prime minister of the Kingdom of Prussia (1862–1890) he unified Germany after three victorious wars and became the first chancellor (1871–1890) of the German Empire. Bismarck was a deeply conservative, aristocratic, monarchist politician. He fought the growing social democratic movement in the 1880s by outlawing several organizations, instituting mandatory old-age pensions, and providing health and accident insurance for workers. He was called the Iron Chancellor and is one of the most important figures in German history. Kaiser Wilhelm II gave Bismarck the title *Count of Lauenberg* when he fired him in 1890. Bismarck told friends that he would only use the honorific if he wanted to travel incognito. Bismarck died in his home in Friedrichsruh, July 30, 1898.

Georg Leo Count von Caprivi, 1890–1894. As Bismarck's successor and Prussian minister president (1890–92) Caprivi decreed a "New Course," including political and social reforms and economic treaties with Russia, Italy, and Austria. Caprivi reduced the import and export duty on wheat. He refused to renew the German-Russian Reinsurance Treaty and the Helgoland-Zanzibar treaty. Caprivi infuriated Bismarck by uprooting many trees in the Reichskanzlerpalais garden. In volume three of his memoirs, Bismarck wrote, "Kaiser Wilhelm I will find no peace in his grave if he discovers that his former guard officer [Caprivi] has cut down his beloved ancient trees, unlike any others in Berlin, merely in order to let in a little more light.... I can overlook other political differences

Leo von Caprivi

with Caprivi, but I cannot sanction the ruthless destruction of old trees." Caprivi died February 6, 1899.

Chlodwig Prince zu Hohenlohe-Schillingsfürst, 1894–1900, was Count Leo von Caprivi's successor as Reich chancellor and Prussian minister president and served from 1894–1900. During his tenure, Germany acquired more colonies and expanded its navy, causing relations with Great Britain to deteriorate. Hohenlohe-Schillingsfürst worked to suppress the Social Democratic Party. By 1900, he had lost influence. Bernhard von Bülow, his state secretary in the Foreign Office, succeeded him. Hohenlohe-Schillingsfürst died in Ragaz, July 6, 1901.

Chlodwik zu Hohenlohe-Schillingsfürst

Bernhard Prince von Bülow, 1900–1909. Working with Kaiser Wilhelm II, Bülow pursued a policy of German aggrandizement in the years preceding World War I. The son of an imperial secretary of state for foreign affairs under Bismarck, Bülow studied law at Lausanne, Berlin, and Leipzig and entered the German Foreign Service in 1874. He held diplomatic posts before becoming German ambassador in Rome in 1893. Bülow's rise to power occurred in June 1897, when Wilhelm II appointed him state secretary for the Foreign Department. He rapidly became a more potent force than the chancellor, Hohenlohe-Schillingsfürst, and after three years he succeeded to the chancellorship. The government hoped that Bülow could prevent the impetuous Kaiser from making a fool of himself. In his foreign policy, both as state secretary and as chancellor, Bülow used what he understood as Bismarckian *Realpolitik* to advance Wilhelm's policy of a "place in the sun" for the Reich among world powers. As state secretary, he had some success in the Pacific, acquiring Chiao-chou (Kiaochow) Bay, China; the Caroline Islands; and Samoa (1897–1900). Bülow actively promoted building the Baghdad Railway to make Germany a power in the Middle East. Germans fearful of the Reich's encirclement praised his success in compelling European acceptance of Austria-Hungary's annexation of Bosnia-Herzegovina (1908). Bülow had less luck in his attempts to prevent the formation of an English-French-Russian combination against Germany. In 1898 and 1901 he tried to negotiate an alliance entailing British guarantees for Austria-Hungary, but the British, concerned over Germany's threat to their naval supremacy, were uninterested. His conclusion of the Treaty of Björkö with Russia in 1905 did not prevent the Russians' adherence to the Anglo-French Entente (1907). The confrontation with France and Britain over Morocco (1905–06) increased international tension.

In the domestic affairs of Prussia and the Reich, Bülow needed the support of the Conservatives and Centrists and, at times, the National Liberals. Though he did not repress the Social Democrats, and even introduced some cautious social measures through his state secretary, Artur Posadowsky, Bülow made sure that the Social Democratic Party gained no real political power. Bülow refused to address several pressing problems: the repeal of the Prussian three-class suffrage laws, the resolution of the dualism between Prussia and the *Reich*, the radical reform of imperial finances, and the imposition of direct taxes. Seeing the necessity of cooperating with the Reichstag, Bülow from 1905 leaned toward liberal constitutionalism. In 1908, Wilhelm's indiscreet remarks, printed in *The Daily Telegraph* of London, that the German people were hostile to Great Britain, led to Bülow's resignation the following year. Bülow admitted that he had not read the proof of the article that the newspaper had submitted to him before publication. Wilhelm believed Bülow had approved the article so that the Kaiser would be humiliated. Bülow died in Rome, October 28, 1929.

Bernhard von Bülow

Everything one size too large. Bruno Paul's satiric view of Prince Bernhard von Bülow in Bismarck's uniform (Deutsches Historisches Museum).

Theobald von Bethmann Hollweg, 1909–1917, was Reich chancellor before and during World War I. A member of a Frankfurt banking family, Bethmann Hollweg studied law at Strassburg, Leipzig, and Berlin and joined the civil service. He was appointed Prussian minister of the interior in 1905 and state secretary in the Imperial Office of the Interior in 1907. He succeeded Prince Bernhard von Bülow, who resigned as chancellor on July 14, 1909. Bethmann's domestic policies were mildly liberal. In foreign policy, his negotiations with the British over reduction of naval armaments (March 1909 and February 1912) came to naught because of the opposition of Admiral Alfred von Tirpitz, supported by Kaiser Wilhelm II. Bethmann's secretary of state, Alfred von Kiderlen-Wächter, created the Moroccan (Agadir) crisis of July–November 1911, in which Germany backed down before France and Great Britain. Bethmann and Sir Edward Grey, the British foreign secretary, worked successfully to prevent the expansion of the Balkan Wars into a major conflict between Austria-Hungary and Russia; this was probably Bethmann's greatest success in foreign affairs. At home, the enactment of his legislation for enlarging the army did not reduce anxiety about Germany's international situation.

Although Bethmann believed that a democratic monarchy based on a Reichstag majority was inevitable, he was not an enthusiast of parliamentary government, and his half-hearted electoral reforms were largely ineffective. Having no desire for war, Bethmann nonetheless probably initiated the July crisis of 1914 with his "blank check" to Austria-Hungary for measures against Serbia. Subsequent German warnings to Austria-Hungary and its prospective opponent Russia could not prevent the outbreak of war. Bethmann finally capitulated to the German general staff, which wanted war immediately. Bethmann worked for a negotiated peace, with no idea of German annexations, and in 1916 tried to obtain the mediation of the United States. Knowing that U.S. entry into the war would be decisive, he resisted in vain the advocates of unrestricted submarine warfare. On April 7, 1917, Bethmann enraged conservative military leaders and civilians with his promise of electoral reforms in Prussia. During the debates on the peace resolution that the Reichstag approved in July 1917, Bethmann was forced to resign. He died January 1, 1921, in Hohenfinow.

Theobald von Bethmann Hollweg. Bethmann Hollweg was Reich Chancellor before and during World War I (AKG Images).

Appendix B: Reich Chancellors

Georg Michaelis, 1917, was Bethmann-Hollweg's successor as German chancellor in July 1917, and was sufficiently unknown that Kaiser Wilhelm II had only the vaguest idea who he was. In fact Michaelis had established his middling reputation chiefly as a civil servant. He spent the first three years of the First World War supervising grain supplies as chairman of national food distribution. In the years prior to the war Michaelis had served as undersecretary of state in the Finance Ministry. With the expulsion of Bethmann-Hollweg, who could no longer command support from either left or right wings of the political and military elite, Michaelis was the surprising choice of the Military Supreme Command for chancellor and president of the Prussian State Ministry. The Supreme Command was by this time the real ruling force in Germany. Paul von Hindenburg and Erich Ludendorff, the heroes of the campaign on the Eastern Front, oversaw a military dictatorship. Michaelis was by no means the first choice of Hindenburg or Ludendorff as replacement for Bethmann-Hollweg. But the Kaiser vetoed their first two nominees, former Chancellor Bernhard von Bulow and ousted naval minister Admiral Alfred von Tirpitz. Because of Michaelis' obscurity he was in some ways an ideal choice for Hindenburg and Ludendorff. Since he could not muster support in the Reichstag he was entirely dependent upon the Supreme Command to keep his job. Michaelis' tenure as chancellor was short. Having shown himself evasive in replying to the Reichstag's peace resolution of 19 July and to Pope Benedict XV's peace proposal of August 1917, his already minimal support shriveled. Less than four months after taking office on 14 July 1917 he was obliged to tender his resignation on 1 November after trying to blame the Social Democratic Party for naval unrest in the autumn. Michaelis was replaced by yet another little-known figure, Count Hertling. Michaelis himself attempted to hold on to his post as Prussian premier, without success. He thereafter became president of the local government of Pomerania (1 April 1918–31 March 1919) and later involved himself in Protestant church groups and projects for student welfare. He joined the National People's Party in 1919. Michaelis died on 24 July 1936 in Bad Saarow-Pieskow at the age of 78.

Georg Count von Hertling, 1917–1918, served as a puppet chancellor of Germany for 11 months from November 1917. Born on 31 August 1843 in Darmstadt, Hertling was a prominent conservative politician and philosopher, and was leader of the conservative wing of the Catholic Center Party in the Reichstag, which he joined in 1875. He served as Bavarian prime minister from 1912 to 1917. He had earlier held theological university chairs at Bonn and Munich. Hertling, who had supported Chancellor Bethmann-Hollweg, reluctantly succeeded the ineffectual and obscure Georg Michaelis as chancellor on 1 November 1917. As chancellor and Prussian minister-president Hertling was wholly subserv-

Georg Michaelis. Michaelis was a virtual puppet of Paul von Hindenburg and Erich Ludendorff, the heroes of the campaign on the Eastern Front, who oversaw a military dictatorship.

Georg von Hertling

ient to the demands of the Supreme Command, a military dictatorship led by Paul von Hindenburg and Erich Ludendorff. Hertling had the unenviable task of trying to reconcile a Reichstag increasingly in favor of a negotiated peace settlement, and a military high command determined to fight on. Like Michaelis, Hertling was unable to call upon a reserve of political goodwill and had no power base within the Reichstag to support his initiatives. He was therefore entirely dependent upon support from Hindenburg and Ludendorff, although he concurred with both in believing in ultimate German victory. With Ludendorff's decision to transfer power back to the Reichstag in September 1918, and resign at the same time, Hertling decided that he would be unable to work constructively with the Reichstag. He therefore resigned, relieved to be leaving office in October 1918. Hertling died the following year in Ruhpolding, on 4 January 1919.

Prince Maximilian von Baden, 1918, became Reich chancellor because his humanitarian reputation made Kaiser Wilhelm II believe that he was capable of bringing World War I quickly to an end. The Germans called him Bademax. He was son of Prince Wilhelm of Baden. In the first years of World War I Prince Max devoted himself to the Red Cross and to work for the welfare of prisoners of war on both sides. On Oct. 3, 1918, when Germany was on the verge of collapse, Max was appointed chancellor of the empire and prime minister of Prussia as successor to Georg Hertling. He quickly supported constitutional changes whereby a genuine parliamentary system was at last brought into being in Germany. Max initiated negotiations for an armistice and arranged for the dismissal of Army Chief of Staff Erich Ludendorff, but too late to save the monarchy. When Kaiser Wilhelm II would give no definite answer to Max's demands that he abdicate in the face of the danger of Communist revolution, Max announced the abdication, Nov. 9, 1918. He then resigned the chancellery in favor of Friedrich Ebert, the leader of the Majority Social Democratic Party.

Friedrich Ebert, Reich chancellor 1918, was head of the Social Democratic movement in Germany and a moderate Socialist. He was a leader in bringing about the Weimar Constitution after the German defeat in World War I and was president of the Weimar Republic from 1919 to 1925. Ebert was the son of a master tailor. He learned the saddler's trade and traveled through Germany as a journeyman saddler. He soon became a Social Democrat and trade unionist. His attention was always directed toward practical improvement in the living conditions of the German working class and, above all, its social and moral betterment. In 1905 Ebert became secretary general of the German Social Democratic Party (SPD). Ebert succeeded August Bebel as party chairman in 1913. Under Ebert's leadership, the Social Democratic movement gained increasing influence in German national politics. On Aug. 3, 1914, Ebert persuaded German Social Democrats to support the war appropriations. The action of the German Social Democratic Party did not differ from that of the other Socialist parties of Europe, in which nationalist feelings remained stronger than internationalist convictions. But Ebert's party gave Germany unconditional support without requiring adoption of a real peace policy. In consequence, Ebert lacked the power to force the government to adopt a policy through which Germany might have escaped the catastrophic defeat that destroyed the Reich and eventually Ebert's postwar policy.

With Ebert's active support, a new government, headed by Prince Max of Baden, was organized in October 1918, through a sweeping constitutional reform that foreshadowed the Weimar Constitution. On November 9, 1918, Prince Max, acting on his own authority, asked

Prince Max von Baden. When Kaiser Wilhelm II would give no definite answer to Max's demands that he abdicate in the face of the danger of Communist revolution, Max announced the abdication, Nov. 9, 1918.

Friedrich Ebert to replace him as chancellor. Ebert, who still hoped to establish a regency for the Kaiser, held office as chancellor for only one day. On November 10th, he formed an entirely Socialist government, with representatives from the Social Democratic Party and the Independent Social Democratic Party. Calling itself the Council of People's Representatives, the government derived its authority from the Workers and Soldiers Council, which claimed to speak for Germany and the German Republic. In fact, the factories and regiments of Berlin alone had elected the government rather arbitrarily. Nevertheless, Ebert was determined to place the power of the Council of People's Representatives and the Workers and Soldiers Council in the hands of a freely elected German parliament as soon as possible. He wished to see a liberal coalition government rather than a Socialist regime in power. The Weimar Republic's first government, under Ebert's fellow party member Philipp Scheidemann, was based on this coalition. The new German constitution, the Weimar Constitution, so called after the town in which it was drawn up, was the work of the coalition. By the votes of the three parties forming the coalition, Ebert was elected the first president of the republic in 1919. Ebert supported Defense Minister Hugo Noske's strenuous efforts to suppress strikes and revolutionary workers' demonstrations. A coup d'état against the republic, the Kapp Putsch, March 13, 1920, collapsed after a few days. On December 23, 1924, a German court ruled that Ebert had committed high treason during the war by his support of a munition workers' strike. Ebert died suddenly in Berlin of a ruptured appendix, February 28, 1925.

Gustav Bauer, 1919–1920. Bauer was born January 6, 1870, in East Prussia, the son of a law court official. After finishing high school, he worked in the office of a lawyer. In 1912 he was elected to the Reichstag as a member of the Social Democratic Party. Under Prince Max of Baden he was appointed state secretary in the labor office. Bauer became Reich chancellor August 14, 1919. Just after the Kapp Putsch had been

Gustav Bauer

put down, Bauer resigned as chancellor. He remained a member of the Reichstag until 1928. In 1933 he was arrested for misappropriation of public funds. He died in Berlin in 1944.

Wolfgang Kapp, 1920. Kapp, the son of a lawyer, allied himself with antidemocratic German elements planning a counter-revolution in 1918. During the Kapp Putsch, March 13, 1920, Chancellor Gustav Bauer and other officials fled Berlin and Kapp named himself Reich chancellor and Prussian minister president. On March 17, the Kapp Putsch was put down and Kapp fled to Sweden. In April 1922, Kapp returned to Germany and was imprisoned. He died of cancer June 12, 1922 in Leipzig.

Hermann Müller, 1920, was a German Social Democratic politician who served as foreign minister (1919–1920), and twice as chancellor of Germany (1920, 1928–1930) under the Weimar

Friedrich Ebert

Wolfgang Kapp (Ullstein Bilderdienst)

Konstantin Fehrenbach

Hermann Müller

Republic. As foreign minister, he was one of the German signatories of the Treaty of Versailles in 1919. His second term as chancellor (1928–30) was as head of the last Weimar government to actually command a majority of the Reichstag, but its "Grand Coalition" fell apart as a result of arguments between the Social Democrats and German People's Party over monetary issues as a result of the onset of the Great Depression. Müller had objected forcefully to his party's decision to leave the government, but was overruled. His death in 1931 was a major blow to the Social Democrats.

Konstantin Fehrenbach, 1920–1921. Fehrenbach was born in 1852, the son of a schoolteacher. He studied law and theology in Breisgau and worked as a lawyer in Freiburg. He joined the Reichstag in 1903 as a member of the Center Party. In 1913 he became a sharp critic of the military and its influence. In 1917 he supported the peace initiative in the Reichstag. Fehrenbach became Reich chancellor June 6, 1920, and tried to work with the victorious Allies, especially the United States. He led the German delegation to reparation conferences in Spa and London. When the Allies decided on German reparations of 132 billion gold marks, the Reichstag recoiled and Fehrenbach resigned as chancellor. He died in Freiburg in 1926.

Dr. Josef Wirth, 1921–1922. Wirth was born in Freiburg, Germany, on 6th September 1879. He studied natural sciences and economics (1899–1906) before becoming a mathematics teacher at Freiburg High School. Wirth joined the Catholic Center Party and was elected to the Reichstag in 1914. During the First World War he fought on the Western Front and the Eastern Front, but in 1917 he contracted pneumonia and was forced to return to Germany. A member of the left wing of the Catholic Center Party, Wirth joined with Matthias Erzberger in calling for peace negotiations. In 1918, Wirth announced he was a republican and urged the abdication of Kaiser Wilhelm II. During the German Revolution Wirth was appointed minister of finance of the republication government of Baden. In 1920 Hermann Müller made Wirth his minister of finance. In May 1921, Wirth became Reich chancellor. Trying to achieve a lasting peace, Wirth joined Walther Rathenau to negotiate the Treaty of Rapallo with the Soviet Union. Wirth was dis-

Joseph Wirth

Wilhelm Cuno

tressed over the gargantuan war reparations that Germany was forced to pay and resigned over this issue in November 1922. He then worked closely with Hans Luther to keep right-wing nationalists out of power. In 1925 he left the Catholic Center Party in protest against its close ties with the Nationalist Party. On 13th April 1929, Wirth acceded to the request of Hermann Müller to become a member of his Social Democratic Party government. The following year Wirth became minister of the interior in Heinrich Brüning's cabinet. Wirth's liberal views made him anathema to right-wing nationalists. When Adolf Hitler took power in January 1933, Wirth was forced into exile. He lived in France until the Second World War, when he moved to Switzerland. After the war, Wirth returned to West Germany. He once again entered politics and helped form the Christian Social Labor Party. Over the next few years he opposed West Germany's rearmament and the country's membership of NATO. Wirth won the Stalin Peace Prize in 1954. He died in Freiburg, Germany, on 3rd January 1956.

Dr. Wilhelm Cuno, 1922–1923. Cuno was born in Suhl in 1876 and studied law in Berlin and Heidelberg. During World War I he served on the Reich grain council and was one of the organizers of the Reich Food Office. On November 1, 1917, Cuno became an official of the Hapag shipping line. He became director of Hapag in 1918 and took part in the negotiations for the peace treaty and reparations. On November 22, 1922, Cuno was recalled to public service as Reich chancellor. When the French and Belgians occupied the Ruhr in January 1923, Cuno called for passive resistance and initiated coal shipments to the two occupying powers. Cuno's resistance to a reparation settlement was one of the factors that led to the German economic collapse and wild inflation of 1923. Cuno incurred the wrath of the German Labor Movement and on August 12 was forced to resign as chancellor. He left politics and went back to Hapag, where he engineered a merger with North German Lloyd to create a giant shipping conglomerate. Cuno died January 3, 1933 in Aumühle, near Hamburg.

Dr. Gustav Stresemann, 1923, was the son of a prosperous owner of a restaurant and tavern. In his early years he helped in the family business and, since he was a lonely boy, assiduously pursued his studies. After attending the Andreas Real Gymnasium in Berlin, Stresemann studied literature, philosophy, and political economy at Berlin and Leipzig. In 1901 at the age of 22, Stresemann became a clerk in the Association of German Chocolate Manufacturers in Dresden. A year later he took over the business management of the local branch of the Manufacturers Alliance, an association of entrepreneurs. With his organizing talent and his persuasiveness, he increased the number of members in the alliance from 180 in 1902 to 1,000 in 1904 and to approximately 5,000 in 1912. Although he represented capital, Stresemann nonetheless supported the idea, novel at the time, that management should accept labor's right to organize and should recognize its representatives as official negotiators

Gustav Stresemann

of collective bargaining demands. In 1906 he was elected to a seat on the town council of Dresden, which he held until 1912; in 1907 he won election to the Reichstag. In 1916, Stresemann supported unrestricted submarine warfare, a disaster for Germany. Later he helped to defeat the government of Reich Chancellor Bethmann-Hollweg and opposed the Treaty of Versailles. Just after the armistice of November 11, 1918, Stresemann formed the German People's Party. He was elected to the national assembly that gathered at Weimar in 1919 to frame a new constitution, and was elected to the Reichstag in 1920.

From August 13 to November 23, 1923, Stresemann was Reich chancellor of a coalition government. He put down an insurrection in Saxony, restored order in Bavaria after Hitler's Beerhall Putsch failed, ended the passive resistance of Germans in the Ruhr to the French occupying forces, and tried to put a stop to the disastrous hyperinflation. In 1924 Stresemann's successor, Wilhelm Marx, chose him as his secretary of foreign affairs. He enjoyed immediate success with the acceptance of the Dawes Plan, which restructured reparations on the basis of Germany's ability to pay. Stresemann took the initiative in arriving at a rapprochement with the Western Allies, especially with France, in guaranteeing the maintenance of the boundaries established at Versailles. After careful preparation for a conference, Stresemann, Aristide Briand of France, and Austen Chamberlain of Great Britain, along with representatives of the other four nations involved, met at Locarno, Switzerland, to draw up mutual security pacts. After initiating the Locarno Pact on October 16, Stresemann rushed home to insure its acceptance by the government. In a speech broadcast to the nation on November 3, 1925, he appealed for support, saying that Locarno signified that the states of Europe at last realized that they could not go on making war upon each other without being involved in common ruin. Stresemann then signed a peace treaty with Russia, called the Treaty of Berlin, in April 1926. He finally saw, on September 8, 1926, the unanimous acceptance of Germany's admission into the League of Nations.

In 1926, Stresemann was awarded the Nobel Peace Prize. His health declined rapidly after Christmas 1927. Against medical advice, Stresemann retained his position as German foreign minister. In 1929 at The Hague, he accepted the Young Plan, which named June 30, 1930, as the final date for the French and Belgian evacuation of the Ruhr. Stresemann died in Berlin of a stroke, October 3, 1929.

Dr. Wilhelm Marx, 1923–1924, 1926–1928. Marx, the son of a headmaster, was born on 15th February 1863. He studied law in Bonn before becoming a lawyer. In 1894 Marx became a judge in Elberfeld. He joined the Catholic Center Party and after serving in the Prussian Parliament he was elected to the Reichstag in 1910. Marx was voted chairman of the Catholic Center Party in 1921 and was appointed Reich Chancellor in 1923. He appointed Hans Luther as finance minister. Luther negotiated the Dawes Plan to restructure German war reparations. In the general election that took place December 1924,

Wilhelm Marx

Marx was forced from office. After serving as prime minister of Prussia, Marx once again became Reich chancellor in May 1926. But after the general election in 1928 Marx resigned as chancellor and as chairman of the Catholic Center Party. He died in Bonn on 5th August 1946.

Dr. Hans Luther, 1925–1926. Luther, the son of a wealthy Berlin businessman, was born on 10th March 1885. He studied law in Kiel and Geneva before joining Berlin's civil service. In 1907 Luther became a town councilor in Magdeburg. He was elected mayor of Essen in 1918. Luther was a competent administrator and in December 1922, Reich Chancellor Wilhelm Cuno appointed him minister of food and agriculture. The next chancellor, Gustav Stresemann, made Luther finance minister. Luther also held this post under Wilhelm Marx and in 1924 was involved in the negotiation of the Dawes Plan. In the general election that took place in December 1924, the decline in the support for the Catholic Center Party forced Wilhelm Marx from office. Luther became Reich chancellor and joined with his foreign minister, Gustav Stresemann, to negotiate the Locarno Treaty (1925). The signing of this treaty prompted the Nationalist Party to withdraw its support for the government and Luther was forced to resign. Luther returned to office in January 1926 when he formed a minority government without the support of rightwing political parties. But after losing a vote of no confidence in May 1926, Luther resigned as chancellor and retired from public life. In 1930 Luther replaced Hjalmar Schacht as president of the Reichsbank When Hitler came to power,

Luther was appointed to be Germany's ambassador to the United States (1933–37). Luther lived in retirement during the Second World War but served as an adviser to the new government of West Germany. He also taught politics at the University of Munich. Hans Luther died in Düsseldorf on 11th May 1962.

Dr. Heinrich Brüning, 1930–1932. Brüning was the son of a wine merchant and was born in Munster, Germany, on 26th November 1885. Brüning studied history in Munich, Strasbourg and London. After obtaining his doctorate in 1915 Brüning joined the German Army and served in a machine-gun company during the First World War. In 1920 Brüning became an official of the German Trade Union Federation. A member of the Catholic Center Party, Brüning was elected to the Reichstag in 1924. He became the party's spokesman on economic matters and in 1929 became leader of the Catholic Center Party. When Müller resigned in March 1930, Brüning was appointed Reich chancellor. Brüning attempted to diminish the unemploy-

Hans Luther

Heinrich Brüning (the "Hunger Chancellor")

ment that followed the Wall Street Crash by increasing taxation and imposing high tariffs on foreign imports. He also reduced government spending by cutting unemployment benefits and was called the "hunger chancellor." Brüning's policies were not successful and by 1930 unemployment reached four million. In the general election that took place in September 1930, the Catholic Center Party won only 87 seats. The party was now much smaller than other parties such as the Social Democratic Party (143 seats) and the Nazi Party (107 seats). Brüning remained in power but now pursued a more nationalistic foreign policy in an effort to appease the growing right wing. Reich President Paul von Hindenburg forced Brüning to resign in May 1932, and Franz von Papen replaced him as Reich chancellor. When Adolf Hitler came to power in 1933, Brüning left Germany and immigrated to the United States. Brüning was appointed as professor of political science at Harvard University (1937–1951). He also worked at the University of Cologne (1951–1955) before returning to the United States. Heinrich Brüning died in Norwich, Vermont, on 30th March 1970.

Franz von Papen, 1932. Papen, the son of a wealthy landowner, was born in Werl, Germany, on 29th October 1879. He joined the German Army and was a general staff officer at the outbreak of the First World War. In 1914 Papen was sent to Washington as a military attaché. While in the United States he helped to arrange for a company in Bridgeport to produce armaments for Germany. But in 1915 he was expelled from the US after being accused of attempting to sabotage American armaments production for the Allies. On his return to Germany, Papen was sent to Palestine where he served as chief of staff of the 4th Turkish Army. He continued his espionage activities and was involved in planning rebellions in Ireland and India and sabotage in the United States. As a result of papers found in Nazareth, some of Papen's agents were arrested and either incarcerated or executed.

After the First World War, Papen joined the Catholic Center Party and in 1921 was elected to the Reichstag. Two years later he bought a controlling interest in its leading newspaper, *Germania*. Papen immediately fired the editor and over the next few years unsuccessfully tried to use the newspaper to foist his right-wing views on the party. Within the Catholic Center Party, Papen was considered an outsider. Thus many people were surprised when Reich President Paul von Hindenburg appointed Papen Reich chancellor on 31st May 1932. Papen immediately tried to win the support of the Nazi Party by lifting the ban on the Sturm Abteilung (SA), Hitler's brownshirt army, which Heinrich Brüning had imposed. Papen added icing to his right wing cake by deposing the Social Democratic Party government in Prussia and making bellicose pronouncements about not keeping to the onerous terms of the Versailles Treaty. Papen's reactionary policies upset Kurt von Schleicher, who wanted a coalition of the center. When Schleicher persuaded several government ministers to turn against Papen, he resigned from office. With Hitler, Papen worked to oust Schleicher, who had become Reich chancellor. With the support of industrial leaders, Papen persuaded President Paul von Hindenburg to appoint Hitler as chancellor. Papen, who became vice-chancellor, told Hindenburg that he would be able to prevent Hitler from introducing extremist policies. After the Night of the Long Knives in 1934, when the Nazis murdered Kurt von Schleicher, Papen sent a letter to Hitler praising him for "crushing the intended second revolution." Soon afterwards Papen resigned as vice-chancellor and was sent as ambassador to Austria (1934–39), where he plotted successfully for Hitler's annexation of the country in 1938. Hitler then made Papen ambassador to Turkey (1939–44).

Papen retired to Westphalia where he was arrested by Allied forces on 10th April 1945. During the Nuremberg trials Papen was charged with scheming to start the Second World War. He was found not guilty, but the German gov-

Franz von Papen (Bayerische Staatsbibliothek)

ernment had him rearrested and charged him with other offenses. On 1st May 1947 Papen was judged to be a "major offender" and sentenced to eight years imprisonment but was released in January 1949. The Allies returned his wealth and property to him but he lost his state pension and his driver's license. Papen died in Obersasbach on 2nd May 1969.

Kurt von Schleicher, 1932–1933. Schleicher, the son of a Prussian army officer, was born in Brandenburg, Germany, on 4th July 1882. He joined the German Army in 1900 and during the First World War was a general on the staff of Paul von Hindenburg.

After the war Schleicher helped organize the Freikorps, the private army that was supposed to defend against Red invasion and revolution. Schleicher remained on good terms with Hindenburg, and after Hindenburg was elected president in 1925, Schleicher served as his political adviser. Schleicher tried to make Heinrich Brüning Reich chancellor in March 1930, but later threw his support to Franz von Papen. Papen's reactionary policies immediately disturbed Schleicher, who wanted a coalition of the center. Schleicher persuaded several government ministers to turn against Papen, forcing him from office in December 1932. Schleicher became chancellor and tried to obtain the support of the center parties to control the activities of the Nazis. Adolf Hitler responded by joining with Papen to get rid of Schleicher. With the support of leading industrialists, Papen persuaded President Paul von Hindenburg to appoint Hitler as chancellor. Papen, who became vice-chancellor, told Hindenburg that he would curb Hitler's extremism. Hitler avenged himself on Schleicher during the Night of the Long Knives, by having him murdered in his Berlin flat on 30th June 1934.

Adolf Hitler, 1933–45.

Joseph Goebbels. In his will, Hitler designated Goebbels his successor as Reich Chancellor. Goebbels was Chancellor for one day, that is, from Hitler's suicide on April 30, 1945, until his own suicide, May 1.

Johann Ludwig Count Schwerin von Krosigk. After Goebbels' suicide, May 1, 1945, Ad-

Kurt von Schleicher (Bayerische Staatsbibliothek)

Johann Ludwig Count Schwerin von Krosigk (Bayerische Staatsbibliothek)

miral Karl Dönitz named Krosigk "Director of the Reich Government" and Reich foreign minister. Krosigk was born in Saxony in 1887. His mother was a countess. He studied law in Halle, Lausanne, and Oxford. Krosigk fought in the First World War, was wounded, and was awarded the Iron Cross. At war's end he was a first lieutenant. Krosigk worked in various governmental positions and in 1924 became a ministerial councilor. In 1925 Count Alfred von Schwerin adopted him, and henceforth he was known as Count Schwerin von Krosigk. In 1932 Franz von Papen named Krosigk finance minister. When Hitler came to power, Krosigk remained finance minister, but after 1938 was no longer politically active. Krosigk was not personally implicated in the July 20, 1944, plot to assassinate Hitler, but he had relatives who were. On April 21, 1945, Krosigk left Berlin. In May he became part of Dönitz's government. On May 23, British troops arrested Dönitz and Krosigk in Flensburg. Krosigk was sent to the Mondorf detention facility and then to Nurmeberg. In 1949, a US military tribunal sentenced Krosigk to 10 years imprisonment for war crimes, but he was released under the terms of a general amnesty in 1951. Krosigk settled in Essen and became a writer. He died March 4, 1977.

Appendix C: Paul von Hindenburg

With Erich Ludendorff, Hindenburg (1847–1934) was in supreme command of the German military during the later years of World War I. In 1925 Hindenburg became president of Germany and moved into the Reich Presidential Palais, Wilhelmstraße 73. From October 1932 until May 1933, Hindenburg resided in the Reichskanzlerpalais while the Presidential Palais was under renovation. Hitler lived in the Chancellery Annex from his appointment as Reich chancellor in January 1933 until renovation of his apartment in the Reichskanzlerpalais was complete in May 1934.

Hindenburg (full name Paul von Beneckendorff und von Hindenburg) was born in Posen (now Poznan, Poland), the son of the Prussian

Paul von Hindenburg receives the diplomats in the Congress Hall of the Reichskanzlerpalais.

aristocrat Robert von Beneckendorff und von Hindenburg and his wife Luise (born Schwickart). After his education at the Wahlstatt and Berlin cadet schools, he fought at the 1866 Battle of Königgrätz and in the 1870–1871 Franco-Prussian War. In 1903, he was promoted to general.

Hindenburg retired from the army in 1911, but returned at the outbreak of World War I, wearing his old Prussian Blue uniform. He was acclaimed for two stunning victories, at the Battle of Tannenberg (1914) and at the Battle of the Masurian Lakes (1915), against the Russian army. In fact, the credit for these victories belongs to Colonel Max Hoffmann, who noticed that the Russian Army's radio communications were not encrypted or poorly encrypted. The Russians sent enough information in a simple and quickly cracked block code that the German Army in the area, under Erich Ludendorff and Field Marshal Hindenburg, knew where the Russians would be. When Hoffmann in later years took visitors over the field of Tannenberg, he would tell them, "This is where the Field Marshal slept before the battle; here is where he slept after the battle; here is where he slept during the battle!"[1]

In late 1916 Hindenburg became chief of the General Staff. But his deputy Ludendorff had the real power. At the end of the war, Hindenburg again retired from the military. In 1925, he succeeded Friedrich Ebert as President of Germany.

In 1932, despite the fact that Hindenburg was lapsing in and out of senility, his supporters persuaded him to run for re-election, as the only candidate who could defeat Hitler. Although Hitler lost the election, the Nazi party won a solid plurality of seats in the Reichstag. Hindenburg remained president after appointing Hitler Reich chancellor in January 1933. He died on August 2, 1934, at his baronial home in Neudeck, East Prussia, which wealthy German industrialists had presented to him. One day earlier, Hitler flew to Neudeck to visit him. Hindenburg, 86 years old and confused, thought he was meeting the Kaiser and called Hitler "Your Majesty."

Appendix D: Interior renovations to the Reichskanzlerpalais, 1875–1878

To convert the Radziwill Palais to the Reichskanzlerpalais, extensive interior renovations were made. The half circular exit of the vestibule was removed and the vestibule was extended to the wall of the garden room. Four columns were added to support the ceiling. The floor of the vestibule was raised to the same level as that of the garden room. The main stairway in the vestibule was removed. In its place two rooms were built, one a kitchen. A hallway led from the vestibule to three offices created during the renovation. To the right of the vestibule a room was created for the chancellery concierge; the room was later used for the telephone switchboard. Behind this room, a new staircase was built which led to the reception rooms on the first floor.

In the north side of the building, adjacent to the garden, the office of the Reich chancellor was built on the first floor. A second floor terrace was placed directly above it. But Bismarck was apparently not pleased with this arrangement, and he used the first floor room for receptions. For his office he used a room directly in front.

In the south wing, a large main stairway was built which led to the delegates' rooms on the second floor. The stairway was accessible directly from the south corridor of the building. The stable in the south wing, adjacent to Wilhelmstraße, was razed. Behind it a larger stable, which could accommodate 12 horses, was built, with adjacent rooms. An exit walkway for large gatherings was added to the honor court.

The imposing ballroom on the second floor was not altered. To an adjacent, spacious three-windowed reception room a vast dining room was annexed, along with a conservatory facing the garden side of the building. A balcony was added, like those on the north and west sides.

The main stairway in the left wing of the building, occupying the entire width, ran along three window axes to the attic, vaulted by window tympani. The stairway provided access to a four-room apartment facing Wilhelmstraße. Count Herbert Bismarck, son of the Reich chancellor, lived here. Between these rooms and the main stairway was a large wardrobe closet.

To the right side of the ballroom in the main wing, the former art gallery was divided into two rooms, one with two windows, the other with three windows. Otto von Bismarck used these rooms for receiving visitors. A four-window dining room was built nearby, which served as an office for Bismarck's successors. In front of the dining room a terrace was built, which led directly into the park via a stairway.

Bismarck's apartment was on the second floor of the right wing of the building. An auxiliary staircase with two windows led to the bedroom, which had a salon with four windows. There were four additional rooms along Wilhelmstraße, each with one window. The corner room of Bismarck's apartment, facing the honor court, was the living room. Adjacent to the market court were two rooms for maids and guests. One of these rooms was later converted to a kitchen.

The renovated attic held more rooms and coat closets. The attic of the main wing was never touched and remained an attic.

Adjacent to the firewalls and open space on the Voß Straße side of the building, a 67-meter long columned hall was built in renaissance style with round, vaulted entrances, a massive posterior, and a flat roof. The first floor was level with the greenhouse of the main building and accessible from it.

The entire Palais was furnished with gas and running water. Hot air heating was installed in the ballroom and main stairway. Hot water radiators were placed in the diplomats' rooms and main dining room. Tile stoves were placed in the other rooms. Gilding was added to decorate the ceilings and walls of the principal rooms, and silk tapestry was also applied. Parquet floors were laid in the diplomats' rooms. The diplomats' stairway was refurbished with French limestone. The stairway to the chancellor's apartment was rebuilt with marble. The decorative oil painting on the palais façade was retained, as well as the slate roof.

The park was completely re-landscaped. The baroque-style symmetric plantings were replaced with lawns and English-style gardens. At the northern boundary wall on Königgrätzer Straße, a greenhouse with planters and a gardener's house were added.

Appendix E: Further renovations to the Reichskanzlerpalais, 1890–1925

Over the years, numerous small changes were made in Bismarck's Reich Chancellery (Reichskanzlerpalais), Wilhelmstraße 77. Many of the alterations were introduced to improve the building's chance of withstanding a fire. But the external appearance was meticulously preserved.

In summer 1890, while visiting Russia, Count Leo von Caprivi, Bismarck's successor, ordered that a garden wall between Wilhelmstraße 76 and Wilhelmstraße 77 be removed. At the same time, renovations were made in the diplomats' rooms and apartments. Bismarck's former bedroom was converted to a bathroom. Kaiser Wilhelm II abruptly sacked Caprivi in 1894. His replacement, Prince Chlodwig zu Hohenlohe-Schillingsfürst, turned Caprivi's bathroom into a bedroom. The bathroom was moved into the dressing room behind the chancellor's office on the first floor. In the basement, directly below the office, Hohenlohe installed a heater to warm the floor. But the floor stayed cold, forcing Hohenlohe to move his office to the warmer second floor. Electric lights were installed in the offices and diplomats' rooms on the ground floor in 1897.

When Bernhard Prince von Bülow became chancellor in 1900, he converted the main dining room on the second floor into a reception room and tea salon. The marble was covered with silk-damask. On the south side of the room a niche was built to hold an Italian-style fireplace. A terrazzo floor replaced the wood floor of the adjacent conservatory. Along the walls were planters with artificial ivy. Bismarck's reception room next to the ballroom became a library with a pine-inlaid ceiling. Bülow had a small dining room remodeled for his office and replaced two tile ovens with a green Renaissance-style oven that was heated externally. The dining room foyer became an anteroom. The dining room in Bismarck's former office was relocated. In the garden room behind the vestibule, 10 Florentine plaster reliefs were installed, along with four iron window frames and mirror glass. Electric lights were added to the ceiling.

In Bismarck's former office on the ground floor, now a dining room, the square inlaid ceiling was removed and replaced with a beamed ceiling supported by iron columns. The oven was replaced with a fireplace. The room in back of the dining room was made into a foyer and the bathtub moved to the second floor. A corridor of iron and glass connected the foyer to the kitchen.

In 1906, more extensive rebuilding was necessary. Dry rot and worms had damaged the roof, which had to be almost completely replaced. Also, more offices were created on the south side of the building out of a kitchen and foyer.

Just after World War I, political unrest and revolution roiled Berlin, resulting in interruptions of electrical power. In 1922, a small building was constructed in the chancellery garden and a generator installed to prevent power failures in the building. Two offices were built in the garden room in 1925. The chancellor's apartment was moved to the north wing of the building and given central heating. The façades in the front and back of the building were restored and repainted.

Appendix F: Notable Gatherings in the Reichskanzlerpalais Before 1914

Congo Conference. At the behest of Reich Chancellor Otto von Bismarck, the Africa Conference, also called the Congo Conference, met in Berlin November 15, 1884 to February 26, 1885, and held its assemblies in the Congress Hall of the Reichskanzlerpalais. Representatives of 13 European nations and the United States discussed African trade activities. The conference decided on free trade in central Africa and freedom of ship travel. Leopold II of Belgium was allowed to keep the Congo. Leopold used slave labor and torture to extract raw materials, mostly rubber, to build his personal fortune, and provided inspiration for Joseph Conrad's novel *Heart of Darkness*. The conference delegates established a framework for the partitioning of Africa among the European powers. Lord Salisbury, who led the British delegation, told the *Times* of London: "[We] have been engaged in drawing lines upon maps where no white man's foot ever trod, we have been giving away mountains and rivers and lakes to each other, only hindered by the small impediment that we never knew exactly where the mountains and rivers and lakes were."

The satirical magazine *Gartenlaube* published a cartoon of the conference with the caption "Africans only as onlookers from the bushes."

Worker-Protection Conference. At the request of Kaiser Wilhelm II, the International Worker-Protection Conference met on March 15, 1890, in the Congress Hall of the Reichskanzlerpalais. The conference discussed work hours, child labor, women's labor, and holiday shifts.

Golden Wedding Anniversary. On the evenings of February 15 and 16, 1897, Reich Chancellor Chlodwig zu Hohenlohe-Schillingsfürst and his wife Maria celebrated their golden wedding anniversary in the Reichskanzlerpalais.

Carl Gottfried von Linde Lecture. On December 17, 1907, Carl Gottfried von Linde (1842–1936) gave a lecture in the Reichskanzlerpalais titled "The Treasures of the Atmosphere." Linde, the son of a pastor, was an engineer and industrialist. He discovered a process for refrigeration and ice production by compressing ammonia, and built one of the largest European manufacturers of refrigerators, which he sold to slaughterhouses, breweries, and wealthy households.

Linde's compressor was the basic element of all electric refrigerators. But Linde's early refrigerators were noisy and sometimes dangerous, because coolants were made of ammonia or sulfur dioxide. In the early 1920s, 41-year-old Albert Einstein read a Berlin newspaper report of a family killed by poisonous gases leaking from a refrigerator. "There must be a better way," said Einstein. Working with his student, Leo Szilard, Einstein devised an improved, inherently much safer, quieter system. Einstein, a patent office clerk when he began his work on relativity theory, advised on the German patent preparation. AB Electrolux licensed the invention for $750. Einstein and Szilard also applied for an American patent. "I would be interested to know," wrote back the U.S. patent examiner, "if Albert

Carl Gottfried von Linde (Ullstein Bilderdienst)

Linde's first refrigeration compressor (Ullstein Bilderdienst)

Einstein is the same person who propounded the theory of relativity." Electrolux purchased a second design, and a Hamburg company bought up a third for a small immersion cooler demonstrated at the Leipzig Fair in 1928. Einstein and Szilard's most successful joint invention was an electromagnetic pump to compress refrigerants. Szilard later fled from the Nazis to Britain where he had a sudden vision of a dangerous "chain reaction" in uranium fission. Szilard took out a patent, which he assigned to the British Admiralty. The result was the atomic bomb.

Development of Islam. In November 1910, missionaries Karl Axenfeld and Julius Richter gave two talks in the Reichskanzlerpalais about the development of Islam in German African colonies and its threat to Christianity.

Medical Missionaries. On December 2, 1910, Dr. Paul Lechler (1849–1925) spoke in the Reichskanzlerpalais on "the medical mission and its meaning for cultural development in regions under our protection (i.e., German colonies)."

Appendix G: Hitler's Speech at the Topping-Out Ceremony of the New Reich Chancellery in the Deutschlandhalle, August 2, 1938

Although excerpts from this speech and the one following were published just after Hitler delivered them, they were not printed in their entirety until 1981, when Angela Schönberger found the complete texts among Albert Speer's papers.

My comrades!

I know that all of you hope to get my signature on your folders. But there are 4,500 people here today, and even if I could write as quickly as you built, it would still take me eight hours to sign my name 4,500 times. So although I cannot sign for all of you, I want to speak to you all.

I am happy that I could come here today to stand among you. I have been coming to the construction site often. If I don't come as often now, it is not because I am disinterested in what you are doing, or because I have become lazier or inured. Rather, I have had much more work recently and much less time to do it. We now have a million more German citizens, and with them have come additional burdens. But despite my new duties, rest assured that I personally experience the building that you, my comrades, are doing, because of my original profession.

I know there are people who feel there shouldn't be so much building, demolishing, and rebuilding, every three or four months something new. I can especially understand this attitude in people who have become politically sluggish. These people should see our construction site now.

I have come into a period in which enormous tasks are everywhere, and these tasks must get done. I don't have the time for everything, as did my predecessors. I have to act quickly. When I came to power, 7,000,000 people in Germany were unemployed. There had been plenty of talking and debating, but the time had come for action. We couldn't let things get the way they are now in America, where 13,000,000 are unemployed. And I was convinced that the best work was construction.

Building is a key industry with enormous significance. That my predecessors did not appreciate this fact was their misfortune and my good fortune. I immediately began two types of building: 1) practical, such as housing, roads, canals, and 2) grand monumental. The practical building was very straightforward, but sometimes when a project was completed, it turned out to be inadequate because it was too small. Take, for example, the streets of Berlin. Everywhere you go you will see the roads dug up and construction going on. I am revamping our highways not for today, but for tomorrow, when there will be vastly more automobile traffic. If we do not build to accommodate this traffic today, tomorrow will be too late. If we need to close off a street for three months, people grumble, they say it is faster to walk than to drive. But what will happen when everyone has a car? I am building for the time when, instead of two million cars, there will be seven, eight, or nine million. I am not building for 1938, 1939, or 1950. I am building for the year 2000 in Germany, even the years 2200 and 2400. If the Berliner of 300 years ago was bold enough, in a city of 37,000, to build Unter den Linden, then we must also be bold enough to create the streets of the future.

Today, because of neglect, our streets are inadequate. We are a country that became a Reich only during the last decades. Until then, all our provinces had their own streets. Now everything must be combined and that will take time. After the streets, we must build canals and numerous other things, for example power plants and factories for our four-year-plan, in other words, a huge amount of construction work. All these buildings will be built for the future.

I will also give the German Volk the governmental buildings that they need. When I put up these buildings, they are not for me. I do not know how long I will live. Perhaps most of these buildings will be finished after I am gone. Their existence does not depend on the life of a single man. I am the Reich Chancellor, but I am also a citizen. As a citizen, I live in the same Munich building I lived in before I came to power. But as Führer and Reich Chancellor, I want Germany represented as well as any other country, in fact, better.

What's more, I don't go into palaces. I'm too proud. The new Reich will not use former palaces as governmental buildings; it will put up new buildings. Russia has the Kremlin, Warsaw has the Belvedere, Budapest has the Königsberg, Prague has the Hradcin. I will put up buildings for the new Reich that will shame these former royal palaces. Above all, the new German republic is neither a boarder nor a vagrant in palaces and castles. Other governments may be housed in the Kremlin or the Hradcin. Our government will occupy a building from its own time. And I will make the German state an object than transcends a single individual.

We are all mortals. Our German capital must endure and be built for the future. I don't know who will be in our buildings. God willing, only the best of our people, no matter from which social class. No one should look down on any of our sons. When someone is called to represent Germany, he is the equal of any foreign king or emperor.

I believe in the future of the German People's Republic, and I would like it to be a worthy representative of the German people. For this reason, I want to build a beautiful, proud German capital. I have already begun something that people might not understand. I have done this with equanimity. The New Reich Chancellery encompasses eternally pure material interests and the really excellent representative tasks of our German people's community. And it is included in our general building program.

Of the 400 million bricks used every year in Berlin buildings, our chancellery required 20 million, a relatively small number. Nevertheless, this structure you are working on will endure for centuries. If in the years to come its purpose becomes dramatically different, we cannot know. In the great rebuilding plan for Berlin, this building will have a somewhat different function in a few years. It will only be a chancellery for the next ten to twelve years, but thereafter it will still serve the needs of the Volk and the Reich. This year our Reich is receiving a magnificent, powerful, large German city, a city rich in our ancient *Kultur* and splendid buildings [Vienna]. Precisely for this reason, it is necessary that the face of Berlin should change as the city adjusts to its new mission. Thus I gave my architect Speer the commission to finish the chancellery on January 10th, 1939. On this day there will be a new reception of diplomats in the new Reich building, the home of the Great German Reich.

Naturally the experts thought it couldn't be done. But my party comrade Speer didn't hesitate for a second. In six hours he had devised a plan and assured me that the old buildings would be razed by March 15th, that the topping out would occur on August 1st, and the new chancellery would be finished January 10th. This is now, my comrades, no longer the American tempo, it is the German tempo, a first in Europe and the world, for that matter, and that is good.

We are an overpopulated country. Our vital needs force new tasks upon us, new stresses, and no one is exempt. I imagine that I achieve more than other statesmen in the so-called democracies. I believe that we are also setting a new political tempo. If it's possible to annex a whole country to the Reich in three or four days, then it must be possible to finish a building in one or two years. I know this is easy to say but hard to accomplish. I know the sweat and toil that has gone into this building; no one gave us anything. But the work has been a source of joy for us all. How many people labor and never get to see what they have produced? That is the wonderful quality of architecture. When something is built, a monument results. How different from a pair of boots, which is also made, but then worn and thrown away in a year or two. A building remains standing and bears witness through the ages to everyone responsible for its construction, including the man who commissioned it, the architect, the engineer, and every workman.

Our chancellery is a memorial to all, the proudest joy anyone can experience. In the beginning there are sour, sour weeks, but when such a work is completed, it is a magnificent accomplishment. People in the future will marvel at it, as we ourselves marvel at works of the past. We know that if our predecessors had not built what they did, we would still be living in the wilds. Therefore, I want to thank all of the gentlemen and ladies who have worked on the chancellery for their diligent labor and dedication. Even had I not visited so frequently, I would have known everything, because when a building begins in January with the razing of old houses and is topped out August 1st, that says it all.

I would also like to thank people who are no longer here, having been called to another construction site. I can speak to them very quietly. I have joked to the western powers that I would fill Germany with steel and concrete to make our country impenetrable to any foreign army. Certainly no one will derive any joy from tampering with us. In any event, our new chancellery is a gigantic work, the likes of which the world has never seen, and many of your colleagues have been called upon to help with it. I want to thank the building supervisors who managed the entire organization, and whose efforts will decide whether the completion date is indeed valid. I especially want to thank my chief architect, the inspector general of buildings, and his associates. They not only put in overtime, but more overtime than has ever been devoted to a single project. They worked not solely on the plans for this one building, but on the plans for the massive reconstruction of Berlin and other German cities. They labored at midnight and one in the morning, going through plans, making revisions, up to their ears in blueprints. It was a huge job that was accomplished here, and this knowledge unites us all. This work is a supreme accomplishment of workers who work with their brains and workers who work with their hands, and therefore, the entire National Socialistic community. I look forward with pleasure to January 10th.

I lead a very modest private and personal life. But I'm proud to be the Führer of the German people. Thus I am pained when, as representative of the German Volk, 75 million strong, I must meet the representatives of foreign countries in unworthy barracks. I must also tell myself that in other lands things are different.

I will be overjoyed January 10th, because I can meet the diplomatic corps in our worthy new chancellery. They'll learn something about the grandeur of the German Reich when they walk down the long corridor from the entrance to the reception hall. On that day I'll think again about you all, who were responsible for this monumental work, even though you may be building houses, other large state buildings, industrial buildings, or who knows what. But I do know that we will always have new jobs, and we will never again have masses of unemployed people. I am placing myself in the center of German life, the German economy, and the German workforce.

People had said to me, OK, where will you get the money? I had no capital, no currency, no gold reserves like the others. I had a single source of capital: the German workforce, the ingenuity of the average German, of the German engineer, the German chemist, the industriousness and diligence of the German worker. That was the only capital I had to work with. Yet with this capital I managed to put seven million people to work. I gave them not only work but bread. I fostered the independence of the German economy. To a significant extent, we no longer rely on imported raw materials.

Without currency and gold reserves I stabilized the German mark. Other countries haven't done the same, even though they are sitting on pots full of gold. Certainly, in this time, I had to speak many hard truths that annoyed people. But there is no use mentioning any particular disappointment.

I always acted on a single principle, and in so doing founded our economic program and banished unemployment. My principle is that money has no intrinsic value; it only gives value to what is produced and is a medium of exchange for what is produced. If nothing is produced, money has no value. I can give someone in the Sahara desert ten million in gold. But if he can't buy anything, then the gold has no value. The democracies are sick because they have not grasped this National Socialist principle.

The decisive element is not the wish for paper currency. I can print as much as I want. The decisive factor is the size of the productive output that is exchanged for money. If there is no production, paper money represents a fantasy and nothing else. Of course, these facts are unpleasant because one always must think about production and labor. Many people wonder if there isn't another way. No, there is no other way, except that which I have described.

One can live his entire life and not produce anything, simply consuming what others have produced. We've done that for a long time. When I came to power, so much had been consumed that nothing was left. I had the thankless task of turning things around, starting up production. We're now in the midst of this process and you can see what we have accomplished, especially the goals that were carried out in the framework of the so-called four-year-plan.

You have no idea of what we discovered. One of our first successes was in the realm of chemistry. In Germany we had always burned the potato vine and potato plant because they were useless. The potato vine has now been turned into a marvelous fiber, the quality of which is superior to Vistra-fiber, a discovery of immense significance. The consequence for us is that we are more able to stand on our own two feet. Foreign capitalists can no longer push us around. They can say, we have the capital, we have the money. Their protestations mean nothing to me. We have the work force and the will to work. We have the talents of our engineers and chemists. We have something else, as far as I am concerned personally, and that is my hard skull and iron will. Thank God, the German Volk stands behind me. The people have accompanied me on my journey and will never abandon me. They will march behind me. I am proud, content, and pleased, no matter what happens in the rest of the world. And I am happy that our people's Reich is getting a new Reich chancellery, which will not only be a central workplace, but a display of the greatness of the German Volk. I don't know how long I will remain in the building, but whoever comes after me will also be proud to use this chancellery the German people have created to represent the millions of our Volk. And you too can be proud, because the new chancellery is a work that doesn't belong to you, and doesn't belong to me. It belongs to all of us, the entire German Volk.

Appendix H: Hitler's Speech in the Berlin Sportpalast, January 9, 1939, on the Occasion of the Completion of the New Reich Chancellery

German comrades! German workers, ladies and gentlemen!

In earlier times, when a monumental building was finished, only the people who worked in it had any further involvement with it. The completion had no meaning to the workers who had created it. But today I have invited everyone who took part in the creation of this marvelous work to celebrate what they achieved, not only the workers from Berlin, but the workers from throughout the Reich. All deserve to be here.

On this great day it is appropriate to look back and reflect. Not upon this work, but upon the conditions that brought the work about. Because it is a stone, a pebble really, no matter how big it appears, in the rebuilding of our great German Reich and its people. In 1933, when I came to power and acquired responsibility for our economy, I found an unattractive situation. I can truly say that I came to power with the National Socialists when every one else was making for the exits. Nobody believed that the country could be rebuilt, and maybe that was why I got my job. People were silently hoping that within a few weeks the National Socialists, too, would be kaput. Then the old parties would return. The experiment would have shown that there was nobody who could do anything. The collapse was total. Only extraordinary measures could remediate the catastrophe. The most difficult aspect was the feeding of 140 people per square meter. That was a work of art, something that no one had ever done before. To feed these 140 people, to clothe them, to provide them with life's necessities, took concerted effort and the whole will of the German people. It could only happen when the whole nation knew its own strength and retained this knowledge. You can't otherwise take on a task like this. There were two causes for the collapse of the Reich. One was a fundamentally wrong domestic policy. The domestic policy bungle shattered our German determination. There was a confusion of parties, organizations, groups, little associations, and points of view, and there was no way they could solve our problems. The country was also a mess economically. You must not forget that our economy was dependent on capital that had been accumulated in former times. In 1933 this capital was gone. By capital I am referring not only to currency reserves, but also to products our workers had produced. They had all been used up. The situation could not be reversed with a fragmented populace. It was necessary to bring new unity to the German people. Today that sounds easy. But the times showed how difficult it was.

The second cause of the collapse was bad foreign policy. This was not our foreign policy. Foreigners had imposed it on us. It was to their benefit, not ours. Yet it filled our people with false hope. The bourgeois stared, as though hypnotized, toward the League of Nations in Geneva. The proletariat looked toward Moscow. They all found something in the world outside of Germany that they thought could help.

But the world outside was egotistical. The outside world thought only of itself. That is self-evident. How else would they think? When you look at the world today, look at all the problems. America, the richest country anywhere, has eleven people per square meter, 13 million unemployed, frightful! Who would think or even hope that from this situation our salvation or even a little help would come?

It took vast effort to restore self-confidence to all the German people. One or the other would say, why does our Führer always announce that our streets must be the biggest? Why is he building superhighways? Why is he enlarging the Berlin streets? Why is he building canals? Why must everything be so huge?

German comrades, I did this building to give Germans back their self-respect. In multiple ways I showed that we were inferior to no one and were the equals of everyone. It's so important that a Volk believe in itself. I want to remove the feeling of inferiority from everyone. Because, German comrades, what have I been doing for the last twenty years? I removed the German worker, bit by bit, from the proletariat. I made him a German citizen, a German comrade. I demolished all prejudices and filled the German people with national pride, not with class pride but with the pride of a German comrade. I have also strived to give our great Reich a worthy capital, a city of which Germans need not be ashamed in front of foreigners. This does not mean that the rest of the Reich will be left out. On the contrary, all Germany will be elevated, but our capital, with its size and splendor, will express our magnificence.

I am vexed and annoyed when I think under what conditions my predecessors had tried to represent the German people.

I stand here today as two beings. One is the representative of the German Volk, the second is a German comrade. As a German comrade I am what I always was, and desire to be no more. If I stepped down, that is what I would be. My private residence is the same as it was before I came to power, and will not change. But here I am the representative of the German Volk. And when I receive anyone in the Reich Chancellery, then I receive them not as Adolf Hitler the private citizen but as Führer of the German nation. Thus I do not receive the visitor, but through me Germany receives him. I want these rooms to attest to this fact. But above all, I have avoided the so-called Reich Presidential Palace. Why is that, comrades? Because the King's Lord High Steward lived there. The Führer of the German nation certainly would not live in the Lord High Steward's residence. I'd rather live in the fifth floor of a private house than in that castle. I simply can't understand our former republic. The gentlemen created a republic, got rid of the old Reich, and then occupied the home of the former Lord High Steward. That is so unworthy, German workers. My predecessors didn't have the strength to immediately give their new state a new face. That was and is my decision, that our new state would have its own reception rooms.

I decided in the beginning of last year to solve a big outstanding question, namely the annexation of the German Ostmark [Austria]. In the last days of January I called our ingenious young architect and said to him, this great German Reich needs a new place for reception rooms. New tasks are on the horizon. I won't have much time to do this work so you don't have much time, either. I know this is unusual. The New Reich Chancellery must be finished, at the latest, by January 10th of the coming year, because I will receive diplomats on that date.

My Inspector General of Buildings asked for some time to reflect. In the evening he came to me with a schedule and said, on such-and-such a day in March, all the old buildings will have been razed, on August 1st we'll have the topping out, and on January 9th, my Führer, I'll report to you that the work has been completed. Such a thing has never happened before. I've been in the construction business myself and I know what a schedule like that means. Nothing similar has ever been done and everyone involved can take pride in this building. Also the achievement shows the capabilities of the German Volk and the German worker. When I receive the diplomats on behalf of the German people on January 12th in these rooms, I will be proud of all of you, my friends, who have made the new chancellery possible.

I would like to thank everyone, including my Inspector General of Buildings, artisans, engineers, technicians, draftsmen, individual companies, etc, and above all the workers, both men and ladies. The work, in the end, speaks for itself. Every individual made his or her contribution to this monumental building, which will endure for centuries and speak of our time, the first construction project of the new German Reich.

I have invited all of you to come together. Many of you have already seen the building as it arose, but others were away in quarries and had no idea what was developing from the work of your industrious hands. Now you can see for yourselves. I have invited you to enjoy yourselves here for a day.

We are a city of four-and-a-half million. We work intensively, diligently. Of the four-and-a-half million, two million are workers. But if all the two million wanted to enjoy themselves once or twice a year, the leisure facilities of Berlin would not be adequate. And those two days would only be modest recompense for what has been accomplished in this metropolis.

Today you should all enjoy yourselves. You should be happy and proud. And I rejoice, German workers, that I may experience this completion and transfer festival. I am happy to see you here before me. I have seen your work. I know that creating such a gorgeous thing required sweat, labor, exertion, and sacrifice. Every glorious work arises from such exertions. But when a work is done, we can take pride in it. The New Reich Chancellery belongs to the year 1938. In that year you built it and it is part of our accomplishments for the year. It is a crowning achievement for the Great German Political Reich. On the occasion of the completion of this German people's work, I close my address with the war cry of the German Volk: To the German Volk and the German People, *Sieg Heil*!

Appendix I: Adolf Hitler Describes His Chancellery Renovations

This essay appeared on German Art Day, July 14–16, 1939, and was reprinted in the Völkischer Beobachter Nr. 198, July 17, 1939.

When Bismarck decided, after the Reich had just been founded, to buy the Reichskanzlerpalais (then the Radziwillpalais), his offices were still in the Foreign Office building. Perhaps the location of the Reichskanzlerpalais, adjacent to the foreign office, was Bismarck's impetus for acquiring the building.

The Reichskanzlerpalais was built in the first half of the eighteenth century. It had almost no office space. It was an old royal palace, with a well-maintained façade. Inside, it had been tastelessly renovated. The embellishment began at the end of the nineteenth century and the building was gradually debased. The splendid interior was spoilt for lack of proper building material, while the original tasteful proportions were concealed. Even the hall where the Congress of Berlin was held could not escape "embellishment." Ugly wall fixtures and a tin chandelier were considered attractive. The paintings on the walls were second-rate borrowings from Prussian State collections. The portraits of the former Reich Chancellors didn't amount to much, with the exception of a Franz von Lenbach painting of Bismarck.

The park outside had become quite overgrown. No one wanted to replace dead trees, and so the trunks had been filled with brick or concrete. The neglect was of such long duration that the grounds resembled the Houthulst Forest in Belgium, after the English had bombarded it for three years during World War I. The Reich Chancellors before 1918 gradually began making improvements, but after the German defeat the place decayed.

In 1934, I moved in despite the poor conditions. The ceiling trusses were sagging and the floor joists were crumbling. Fearing collapse of the floor, the police had limited occupancy of the Congress Hall, where diplomatic receptions took place, to sixty people. A few months earlier, Reich President Paul von Hindenburg had held a reception for a hundred people in another room. Shortly thereafter, the entire floor had to be replaced because the joists were so rotten a fist could punch through them. When it rained, water came flowing in from Wilhelmstraße, up through the floors, as well as down from the ceiling. The ground floor rooms became a brook that flowed into the adjacent lavatories. Because my immediate predecessors as chancellor had remained in office for three to four months at most, none had bothered to clean up the filth or make repairs. They had no concern at all for their successors. And they had conducted so little foreign diplomacy that no one visiting the building remarked on its condition.

The interior was completely decayed. The ceilings and floors were moldering, carpets and floor coverings spoilt, and an evil smell permeated the rooms. The new chancellery Annex on Wilhelmplatz looked like a warehouse or city

Appendix I: Adolf Hitler Describes His Chancellery Renovations

Old trees in Reichskanzlerpalais garden

firehouse, and on the inside resembled a tuberculosis sanatorium. Indeed, if someone in the building had been ill, the people working nearby probably would not have noticed.

In order to be able to use the chancellery again, I decided to undertake a complete renovation. The state did not pay for this work. I arranged to cover it personally. Professor Troost, the architect, had the following tasks:

1. Relocate the apartments and reception rooms to the ground floor, so far as possible.
2. Renovate the second floor for Chancellery offices.

These alterations were necessary because my office was too close to Wilhelmplatz. Moreover, its size and decoration were reminiscent of the tasteless workplace of a middle manager in a middling tobacco company. When the windows were closed I could not remain in the room because of the heat; when they were open the noise was intolerable. Not only the receptions of the Reich Chancellor were held in the chancellery. The elderly Reich President also lived there because of the renovation of the Presidential Palace, and he held his own receptions in the second floor rooms of the chancellery. But for most of the year these rooms stood empty. I decided to move the reception rooms to the ground floor so that the second floor rooms facing the garden could be converted to offices. The congress hall, which was empty most of the year, became the cabinet meeting room. I commissioned Professor Gall to build a wing for large diplomatic and state receptions. It would be possible to do this with only modest alterations of the adjacent rooms. The offices of Reich President and Reich Chancellor were combined in 1934. We then needed new rooms for the presidential chancellery and Wehrmacht Adjutantur, as well as more rooms for state receptions. To fulfill these requirements the Borsig Palais was acquired. This building was certainly not an architectural masterpiece but its interior was far superior to the 90's style of the Reichskanzlerpalais.

With the Borsig Palais came Albert Speer's first commission for Reich Chancellery renovation. In a short time and without modifying the facade, Speer connected architect [Richard] Lucae's building to the factory building on Wilhelmstraße [i.e. the Chancellery Annex] and elegantly renovated the interior. At least for the present, the presidential chancellery, the Wehrmach Adjutantur, and the SA leadership would have their own space. In addition, the party chancellery, directed by [Philipp] Bouhler, got a few rooms. A balcony overlooking Wilhelmplatz, the first architecturally respectable element, was added to the former Reich Chancellery office building.

These renovations were only temporary measures, since nothing had been done to eliminate the most pressing deficiency. I needed only two months in 1938 to come up with an immediate solution.

To lighten the east-west traffic in Berlin, the Highway Office had decided to lengthen Jägerstraße so that it traversed the ministry garden and the Tiergarten, thereby creating a connection to Tiergartenstraße. I recognized that these plans were ill conceived. I therefore commissioned Professor Speer to lighten the traffic on Leipzigerstraße and Unter den Linden by creating a direct western connection to Wilhelmplatz. This would deprive Voß Straße of its narrow character and convert it to a through street. And the widening could not be accomplished at the expense of the Wertheim Department Store. It would need to be done by altering the part of the Reichskanzlerpalais garden adjacent to the street, breaking it up and altering it completely.

In December and January, 1937/38, I decided to resolve the Austrian question, thereby creating the Great German Reich. Under no circumstances would the Old Reich Chancellery be adequate, either for offices or representative activities. For this reason, on January 11, 1938, I commissioned General Inspector of Buildings Professor Speer to build the Reich Chancellery on Voß Straße. I set a completion date, January 10, 1939, when the new building was to be handed over. Even if we had spoken extensively about the project, the task would have been formidable.

But the completion date was even more pressing. Building could not begin on January 11, 1938, since the houses on Voß Straße had to be razed. Actual construction did not commence until the end of March. Therefore, the actual time allotted for building was scarcely nine months. The successful completion of the New Chancellery within the designated period was wholly the accomplishment of the ingenious architect, an artist with incredible organizational talent, and his industrious co-workers.

The Berlin worker had outdone himself during this project. I think that nowhere else in the world could such a feat have been conceivable. Only the diligence of the Berlin workers allowed timely completion of the project, given the winter and late heavy frost. I do not need to add that naturally, in regard to the social welfare of those involved with the construction, we have done everything possible.

The design of the New Chancellery makes clear and generous use of the construction area. The enormous linear extension along Voß Straße is both functional and aesthetic. The grouping of the rooms, from the honor court to the innermost recess, is not only purposeful and satisfying but truly splendid. The appointment of the interior is superb, thanks to the efforts of interior decorators, sculptors, painters, etc. Their work bears witness to the excellence of German art. The landscaping of the park is complete, save for that part which was used during construction. The rapidity of the work did not allow for the total completion of the ballroom at the end of the great hall. Interim measures have been taken to make the entire building usable. Within two years all the work will be done. Although by 1950 another use for the Reichskanzlei is foreseen, the building represents a supreme artistic triumph, which speaks volumes for its resourceful creator and architect, Albert Speer.

Appendix J: Text of Hitler's Agreement to Occupy Czechoslovakia, Signed in the New Reich Chancellery

The Führer and Reich Chancellor today received Czech State President Dr. Hacha and Czech Foreign Minister Dr. Chvalkovsky, at their request, in the presence of Reich Foreign Minister von Ribbentrop. The serious situation of the past months in the up-to-now Czech regions has been quite public. The Czechs and the Germans are agreed that quiet, order, and peace must prevail in this portion of middle Europe. The Czech President has expressed his desire for these goals and the pacification of his country. He is therefore placing the destiny of the Czech Volk and his country trustingly in the hands of the Führer of the German Reich. The Führer has accepted this offer and has agreed to put the Czech Volk under the protection of the German Reich to allow the Czech Volk to develop their way of life on their own. To authenticate this agreement two copies of this document have been signed. Berlin 15 March 1939.

[A. Hitler, Ribbentrop, Dr. E Hacha, Chvalkovsky]

Appendix K: Heinrich Himmler's Heydrich Eulogy

Heinrich Himmler was born October 7, 1900, in Munich. The second most powerful man in the Third Reich, he controlled the police, the SS, and, toward the end of World War II, even parts of the army. In notorious speeches at Posen to generals of the Waffen SS (October 4, 1943) and at Sonthofen to Wehrmacht generals (June 21, 1944), Himmler announced the wholesale plundering and murder of the Jews. Captured by the British in 1945, he committed suicide by taking poison (or was murdered by his British captors) and was buried on the Lüneberg Heath, near Hamburg, in an unmarked grave. On June 9, 1942, in the Mosaic Hall of the New Reich Chancellery, Himmler delivered this verbose eulogy for Reinhard Heydrich, discreetly omitting any mention of Heydrich's expulsion from the navy, chronic womanizing, or the inconvenient fact that Bruno Heydrich, Reinhard's father, might have been Jewish.

My Führer!
Dear Heydrich Family!
Honored mourning guests!

With the death of SS Obergruppenführer Reinhard Heydrich, the Deputy Reichsprotektor of Bohemia and Moravia, Chief of the SD and security police, the National Socialist Movement has made a tragic contribution to the fight for freedom of our people.

How incomprehensible to us is the thought that this shining, great human, scarcely 38 years old, is no longer with us and unable to battle along with his friends. His unique abilities and pure character, his mind, his logic and clarity, are irreplaceable. We would not be abiding by his wishes were we not here with his coffin, heroic thoughts of living and dying investing us, as they once did when our Volk confronted the death of its dearest.

In this spirit we devote our ceremony to honoring him, recounting his life, his deeds, and then returning his mortal remains to the earth.

We will fight as he fought during his life and seek to fulfill his role.

Reinhard Heydrich was born March 7, 1904, in Halle on the Saale. He attended Volksschule and a Reform High School. During his school years, in 1918 after the great break up of our Volk, the 16-year-old student demonstrated his ardent love for Germany by volunteering for the Freikorps "Maercker" and Freikorps "Halle," which were active in the red regions of mid–Germany. In 1922, an epoch when soldiering was despised, he enlisted in the navy. In 1926 he was a lieutenant, 1928 Oberleutnant zur See. He served as a radio and communications officer and broadened his horizons with foreign duty and travel. In 1931 he left the navy.

Through one of his friends, SS Oberführer [Friedrich Karl] von Eberstein, I met him and inducted him that July into the Schutzstaffel. Heydrich, who had been a lieutenant, became a simple SS man on the small Hamburg staff, together with other noble, mostly unemployed, young men, who found there a true calling. Their duty was the Saal war and they were involved with propaganda in the predominantly red quarters of the city. Soon after, I brought Heydrich with me to Munich and gave him new duties in the little Reichsführung SS.

During the politically difficult autumn of 1932, he served loyally and steadfastly, despite the many demands upon him.

After we came to power, I became Munich police chief on March 12, 1933. I immediately gave Heydrich the so-called political division of the presidium. In no time he reorganized the division, and in a few weeks transformed it into the Bavarian Political Police. Soon the division became a model for political police departments in non-Prussian German territory. On April 20, 1934, the Prussian Minister President, our Reichsmarschall Hermann Göring, appointed me to lead the State Police of Prussia and appointed SS Brigadeführer Heydrich as my deputy. In 1936 the Führer appointed 32-year-old Heydrich chief of the newly created Security Police. Besides the secret police, he was responsible for all of the criminal police.

The years 1933, 34, 35, 36 were filled with work and innumerable startup problems. We had to deal with expelling immigrants and traitors. These difficult, painful duties fell to Heydrich's security police and the SD, which had to earn the respect of the states and the entire Reich. By the beginning of 1938 the security police was a strong organization that could carry out all tasks. Heydrich rendered a great, though unobtrusive, service during the bloodless march into Austria [Ostmark], the Sudetenland, and Bohemia-Moravia, as well as the liberation of Slovakia, by arresting opponents and keeping a watchful eye on enemies in these places.

I would like to mention here publicly the thoughts of this man, who was feared, hated, and denounced by sub-humans, such as Jews and miscellaneous criminals. Even many Germans did not understand him.

All measures and actions he took were the deeds of a National Socialist and SS man. From the depths of his heart and blood he made the world-view of Adolf Hitler a reality. All problems Heydrich solved from a racial point of view. His ultimate goal was the maintenance, protection, and preservation of our blood.

To carry out his difficult task, he had to build and lead an organization, which dealt with evil, criminal, anti-social elements in our society. There was little joy in this work.

Heydrich's view was that only the best of our Volk, the racially pure of exceptional character, were able to battle the negative social elements with sufficient hardness. He himself was incorruptible. Flatterers and toadies elicited only scorn from him. But truthful, upstanding people, even if guilty, could rely on his knightly nobility and human understanding. Yet he never let anything happen that could damage the whole nation or the future of our blood.

No one should forget his truly revolutionary creativity in the criminal police. He approached the question of criminality with a healthy, sober human understanding. But at the same time he tried to make the German criminal police a modern and scientific force. As chief of the International Criminal Police Commission [today Interpol] he gave to the policemen of the world his wisdom, his experience, and his comradeship. After 1936, when his service began, there was a continuous decrease in crime. Despite three years of war, crime incidence has now reached its lowest level ever. People in Germany can walk down the streets in peace, unmolested, even in the hardest times, in contrast to the "splendid, humane, democratic countries." Germans can thank Reinhard Heydrich from the bottom of their hearts for this security. Both criminal and political miscreants have been severely handled and our security police will continue to do so.

Yet after innumerable conversations with Heydrich, I learned that this man, who was externally hard and strict, suffered deeply on account of his duty. But no matter, according to SS law, he was not allowed to spare foreign or German blood when the life of the nation was in question. He was one of the best teachers of National Socialist morals and educated the SS Führerkorps of the security service and led it with unimpeachable purity.

To the men he commanded, he devoted love and attention, even in the most difficult matters, and showed himself to be a born and bred gentleman. He was a shining example in his willingness to accept responsibility and was a model of modesty. He let his work speak for itself and never blew his own horn. Many people were surprised that he took an interest in all the intellectual endeavors of the security service, no matter what their nature. There was not a trace in him of the fusty old policeman. He worked out the scientific basis for everything and applied his findings to everyday questions.

The war came with its many tasks in the newly occupied areas, in Poland, Norway, the Netherlands, Belgium, France, Yugoslavia, Greece, and above all, Russia.

It was difficult for him, this fighter and doer, not to be right at the front. Besides his tireless devotion to assigned tasks, which he accomplished day and night as the most diligent man in the Reich, he spent the early mornings of weeks and months gradually obtaining certification as a pilot and passing his examination as a combat flier. In 1940 he flew combat missions in the Netherlands and Norway. He was awarded the bronze flying medal and the Iron Cross second class. But he was not satisfied.

In 1941, at the beginning of the Russian campaign, he flew combat missions, without my knowledge, and I can confirm this fact with joyous pride and certainty. It was the one secret he kept from me in the eleven years we worked together. He was a fighter pilot in a German squadron in southern Russia, and won the silver front flyer's medal and the Iron Cross first class. At this time, destiny reached out to him. Russian flak downed his plane, but luckily he landed between the two lines and dragged himself to the German side, only to go up again the next morning in another plane.

I always held to the view that Heydrich was more important here than as a far-off front soldier, even though I understood his need to do what he did. He was abiding by the law: "do not spare your own blood," and proved himself in combat, even though his duty as security police chief was in fact much more dangerous.

In September last year came his greatest task, and, as we now know, his last great task. The Führer made him Deputy Reichsprotektor of Bohemia and Moravia when Reichsprotektor [Konstantin] von Neurath became ill. Many Germans and Czechs thought: here comes the fearsome Heydrich, who will rule with blood and terror. But during these months, he showed the world his positive creative qualities and applied his genial abilities in the fullest measure. He was firm, pursued the guilty, and engendered enormous respect for German power and law. Yet he gave those who were willing the opportunity to work with him. There wasn't a problem in the many-faceted life of Bohemia and Moravia that this young deputy Reichsprotektor didn't solve with aplomb, guided by his understanding of our laws and our Reich.

On May 27th, an English bomb hit him from behind. A paid person from the ranks of the most worthless subhumans had brought him low. Fear and excessive caution were foreign to him, the greatest sportsman of the SS, a bold fencer, rider, pentathlon champion, and swimmer. With courage and energy he defended himself and shot twice at his attackers, though he had been gravely wounded.

For days we hoped that his hereditary strength and disciplined, healthy body would overcome his horrible injury. On the seventh day, June 4, 1942, destiny, almighty God the ancient, ended the life of Heydrich, a deep believer but the greatest opponent of the use of religion for political purposes.

All of us, foremost the Reich Führer, whom he served so loyally, are now gathered to honor Heydrich. He was at the time of his death a paragon of happy family life, and his two young sons are here to represent his courageous wife, who is expecting another child.

The Führer is awarding Heydrich the gold wound badge, and named, on the day of his death, a Waffen SS unit on the eastern front, the 6th SS infantry, "Reinhard Heydrich."

Heydrich will live on in our holy convictions, which were also his. He honored and advanced the cause of those who shared his blood. He will endure on account of his talents. He was a musical person and a bold warrior, happy and earnest, an unvanquished spirit, a character of unblemished noble purity, upstanding and unsullied. He has transmitted these virtues to his sons, who honor his blood and heritage. His wife and these children deserve our attention and loving care. The SS will look after them well.

He will live on in our SS society. His memory will aid us when we have tasks to carry out for the Führer and the Reich.

He will fight along with us, if we remain true to the law until the end. He will be our companion in good times and bad.

He will also be present when we are celebrating with our comrades. For the security police and security service that he created and founded, he will be a model that will never be forgotten, a goal we can aspire to but never reach.

For all Germans he will bear witness as a martyr that Bohemia and Moravia are and always will be German lands, as they have been since time immemorial. There, in the world beyond, he will abide among the great battalions of dead SS men. He will be with his old comrades: [Fritz] Weitzel, [Paul] Moder, [Richard] Herrmann,

[Arthur] Mülverstedt, [Dr. Walter] Stahlecker, and many others who in spirit are still fighting with us.

But it is our holy duty to atone for his death, to take up his tasks, and to pitilessly destroy, without any sign of weakness, the enemies of our Volk.

I have one last thing to say: You, Reinhard Heydrich, were truly a good SS man. On a more personal level I thank you for your unwavering loyalty and wonderful friendship, which united us in this life and which death cannot obliterate!

Notes

Introduction

1. Karl Heinz Krüger. "Die entnazifizierung der Steine," *Der Spiegel* 4 (1989).

Chapter I

1. Silke Böttcher. "Die Wilhelmstraße," *Berliner Morgenpost*, July 28, 2002.
2. Peter Schubert. "Umzug ins 'Haus der Lügen,'" *Berliner Morgenpost*, June 3, 1997.
3. *Allgemeines lexikon der bildenden Künstler*, p. 284.
4. Robert Asprey. *Frederick the Great*, p. 201.
5. Laurenz Demps. *Berlin Wilhelmstraße*, p. 64.
6. Adam Gopnik. "The big one."
7. Bundesarchiv Berlin, Bestand R2:27452.

Chapter II

1. Chris Hedges. "Warning from a student of democracy's collapse," *New York Times*, Jan. 6, 2005.
2. Albert Speer. *Inside the Third Reich*.
3. Bundesarchiv Berlin, Bestand R2:27452.
4. Bundesarchiv Berlin, Bestand R2:27452.
5. *New York Times*, Feb. 5, 1937.
6. Anne O'Hare McCormick. "Hitler seeks jobs for all Germans," *New York Times*, July 10, 1933.
7. *New York Times*, March 25, 1935.
8. Ian Kershaw. Jan. 1999.
9. *New York Times*, March 29, 1935.
10. *New York Times*, July 17, 1945.
11. *New York Times*, June 27, 1936.
12. *New York Times*, Aug. 17, 1936.
13. *New York Times*, Nov. 13, 1936.
14. *New York Times*, Feb. 18, 1938.
15. *New York Times*, April 21, 1937.
16. *New York Times*, Dec. 7, 1937.
17. *New York Times*, March 9, 1938.
18. *New York Times*, Dec. 5, 1937.

Chapter III

1. Christiane Kohl. "Eine Schuld, die nicht verjährt."
2. Jola Merten. "Gedenken an zivilen Protest gegen Fabrikaktion 1943," *Berliner Morgenpost*, March 1, 1999.
3. Erica Fischer and Simone Ladwig Winters. *Die Wertheims*.
4. Cornelia Höhling. "Mit der Schaufel den Weltwundern auf der Spur," *Berliner Morgenpost*, Jan. 24, 1998.
5. John Shiffman. "Grandmother in middle of tale of Nazis," *Philadelphia Inquirer*, June 15, 2003.
6. Laurenz Demps. *Berlin Wilhelmstraße*, p. 117.
7. *New York Times*, Jan. 10, 1939.
8. Oliver Kniess. "Geheimnis um roten Marmor wird gelüftet," *Berliner Morgenpost*, March 2, 1998.
9. Ernst Schumacher. "Von der Rekonstruktion zur Dekonstruktion," *Berliner Zeitung*, April 21, 2004.
10. *New York Times*, Jan. 13, 1939.
11. G.M. Gilbert. *Nuremberg diary*, p. 144.
12. *New York Times*, Jan. 17, 1939.
13. *New York Times*, Dec. 22, 1939.
14. "Der Griff nach dem letzten Grasbüschel." *Der Spiegel*.
15. *New York Times*, May 23, 1939.
16. *New York Times*, Oct. 19, 1939.
17. Ian Kershaw. *Hitler 1936–1945: Hubris*, p. 277 ff.
18. *New York Times*, March 2, 1940.
19. Ian Kershaw. *Hitler 1936–1945: Hubris*.
20. Simon Sebag Montefiore. *Stalin*.
21. Felix Chuev and Albert Resis. *Molotov remembers*.

22. "Barbie Called One of Many Ex-Nazis Aided by U.S." *New York Times*, Feb. 20, 1983.
23. *New York Times*, Feb. 2, 1941.
24. *New York Times*, March 28, 1940.
25. *New York Times*, Nov. 27, 1941.
26. *New York Times*, Feb. 13, 1942.
27. *Berliner Morgenpost*, Sept. 29, 2004.

Chapter IV

1. Vanessa Thorpe. "Revealed," *The Observer*, Oct. 9, 2004.
2. Ernst Günther Schenck. *Patient Hitler*.
3. Susann Loof. "Nazis gassed Hitler's relative," *Guardian*, Jan. 19, 2005.
4. Brigitte Hamann. *Hitlers Wien*.
5. Ian Kershaw. *Hitler, 1936–45*.
6. Joachim Fest. *Inside Hitler's bunker*.
7. Helmut Börsch-Supan. "Meditationsbild für den Untergang." *Frankfurter Allgemeine Zeitung*, Oct. 13, 2004.
8. *Times* (London), May 8, 1999.
9. Howard Taubman. "Original scores of Wagner music feared lost at Hitler's bunker," *New York Times*, July 27, 1958.
10. Richard Cohen. "Guess who's on the backlist," *New York Times Book Review*, June 28, 1998.
11. Klaus Wiegrafe. "Hitlers Nachlass," *Der Spiegel*.
12. Winston Churchill. *Triumph and tragedy: The Second World War*, vol. 5, 1953.
13. Uwe Schmitt. "Ich rauchte Görings Zigarren," *Berliner Morgenpost*, Nov. 16, 2003.
14. Hannah Cleaver. "Nazi Speer's daughter is banned from synagogue," *Daily Telegraph*, March 7, 2004.
15. Toby Helm. "This is my master plan," *Daily Telegraph*, June 3, 2000.

Appendix C

1. Barbara Tuchman. *The Guns of August*.

References

Allgemeines lexikon der bildenden Künstler. H. Vollmer, ed. Leipzig: EA Seeman, 1934.

"Anne O'Hare McCormick is dead; Member of Times Editorial Board." *New York Times,* May 30, 1954.

Arnold, Dietmar. *Neue Reichskanzlei und Führerbunker.* Berlin: Ch. Links Verlag, 2005.

Asprey, Robert. *Frederick the Great.* New York: Ticknor & Fields, 1986.

Axelsson, George. "13 regimes sign anti-red pact." *New York Times,* Nov 26, 1941.

"Barbie called one of many ex–Nazis aided by U.S." *New York Times,* Feb. 20, 1983.

Beevor, Anthony. *The fall of Berlin.* New York: Penguin Books, 2003.

Bernstein, Richard. "German court awards Jewish heirs of Nazi-seized emporium." *New York Times,* March 5, 2005, A5.

Bismarck, Otto v. *Gedanken und Erinnerungen.* Herbig. Munich 2004.

Black, Edwin. *IBM and the Holocaust.* New York: Crown, 2001.

Boldt, Gerhart. *Hitler's last ten days.* Translated by Sandra Bance. London: Sphere Books, 1973.

Bönisch, Georg, and Mathias Müller von Blumencron. "Trophäen des Sieges." *Der Spiegel,* 5:50–54, 1999.

Börsch-Supan, Helmut. "Meditationsbild für den Untergang; Ein Monarch ohne Feldherrnblick: Die Geschichte des Bildnisses Friedrichs des Großen in Hitlers Reichskanzlei." *Frankfurter Allgemeine Zeitung,* Oct. 13, 2004.

Botstein, Leon. "Die Walküre analysis." Texaco-Metropolitan Opera International Radio Network, 1997.

Böttcher, Silke. "Die Wilhelmstraße — ein Buch der deutschen Geschichte." *Berliner Morgenpost,* July 28, 2002.

"Chancellery bronze trim goes to Nazis' war chest." *New York Times,* April 5, 1940.

Chuev, Felix, and Albert Resis. *Molotov remembers.* Chicago: Ivan R Dee, 1991.

Churchill, Winston. *Triumph and tragedy: The Second World War,* vol. 5. Boston: Houghton Mifflin, 1953.

Cleaver, Hannah. "Nazi Speer's daughter is banned from synagogue." *Daily Telegraph,* March 7, 2004.

Cohen, Richard. "Guess who's on the backlist." *New York Times Book Review,* June 28, 1998.

Cohen, Roger. "Exhibiting the art of history's dustbin." *New York Times,* Aug. 17, 1999.

Dannen, Gene. "The Einstein-Szilard refrigerator." *Scientific American,* Jan. 1997.

Demps, Laurenz. *Berlin Wilhelmstraße. Eine Topographie Preußisch-Deutscher Macht.* Berlin: Ch. Links Verlag, 2000.

Duffy, Michael. *http://firstworldwar.com*

Erlanger, Steven. "Hitler, it seems, loved money and died rich." *New York Times,* Aug. 7, 2002.

Fest, Joachim. *Inside Hitler's Bunker.* Translated by Margaret Bettauer Dembo. New York: Farrar, Straus and Giroux, 2004.

Fischer, Erica, and Simone Ladwig Winters. *Die Wertheims.* Berlin: Rowohlt, 2004.

Fischer, Vera. "Senat lenkt ein: Zusätzliches Honorar für Bildhauerin." *Berliner Morgenpost,* Dec. 19, 1997.

Gernert, Johannes. "Der Besuch der alten Dame; Ein Anruf verändert Barbara Principes Leben — aber nicht die Zeitläufe des Unrechts. Seit Jahren kämpft die Erbin mit dem Karstadt-Konzern um den einstigen Besitz der Gebrüder Wertheim. Ein schändliches Kapitel Berliner Geschichte." *Frankfurter Allgemeine Zeitung,* Oct. 7, 2004, p. 28. (This article purposely has the same title as Friedrich Dürrenmatt's play, *The Visit of the Old Lady,* known in English as *The Visit.*)

Gerhart, Ann, and Annie Groer. "The reliable source." *Washington Post,* Nov. 8, 1995.

Gersdorff, Dagmar v. *Bettina und Achim von Arnim.* Rowohlt. Berlin 2002.

Gilbert, G.M. *Nuremberg diary.* New York: Da Capo, 1974.

Goebbels, Joseph. *Tagebücher 1924–1945.* Munich: Piper Verlag, 2003.

"Goebbels' bunker found at Holocaust memorial site." *The Guardian* (Manchester), Jan. 27, 1998, p. 13.

"Goebbels' bunker possibly located." *Washington Post*, Jan. 28, 1998, p. A13.

Gopnik, Adam. "The big one." *The New Yorker*, Aug. 23, 2004.

Greenough, Richard. "'First ladies' of Hitler's Reich live on as recluses, stripped of wealth and esteem." *New York Times*, Aug. 21, 1955.

"'Der Griff nach dem letzten Grasbüschel.' München 1938: Hitler's Triumph über die Westmächte — Der Schacher um die Tschechoslowakei." *Der Spiegel*, 39:51–60, 1988.

Grundberg, Andy. "Erich Salomon: A chronicler in the citadels of power." *New York Times*, Aug. 1, 1982.

Hamann, Brigitte. *Hitlers Wien*. München: Piper Verlag, 1996.

Haythornthwaite, Philip. *Napoleon's commanders*. 1, c1792–1809. Oxford: Osprey Military, 2001.

Hedges, Chris. "Warning from a student of democracy's collapse." *New York Times*, Jan. 6, 2005, B2.

Helm, Toby. "This is my master plan." *Daily Telegraph*, June 3, 2000.

Hilger, Gustav, and Alfred G. Meyer. *The incompatible allies: A memoir-history of German-Soviet relations, 1918–1941*. New York: Macmillan, 1953.

"Hitler's Höllenfahrt." *Der Spiegel*, 14:170, 1995.

Hoffmann, A. *Missionsarbeit unter primitiven Völkern: Vortrag, gehalten im Reichskanzlerpalais zu Berlin am 9. Dezember 1910*. Berlin: Buchhandlung der Berliner Ev. Missionsgesellschaft, 1911.

Höhling, Cornelia. "Mit der Schaufel den Weltwundern auf der Spur. Seit 100 Jahren ermöglicht die Deutsche Orient-Gesellschaft Grabungen in Ruinenfeldern." *Berliner Morgenpost*, Jan. 24, 1998.

Holtzman, Elizabeth. "Examine U.S. aid to Nazi criminals." *New York Times*, April 23, 1983.

Horowitz, Joseph. The "specter of Hitler in the music of Wagner." *New York Times*, Nov. 8, 1998, section 2, page 1.

http://www.Spartacus.schoolnet.co.uk

Huss, Pierre J. *The foe we face*. New York: Doubleday, 1942.

Hyngar, Michael. "12,360 Tonnen Beton: Investor verzweifelt gesucht. Hinterlassenschaft Albert Speers steht unter Denkmalschutz — Wie der 'Großbelastungskörper' künftig genutzt wird, ist unklar." *Berliner Morgenpost*, Jan. 5, 2000.

Irving, David. *Hitler's war*. New York: Viking, 1977.

"John F. Kennedy's 1945 visit to Germany." *Journal for Historical Review* 18(3): (May/June 1999): 30.

Junge, Traudl. *Until the final hour*. New York: Arcade, 2004.

Kellerhof, Sven Felix. *Mythos Führerbunker*. Berlin: Berlin Story, 2004.

Kennedy, John F. *Prelude to leadership: The postwar diary of John F. Kennedy*. Washington, DC: Regnery, 1995.

Kershaw, Ian. *Hitler 1889–1936*. New York: Norton, 1999.

_____. *Hitler 1936–1945: Hubris*. New York: Norton, 2000.

_____. *Making friends with Hitler: Lord Londonderry and Britain's road to war*. New York: Penguin, 2004.

Kinzer, Stephen. "Retrieve the lurid past? (Some Germans recoil)." *New York Times*, Feb. 12, 1992.

Kniess, Oliver. "Geheimnis um roten Marmor wird gelüftet. Neue Belege: Edler Stein in der Humboldt-Uni stammt wohl doch aus der Reichskanzlei." *Berliner Morgenpost*, March 2, 1998.

Kohl, Christiane. "Eine Schuld, die nicht verjährt. Zwangsarbeiter: Die juedische Familie Meyer, auf deren Grundstück Hitler seine Reichskanzlei baute." *Süddeutsche Zeitung*, June 14, 2000, p. 3.

Kohn, Hans. "A German in Moscow." *New York Times*, Nov. 15, 1953.

Krüger, Karl Heinz. "Die entnazifizierung der Steine." *Der Spiegel*, 4:64–81, 1989.

Kubizek, August. *Adolf Hitler, mein jugendfreund*. 6th edition. Graz and Stuttgart: Leopold Stocker Verlag, 1995.

Lechler, Paul. *Die ärztliche Mission und ihre Bedeutung für die kulturelle Entwicklung unserer Schutz-Gebiete: Vortrag, gehalten im Reichskanzlerpalais zu Berlin am 2. Dezember 1910*. Berlin: Buchhandlung der Berliner Ev. Missionsgesellschaft, [circa 1910].

Leff, Laurel. *Buried by the Times: The Holocaust and America's most important newspaper*. New York: Cambridge University Press, 2005.

Lehmann, Armin D. *Hitler's last courier*. Xlibris 2000.

Lehrer, Steven. *Hitler sites*. Jefferson, NC: McFarland, 2002.

_____. *Wannsee House and the Holocaust*. Jefferson, NC: McFarland, 2000.

"Leser-Frage: Wer war General von Pape?" *Berliner Morgenpost*, Nov. 14, 1999.

"Leser-Frage: Wo liegt der Betonklotz für Messungen der Nazis?" *Berliner Morgenpost*, July 3, 1999.

Linde, Carl v. Die Schätze der Atmosphäre: Fest-Vortrag, gehalten im Reichskanzler-Palais in Berlin am 17. Dez. 1907. Munich 1907.

Loof, Susanna. "Nazis gassed Hitler's relative." *Guardian*, Jan. 19, 2005.

Lorant, Stefan. *Sieg heil*. New York: Norton, 1974.

Margolick, David. "Max Schmeling, heavyweight champion caught in the middle of Nazi politics, dies at 99." *New York Times*, Feb. 5, 2005.

"Max Schmeling, German boxing legend, dies at 99." *New York Times*, Feb. 4, 2005.

McCormick, Anne O'Hare. "Hitler seeks jobs for all Germans." *New York Times*, July 10, 1933.

_____. "Thoughts on visiting Hitler's Chancellery." *New York Times*, March 21, 1948.

McCullough, David. *Truman*. New York: Simon & Schuster, 1993.

Merten, Jola. "Auf der Spur moralischer Größe. Eine Führung zu den Orten der Hitler-Verschwörung." *Berliner Morgenpost*, July 21, 1999.

———. "Erfolg der 'Bunkerküsser.' Die Schaustelle führt erstmals in die Unterwelt." *Berliner Morgenpost*, June 6, 1999.

———. "Gedenken an zivilen Protest gegen Fabrikaktion 1943." *Berliner Morgenpost*, March 1, 1999.

———. "Schrott — oder Zeugnis der Zeitgeschichte? Wilfried Menghin, Leiter des Archäologischen Landesamtes, zum Thema 'ausgegrabene Nazi-Bunker.'" *Berliner Morgenpost*, Feb. 2, 1998.

———. "Torfklo und armdicke Telefonkabel: was Goebbels im Bunker hinterließ." *Berliner Morgenpost*, Jan. 29, 1998.

———. "Was soll aus Goebbels Bunker werden? Verein 'Berliner Unterwelten' warnt vor Zerstörung und regt Diskussion an." *Berliner Morgenpost*. Jan. 31, 1999.

Mertens, Melanie. *Berlier Barockpaläste: Die Entstehung eines Bautyps in der Zeit der ersten preußischen Könige*. Berlin: Gebr. Mann, 2003.

Miller, William J. "I am a jelly-filled doughnut." *New York Times*, April 30, 1988.

Montefiore, Simon Sebag. *Stalin*. New York: Knopf, 2004.

Montgomery, Paul. "Schmeling still battles to grasp the past." *New York Times*, Jan. 19, 1988.

Moran, Lord. *Churchill at war*. New York: Carroll & Graf, 2002.

Neun, Hubert (pseudonym of Erich Peter Neumann). "Ein Tag in der Reichskanzlei." *Das Reich*, no. 14, April 6, 1941.

Nicolai, Friedrich. *Beschreibung der königlichen Residenzstädte Berlin und Potsdam, aller daselbst befindlicher Merkwürdigkeiten und der umliegenden Gegend*. 1768. Reprint, Berlin: Haude und Spenersche, 1968.

O'Donnell, James P. *The bunker*. Boston: Houghton Mifflin, 1978.

Pietro, Guido. *Führer Bunker*. Editions ISEM, No date.

Pünder, Hermann. *Zur Geschichte des Reichskanzlerpalais und der Reichskanzlei*. Berlin: Zentralverlag Gmbh, 1928.

Radford, Tim. "Einstein and a chilling theory." *The Guardian* (London), Jan. 6, 1997.

Read, Anthony, and David Fisher. *Berlin Rising*. New York: W.W. Norton, 1994.

Richter, Julius, and Karl Axenfeld. *Vom Kampf des Christentums um Asien und Afrika: zwei Vorträge gehalten im Reichskanzlerpalais zu Berlin im November 1910*. Berlin: Buchhandlung der Berliner Evangelischen Missionsgesellschaft, 1912.

Riefenstahl, Leni. *Leni Riefenstahl: A memoir*. New York: St. Martin's Press, 1993.

Ritzmann, Kai. "Entscheidung vor 50 Jahren: Nofretete is Berlinerin. Als die Amerikaner den Rückgabestreit um die ägyptische Skulptur beendeten." *Berliner Morgenpost*, Jan. 29, 1997.

Rosenbaum, Ron. *Explaining Hitler*. New York: Random House, 1998.

Ryback, Timothy W. "Hitler's forgotten library: The man, his books, and his search for God." *Atlantic Monthly*, May 2003.

Sailer, Gerhard. "Austria." *Spoils of War* No. 3 (1996): 35–37. (Loss of the Gobelin tapestries).

Salomon, Erich. "On the hunt with an indiscreet camera." *New York Times*, June 26, 1932.

Schenck, Ernst Günther. *Das Notlazarett unter der Reichskanzlei*. Wiesbaden: VMA Verlag, 2000.

———. *Patient Hitler*. Augsburg: Bechtermünz Verlag, 2000.

Schmidt, Paul. *Hitler's interpreter*. New York: Macmillan, 1951.

Schmidt, Uwe. "Ich rauchte Görings Zigarren." *Berliner Morgenpost*, Nov. 16, 2003.

Schönberger, Angela. *Die Neue Reichskanzlei von Albert Speer*. Berlin: Gebr. Mann, 1981.

"Die schönen und das Biest." *TAZ*, May 12, 2001.

Schubert, Peter. "Umzug ins 'Haus der Lügen.' Die Last der Altbauten: Vom schwierigen Umgang mit der NS-Architektur." *Berliner Morgenpost*, June 3, 1997.

Schumacher, Ernst. "Von der Rekonstruktion zur Dekonstruktion." *Berliner Zeitung*, April 21, 2004.

Sereny, Gitta. *Albert Speer: His battle with truth*. New York: Vintage, 1996.

Shiffman, John. "Grandmother in middle of tale of Nazis, fraud, riches." *Philadelphia Inquirer*, June 15, 2003.

Simon, John. "The Führer's movie maker." *New York Times*, Sept. 26, 1993.

Soltis, Andy. "New embassy in Berlin raises historic Führer." *New York Post*. Nov. 24, 2000.

Speer, Albert. *Inside the Third Reich*. Translated by Richard and Clara Winston. New York: Macmillan, 1970.

"Stasi im Führerbunker." *Der Spiegel*, 10:18, 1997.

"Streider: Hitler-Bunker nicht öffnen." *Berliner Morgenpost*, Oct. 16, 1999.

Sullivan, Walter. "Relativity in the kitchen." *New York Times*, April 9, 1972.

Taubman, Howard. "Original scores of Wagner music feared lost at Hitler's bunker." *New York Times*, July 27, 1958.

Terrance, Marc. *Concentration camps: A traveler's guide to World War II sites*. [Parkland, FL]: Universal, 1999.

Thorpe, Vanessa. "Revealed: The man who wed Hitler and Eva." *The Observer*, Oct. 9, 2004.

Tuchman, Barbara. *The Guns of August*. New York: Macmillan, 1962.

Ulshöfer, Helmut (ed). *Liebesbriefe an Adolf Hitler — Briefe in den Tod*. Frankfurt a.M.: VAS, 1996.

Walsh, Mary Williams. "Heirs' Angst upstages Wagner. The Bayreuth Festival, Germany's new showcase for the composer's works, has become a gothic tale of infighting. Control of the operas, new revelations of Third Reich ties figure in the generational face-off." *Los Angeles Times*, July 31, 1998, p1.

_____. "A witness to Hitler's last stand as Germany debates sealing the Berlin bunker where the Nazi leader killed himself; one of its last occupants describes the intrigues and tension of the final days." *Los Angeles Times*, April 29, 1995, p1.

Welles, Benjamin. *Sumner Welles: FDR's global strategist*. New York: St. Martin's Press, 1997.

White, Michael, and Kevin Scott. *Introducing Wagner*. New York: Totem Books, 1995.

Wiegrafe, Klaus. "Hitlers Nachlass." *Der Spiegel*, 52:35, 2001.

Wilderotter, Hans, and Klaus D. Pohl. *Der letzte Kaiser: Wilhelm II. im exil*. Berlin: Bertelsmann Lexikon Verlag/ Deutsches Historisches Museum, 1991.

Zentner, Christian, and Friedemann Bedürftig, eds. *The encyclopedia of the Third Reich*. English translation edited by Amy Hackett. New York: Macmillan, 1991.

Zur Feier der Goldenen Hochzeit im Reichskanzler-Palais zu Berlin am Abend des 15. und 16. Februar 1897. Berlin, 1897.

Index

Adlon Hotel 36, 90, 96
Albertinum (Dresden) 66
Alexis, Wilibald 3
Amenhotep IV 71
Der Angriff 3
Anhalter Station 3, 99, 197
Anti-Comintern Pact 108, 109
Au Bon Marché 70
August Ferdinand of Prussia 9
Axenfeld, Karl 181
Axmann, Arthur 137

Baden, Maximilian von 166
Baldwin, Stanley 48
Ball, Rudy 50
Ballin, Albert 71
Barthelmes Drill Company 66
Bauer, Gustav 167
Baumgarten, Paul 71
Baur, Hans 129
Beecham, Sir Thomas 54
Begas, Reinhold 26
Bell, Johannes 22
Below, Nikolaus von 130
Benes, Eduard 57, 91
Berchtesgaden 32, 57, 137, 141, 150
Berliner Morgenpost 122, 199, 200, 201, 202, 203, 204
Bethmann Hollweg, Theobald von 164
Bismarck, Otto von 3, 15, 16, 17, 18, 20, 25, 26, 27, 88, 99, 128, 162, 163, 164, 177, 179, 180, 189, 201
Bismarck Museum 26
Black, Edwin 56
Blomberg, Werner von 140
Boldt, Gerhard 114, 115, 116, 201
Borchardt, Ludwig 71, 198
Borgmann, I.G. 114
Bormann, Martin 115, 116, 128, 135, 136, 148, 152; orders red carpet for Führerbunker 125
Borsig Palais 23, 25, 37, 38, 84, 190
Botstein, Leon 147
Bourke White, Margaret 27
Brandenburg Gate 18, 30
Brandt, Karl 54, 134

Braun, Eva 1, 125, 126, 129, 133, 135, 136, 137, 139, 149; marries Hitler 136; remonstrates Hitler for wearing dirty clothes 131; room in Führerbunker of 125; SS burns body of 137; suicide of 137
Braun, Gretl 149
Breker, Arno 75, 113
Briand, Aristide 28, 102, 170
British Embassy 3, 44
Brückner, Wilhelm 42
Brüning, Heinrich 26, 27, 28, 169, 171, 172, 173
Buber, Martin 69
Bülow, Bernhard von 163
Burgdorf, Wilhelm 115

Caprivi, Leo von 162
Carinhall 58, 85, 97, 98, 103
Carlyle, Thomas 144
Castlereagh, Lord 48
Chamberlain, Neville 10, 48, 91, 170
Chancellery Annex 20, 24, 25, 26, 32, 38, 40, 41, 63, 64, 75, 77, 94, 98, 103, 155, 175, 191, 197
Charité Hospital 134
Charles IX 151
Chekhov, Anton 18
Christian, Gerda 129
Churchill, Winston 1, 22, 45, 46, 47, 48, 91, 94, 151, 152, 198, 199, 201, 204
Chvalkovsky, Frantisek 90
Ciano, Galeazzo 92, 94, 110
Clauren, Heinrich 11
Clausewitz, Carl von 11, 95
Clemenceau, Georges 17, 22
Coca-Cola 50
Cohen, Roger 146
Congress of Berlin 18, 189
Conrad, Joseph 180
Coolidge, Calvin 102
Corinth, Lovis 66
Coste, Waldemar 146
Craig, Gordon 143
Csaky, Stephen 89
Cuno, Wilhelm 169

Daily Telegraph 57
Daladier, Edouard 91
Dekanozov, Vladimir 99
Delp, Alfred 150
Destailleur, Hippolite 23
Deutschland über Alles 50
Deutschlandhalle 84
Dietrich, Otto 90
Dönhoff, Friedrich Wilhelm von 10
Dönhoff, Sophie von 10, 11
Dönitz, Karl 130
Dunnage, Wally 158, 159
Dyckerhoff & Widmann 60

Ebert, Friedrich 3, 166, 167, 176
Eden, Anthony 28, 44, 45, 46, 198
Einstein, Albert 27, 28, 143, 180, 181, 201, 204
Eisenhower, Dwight D. 42
Emker, W.C. 138
Encke, Wilhelmine 10
Enderis, Guido 88, 198
Erlanger, Steven 149
Evangelisches Gymnasium zum Grauen Kloster 27

Farley, James G. 50
Faust (Goethe) 2, 88
Fegelein, Hermann 130, 131
Fehrenbach, Konstantin 168
Fichte, Johann Gottlieb 144
Fischer, Erica 70
Fleming, Alexander 159
Forrestal, James 152
Frank, Hans 88
Frank, Heike 139
Frederick the Great 5, 8, 9, 10, 20, 23, 125, 131, 144, 145, 200, 201
Freytag-Loringhoven, Bernd von 114, 115, 116
Frick, Wilhelm 31, 53, 54, 101
Friedrich III 18
Friedrich Wilhelm I 5, 7, 8, 20, 23, 161
Friedrich Wilhelm II 10
Fritsch, Werner von 139
Führerbau (Munich) 1
Führerbunker 1, 114, 117, 119, 122, 123, 124, 125, 126, 127, 129,

130, 131, 132, 133, 137, 144, 145, 148, 150, 151, 152, 155, 157, 200, 202
Fürstenberg, Carl 72
Fürstner, Wolfgang 50, 53; suicide of 53, 54

Gabčík, Josef 112
Gall, Leonhard 117, 118, 123, 128, 190
George, Stefan 65
German Girls' League (BDM) 67
Germania 58, 61, 62, 172
Giessler, Herman 151
Gilbert, G.M. 88
Gneisenau, August Wilhelm von 11
Goebbels, Joseph 3, 5, 9, 30, 31, 37, 43, 54, 90, 99, 105, 115, 122, 126, 135, 136, 137, 138, 144, 155, 157, 159, 173, 174, 200, 202, 203; Berlin bunker of 122; death of 137; diary pages found in Führerbunker 157; moves into Führerbunker 125
Goebbels, Magda 138
Goethe, Johann Wolfgang von 2, 3, 11, 12, 65, 88
Göhre, Paul 69
Göring, Hermann 3, 31, 33, 41, 48, 84, 90, 97, 98, 100, 103, 104, 119, 130, 135, 159, 194; asks Speer to renovate his residence 33; changes name of Wertheim Department Store 73; plays host to Hoover 58; takes Gobelins from Vienna 85; threatens Hacha 91; visited by Sumner Welles 97
Graff, Anton 144
Grand Mufti of Jerusalem 110
Großbelastungskörper *see* large load body
Grunewald Station 127, 129
Guderian, Heinz 114, 115, 116, 144
Günsche, Otto 115, 129, 136
Gürtner, Franz 101

Haase, Werner 134
Hacha, Emil 90, 91, 92, 192, 199
Haussmann, Georges 60
Hearst, William Randolph 28
Heart of Darkness (Conrad) 180
Helm, Ingo 149
Helm, Toby 160
Helmis, Arno 48
Hentschel, Johannes 129
Herrmann, Richard 195
Hertling, Georg von 165
Hess, Rudolf 100
Hewel, Walter 130
Heydrich, Bruno 112
Heydrich, Reinhard 3, 71, 101, 112, 113, 114, 140, 193, 194, 195, 196; inaugurates Prague music festival 112; named governor of Czechoslovakia 112
Hilz, Sepp 145

Himmler, Heinrich 3, 99, 101, 110, 112, 113, 130, 131, 157, 159, 193
Hindenburg, Paul von 24, 30, 32, 48, 88, 165, 166, 172, 173, 175, 176, 189
Hitler, Adolf 1, 3, 22, 29, 30, 31, 32, 33, 35, 36, 37, 38, 39, 40, 41, 42, 43, 44, 45, 46, 47, 48, 49, 50, 51, 52, 53, 54, 55, 56, 57, 58, 59, 60, 62, 63, 64, 65, 66, 71, 72, 74, 75, 77, 79, 84, 85, 86, 87, 88, 89, 90, 91, 92, 94, 95, 96, 97, 98, 99, 100, 101, 102, 103, 105, 108, 109, 110, 111, 112, 113, 114, 115, 116, 117, 118, 119, 121, 122, 125, 126, 127, 128, 130, 131, 132, 133, 134, 135, 136, 137, 138, 139, 140, 141, 142, 143, 144, 145, 146, 147, 148, 149, 150, 151, 152, 153, 155, 157, 158, 159, 169, 170, 171, 172, 173, 174, 175, 176, 182, 186, 187, 189, 192, 194, 197, 198, 199, 200, 201, 202, 203, 204, 205; annoyance with Hungary of 89; appoints Albert Speer Inspector General of Berlin Buildings 58; on architecture 1, 197; autopsy of 137; becomes Reich Chancellor 30; Bismarck Museum and 26; breaks Anti-Comintern Pact 108; browbeats Czech President Hacha 91; buys villa for Eva Braun 149; commissions Paul Troost to renovate Chancellery 32; commissions Speer to add a Chancellery balcony 38; eulogizes Fritz Todt 111; eulogy for Reinhard Heydrich 112; favorite opera of 54; Gerhard Boldt's impression of 115; hatred of foreign reporters 57; inspects chancellor's residence 33; inspects Czech border fortifications 92; invites Speer to dinner 36; Karl May's influence on 143; last meal of 137, 199; leads 1936 Olympic parade 50; Leni Riefenstahl and 42; Lord Londonderry's description of 48; meets Sir John Simon and Anthony Eden 44; New Reich Chancellery sketch of 63; promises help to Arabs in struggle against the Jews 110; propagates New Reich Chancellery myth 63; relocates SA leadership to Borsig Palace 38; reveals war plans to army chiefs, 1937 74; sketches triumphal arch design 60; suicide of 136; views about black athletes 51, 53; visits completed New Reich Chancellery 75; Wagner and 147; warning to Sumner Welles 97
Hitler, Paula 150
Hodler, Ferdinand 66
Hoffmann, Heinrich 149
Hofmannsthal, Hugo von 65
Högl, Peter 129

Hohenlohe-Schillingsfürst, Chlodwig 162
Holocaust Memorial (Berlin) 122
Hoover, Herbert 28, 57, 58, 141, 198
Horst, C.H. 6, 50
Horst Wessel Lied 50
Hoßbach, Friedrich 74
Hoßbach protocol 74
Hotel Kaiserhof 31
Huch, Ricarda 65
Humboldt, Wilhelm von 11
Husseini, Haj Amin al *see* Grand Mufti of Jerusalem

IBM 55, 201
Inside the Third Reich (Speer) 157

Jacobs, Joe 50
Jandorf, Adolf 70
Jodl, Alfred 115
Junge, Traudl 129, 135, 136, 202

KaDeWe 70
Kampf, Arthur 145
Kanya, Coloman 90
Kapp, Wolfgang 167
Karstadt, Rudolph 70
Karstadt-Quelle 73, 74
Keitel, Wilhelm 90, 91, 98, 99, 115, 116
Kellerhof, Sven Felix 117, 119, 123, 125, 202
Kellogg, Frank B. 102
Kempka, Erich 129
Kennedy, John F. 152
Kershaw, Ian 30, 47, 197, 199, 200, 202
Klinger, Max 65, 69
Kohl, Christiane 65, 66, 69, 198, 203
Kreis, Wilhelm 113
Kristallnacht 48
Krosigk, Schwerin von 63
Krüger, Else 129
Kubiš, Jan 112
Kubizek, August 141, 147, 203

Ladwig-Winters, Simone 70
Lafferentz, Bodo 148
Lafferentz, Verena 148
Lagarde, Paul 141
Lammers, Hans Heinrich 40, 57, 117, 124
Landsberg Prison 147
Langer, Walter 144
Large load body (Berlin) 60
Laval, Pierre 28
Leander, Zarah 66
Lechler, Paul 181
Lehár, Franz 54
Lenbach, Franz von 15, 26, 65, 66, 88, 189
Lenthe, Ernst von 9
Leopold, King of Belgium 57
Leopold II 180
Lepsius, Reinhold 65
Liebermann, Max 66
Linde, Carl Gottfired von 180

Index

Lindgens, Arthur 72, 73
Linge, Heinz 129
Londonderry, Lord 46, 47, 48, 202
Louis, Joe 48
Luehmann, Johann Hinrich 67
Luther, Hans 171

MacDonald, Ramsay 27, 28, 47, 48
Making Friends with Hitler (Kershaw) 47
Mann, Golo 15
Manziarly, Constanze 129, 136
Märkisches Museum 26
Marschall, Samuel von 23, 161
Marx, Wilhelm 170
Maser, Werner 150
Mastny, Voytec 90
Matsuoka, Yosuke 97, 101, 102, 103, 104, 199
May, Karl 143
McCormick, Anne 42, 155, 197, 200, 203
Mein Kampf (Hitler) 58, 88, 141, 147, 149, 150, 200
Meissner, Otto 44, 90, 109, 135
Die Meistersinger (Wagner) 54
Mendelssohn, Felix 11
Menzel, Adolf von 66
Merekaloff, Alexei 88
Merry Widow (Lehár) 54
Mertens, Melanie 6, 203
Messel, Alfred 70, 71
Meyer, Adolph Ernst Joachim 66
Meyer, Albert 159
Meyer, Helene 50
Meyer, Reinhold 65
Meyer, Richard Moritz 65
Michaelis, Georg 165
Misch, Rochus 129
Moder, Paul 195
Modersohn-Becker, Paula 66
Mohnke, Wilhelm 121, 132
Molotov, Vyacheslav 98, 99, 100, 101, 108, 199, 201
Montgomery, Paul 49
Moore, David 141
Morell, Theodor 91, 92
Müller, Hermann 22, 168
Müller, Ray 44
Mülverstedt, Arthur 196
Mussolini, Benito 29, 42, 84, 92, 94, 136

Napoleon 11, 12, 113, 202
Nefertiti 71
Neumann, Elisabeth Noelle 107
Neumann, Erich Peter 105, 107, 108, 204
Neumann, Georg 18
Neun, Hubert *see* Neumann, Erich Peter
Neurath, Constantin von 44, 112, 195
New Reich Chancellery 1, 36, 62, 63, 64, 75, 76, 77, 79, 84, 85, 86, 87, 88, 89, 90, 91, 92, 94, 95, 96, 97, 100, 101, 102, 105, 109, 111, 112, 113, 114, 121, 123, 127, 128, 130, 133, 138, 141, 142, 155, 182, 183, 186, 187, 188, 192, 193
New York Times 27, 40, 42, 44, 49, 55, 57, 88, 89, 92, 96, 146, 149, 155, 197, 198, 199, 200, 201, 202, 203, 204, 205
Nicolai, Friedrich 5, 6, 7, 145, 204
Niemoeller, Martin 66
Nietzsche, Friedrich 65
Nuremberg Laws 147

O'Donnell, James P. 150, 151, 204
Old Reich Chancellery 5, 77, 191; *see also* Reichskanzlerpalais
Olympia 43
Olympic Village 50
On Religion (Schleiermacher) 3
On War (Clausewitz) 11
Orsenigo, Cesare 88, 89
Osen, Gary 73
Oshima, Hiroshi 102, 109, 110
Osram 67, 69
Owens, Jesse 51, 53

Pact of Steel 92
Pannewitz, Wolf 5, 161
Papen, Franz von 30, 38, 101, 172, 173, 174
peat toilet *see* Torfklo
Philadelphia Inquirer 73, 204
Piepenburg, Carl 122, 123, 124, 155
Pietro, Guido 157
Planck, Max 27, 28
Pleß, Prince of 23
Posse, Hans 66
Preiss, Achim 146
Prelude to Leadership: The Post-War Diary of John F. Kennedy 152
Prien, Günther 94, 95, 199
Princip, Gavrilo 18
Principe, Barbara 73, 74, 198
Principe, Dominick 73
Protzen, Carl Theodor 146
Pünder, Hermann 18, 26, 197, 204

Radziwill, Anton 11, 12, 14, 15, 18, 177
Radziwill, Elisa 12, 14
Radziwill, Michael 11
Rathenau, Emil 72
Rathenau, Walter 72
Rattenhuber, Johann 130
Raubal, Angela 150
Rauch, Christian Daniel 11
Das Reich 105
Reich Chancellery 155
Reich Ministry for Enlightenment of the People and Propaganda 3
Reich Party District (Nuremberg) 1
Reichskanzlerpalais 3, 5, 8, 15, 18, 20, 22, 23, 24, 25, 26, 27, 30, 33, 35, 36, 42, 57, 63, 75, 95, 114, 117, 118, 128, 130, 135, 139, 144, 145, 155, 162, 175, 176, 177, 179, 180, 181, 189, 190, 191, 197, 202, 203, 204
Ribbentrop, Joachim von 46, 47, 48, 74, 89, 90, 91, 92, 99, 100, 102, 108, 109, 110, 130, 192
Richter, C.F. 5, 6, 197
Richter, Hans 148
Richter, Julius 181, 204
Richter, Kurt 66
Riefenstahl, Leni 42, 43, 44, 51, 144, 204
Rienzi (Wagner) 147, 148
Ringlin, Jean George 6
Roosevelt, Franklin D. 42, 96, 97, 98, 139, 144
Royal Oak 94
The Royal Residences of Berlin and Potsdam (Nicolai) 5, 7
Ryback, Timothy 139, 141, 144, 204

Sahm, Heinrich 27
Salisbury, Lord 180
Salomon, Erich 27, 28, 29, 202, 204
Schadow, Johann Gottfried 18
Schall, Count von 9
Schenck, Ernst Günther 133, 134, 135, 199, 204
Schicklgruber family 139
Schinkel, Karl Friedrich 11
Schkarawski, Faust Jossifowitsch 137
Schleicher, Kurt von 172, 173
Schleiermacher, Friedrich 3
Schmeling, Max 48, 49, 50, 198, 203, 204
Schmidt, Hans 139
Schmidt, Paul 44, 45, 55, 90, 96, 99, 102, 103, 104, 204
Schnierbel, Gerhard 66
Schönberger, Angela 63, 87, 182, 204
Schorfheide 104
Schröder, Christa 129, 135, 136
Schubert, Franz 12
Schulenburg, Adolf Friedrich 5, 6, 7, 8, 10, 11, 12, 161, 197
Schulenburg, Friedrich Werner Graf von 100
Schulenburg, Gebhard Werner 8, 9
Schulenburg, Karl Friedrich 9
Schulenburg Palais 5, 6, 7, 9, 12, 197
Schult, Johann 145
Sereny, Gitta 112, 157, 158, 204
Sharkey, Jack 49
Shaw, George Bernard 27
Shiffman, John 73
Sidey, Hugh 153
Siedler, Eduard Jobst 24, 25, 40, 197
Skoda Works 91
Smith, Paul 57
Spandau Diaries (Speer) 143
Speer, Albert 25, 33, 35, 36, 37, 38, 40, 41, 51, 58, 59, 60, 62, 63, 64, 74, 75, 76, 84, 85, 86, 87, 91, 103, 105, 111, 112, 118, 122, 124, 126, 128, 141, 143, 144, 151, 155, 157, 158, 159, 160,

182, 183, 190, 191, 197, 200, 201, 204; appointment as armaments minister 110; death of 158; finishes most of plans for new chancellery 63; impression of Führerbunker 127; meets Hitler 33; new building plans for Linz of 133; proposes theory of ruin value 86; renovates Hitler's office 36
Speer, Albert, Jr. 160
Speer, Hilde 158, 159, 160
Speer, Margret 157, 158
Spontini, Gaspare Luigi 11
Sportpalast 85, 186
Stahlecker, Walter 196
Stalin, Josef 42, 99, 100, 102, 127, 137, 151, 169, 199, 203
Stern, Fritz 30
Strauss, Richard 50
Streicher, Julius 50
Stresemann, Gustav 3, 169, 170, 171
Stumpfegger, Ludwig 129
Der Stürmer 50
Suttner, Bertha von 143
Szilard, Leo 180

Taylor, A.J.P. 18
Tempelhof Airport 133
Therbusch, Anna Dorothea 9
Tietz, Hermann 70
Tietz, Leonhard 70
Time magazine 101, 121
Tissot Victor 17
Tivoli, Th. Roosgen von 7
Todt, Fritz 38, 110, 111, 112, 159, 199

Todt, Ilsebill 112
Tolischus, Otto D. 92, 96, 199
Topographie des Terrors 3, 4
Torfklo 122
Treaty of San Stefano 18
Trevisani, Francisco 7
Triumph of the Will 43
Troost, Paul Ludwig 32, 33, 36, 190
The Trousers of Herr von Bredow (Alexis) 3
Truman, Harry S. 42, 151, 203

U-47 94
Unter den Linden 38, 102, 153, 183, 191

Van Dyck, Anthony 7
Veit, Aloisia 139
Vernois, Adrian 10
Veronese, P. 7
Victor, Marshal 12
Villa Wahnfried 147
von Arnim, Achim 3
von Arnim, Bettina 3, 75, 202
von John, Hasso 116
Vorbunker 117, 122, 123, 125, 126, 128, 150, 155, 157
Voss, Erich 130
Voß Strasse 1, 37

Wagner, Richard 147
Wagner, Walter 136
Wagner, Wieland 148
Wagner, Winifred 147
Die Walküre (Wagner) 147
Warsaw Ghetto 107
Watson, Thomas J. 55

Weitzel, Fritz 195
Weizmann, Chaim 72
Welles, Sumner 96, 97, 98, 205
Werner, Rudolf 145
Wertheim, Abraham 69
Wertheim, Franz 72
Wertheim, Fritz 73
Wertheim, Georg 70
Wertheim, Günther 72
Wertheim, Ursula 70
Wertheim Department Store 69, 72, 74, 79, 191
Wilhelm I 14, 16, 17, 18, 38, 162
Wilhelm II 8, 10, 11, 18, 20, 21, 23, 31, 70, 149, 162, 163, 164, 165, 166, 167, 168, 179, 180, 205
Wilhelmstraße 1, 3, 4, 5, 6, 7, 8, 9, 10, 15, 17, 18, 23, 24, 30, 31, 32, 33, 37, 38, 39, 64, 75, 79, 87, 117, 119, 121, 122, 151, 152, 155, 157, 161, 175, 177, 179, 189, 191, 197, 198, 201
Wilke, Dorle 63, 65, 66, 69, 198
Wilson, Hugh R. 57
Windsor, Duchess of 104
Windsor, Duke of 104
Winter Help Campaign 55
Wirth, Josef 168
Wittenberg, Tauentzien von 113
Wittgenstein, Prince Ludwig Adolf Peter 14
Wolf, Johanna 129, 136
Wölke, Hans 51
The Wool Market (Clauren) 11
World War II 112
Wortham, Martin 74

www.ingramcontent.com/pod-product-compliance
Ingram Content Group UK Ltd.
Pitfield, Milton Keynes, MK11 3LW, UK
UKHW051827021125
3462IPUK00012B/28